Mapping Modernity in Shanghai

This book argues that modernity first arrived in late nineteenth-century Shanghai via a new spatial configuration. This city's colonial capitalist development ruptured the traditional configuration of self-contained households, towns, and natural landscapes in a continuous spread, producing a new set of fragmented as well as fluid spaces. In this process, Chinese sojourners actively appropriated new concepts and technology rather than passively responding to Western influences. Liang maps the spatial and material existence of these transient people and reconstructs a cultural geography that spreads from the interior to the neighborhood and public spaces.

In this book the author:

- discusses the courtesan house as a surrogate home and analyzes its business, gender, and material configurations;
- examines a new type of residential neighborhood and shows how its innovative spatial arrangements transformed the traditional social order and hierarchy;
- surveys a range of public spaces and highlights the mythic perceptions of industrial marvels, the adaptations of colonial spatial types, the emergence of an urban public, and the spatial fluidity between elites and masses.

Through reading contemporaneous literary and visual sources, the book charts a hybrid modern development that stands in contrast to the positivist conception of modern progress. As such it will be a provocative read for scholars of Chinese cultural and architectural history.

Samuel Y. Liang is Lecturer in Chinese Cultural Studies at the University of Manchester, UK.

Asia's Transformations

Edited by Mark Selden, Cornell University, USA

The books in this series explore the political, social, economic and cultural conse-
quences of Asia's transformations in the twentieth and twenty-first centuries. The
series emphasizes the tumultuous interplay of local, national, regional and global
forces as Asia bids to become the hub of the world economy. While focusing on the
contemporary, it also looks back to analyse the antecedents of Asia's contested rise.

This series comprises several strands:

Asia's Transformations

Titles include:

Debating Human Rights*
Critical essays from the United States
and Asia
Edited by Peter Van Ness

Hong Kong's History*
State and society under colonial rule
Edited by Tak-Wing Ngo

Japan's Comfort Women*
Sexual slavery and prostitution during
World War II and the US occupation
Yuki Tanaka

**Opium, Empire and the Global
Political Economy***
Carl A. Trocki

Chinese Society*
Change, conflict and resistance
*Edited by Elizabeth J. Perry and
Mark Selden*

Mao's Children in the New China*
Voices from the Red Guard generation
Yarong Jiang and David Ashley

Remaking the Chinese State*
Strategies, society and security
*Edited by Chien-min Chao and Bruce
J. Dickson*

Korean Society*
Civil society, democracy and
the state
Edited by Charles K. Armstrong

The Making of Modern Korea*
Adrian Buzo

The Resurgence of East Asia*
500, 150 and 50 year perspectives
*Edited by Giovanni Arrighi,
Takeshi Hamashita and Mark Selden*

Chinese Society, second edition*
Change, conflict and resistance
Edited by Elizabeth J. Perry and
Mark Selden

Ethnicity in Asia*
Edited by Colin Mackerras

The Battle for Asia*
From decolonization to globalization
Mark T. Berger

State and Society in 21st-century
China*
Edited by Peter Hays Gries and
Stanley Rosen

Japan's Quiet Transformation*
Social change and civil society in the
21st century
Jeff Kingston

Confronting the Bush Doctrine*
Critical views from the Asia-Pacific
Edited by Mel Gurtov and
Peter Van Ness

China in War and Revolution,
1895–1949*
Peter Zarrow

The Future of US–Korean
Relations*
The imbalance of power
Edited by John Feffer

Working in China*
Ethnographies of labor and workplace
transformations
Edited by Ching Kwan Lee

Korean Society, second edition*
Civil society, democracy and the state
Edited by Charles K. Armstrong

Singapore*
The state and the culture of excess
Souchou Yao

Pan-Asianism in Modern
Japanese History*
Colonialism, regionalism
and borders
Edited by Sven Saaler and
J. Victor Koschmann

The Making of Modern Korea,
second edition*
Adrian Buzo

Re-writing Culture in Taiwan
Edited by Fang-long Shih,
Stuart Thompson, and
Paul-François Tremlett

Reclaiming Chinese Society*
The new social activism
Edited by You-tien Hsing and
Ching Kwan Lee

Girl Reading Girl in Japan
Edited by Tomoko Aoyama and
Barbara Hartley

Chinese Politics*
State, society and the market
Edited by Peter Hays Gries and
Stanley Rosen

Chinese Society, third edition*
Change, conflict and resistance
Edited by Elizabeth J. Perry and
Mark Selden

Mapping Modernity in Shanghai
Space, gender, and visual culture in
the sojourners' city, 1853–98
Samuel Y. Liang

Asia's Great Cities

Each volume aims to capture the heartbeat of the contemporary city from multiple perspectives emblematic of the authors' own deep familiarity with the distinctive faces of the city, its history, society, culture, politics and economics, and its evolving position in national, regional and global frameworks. While most volumes emphasize urban developments since the Second World War, some pay close attention to the legacy of the longue durée in shaping the contemporary. Thematic and comparative volumes address such themes as urbanization, economic and financial linkages, architecture and space, wealth and power, gendered relationships, planning and anarchy, and ethnographies in national and regional perspective.

Titles include:

Bangkok*
Place, practice and representation
Marc Askew

Representing Calcutta*
Modernity, nationalism and the
colonial uncanny
Swati Chattopadhyay

Singapore*
Wealth, power and the culture of control
Carl A. Trocki

The City in South Asia
James Heitzman

Global Shanghai, 1850–2010*
A History in Fragments
Jeffrey N. Wasserstrom

Hong Kong*
Becoming a global city
*Stephen Chiu and
Tai-Lok Lui*

Asia.com is a series which focuses on the ways in which new information and communication technologies are influencing politics, society and culture in Asia.

Titles include:

Japanese Cybercultures*
*Edited by Mark McLelland and
Nanette Gottlieb*

Asia.com*
Asia encounters the Internet
*Edited by K. C. Ho, Randolph Kluver
and Kenneth C. C. Yang*

**The Internet in Indonesia's New
Democracy***
David T. Hill and Krishna Sen

Chinese Cyberspaces*
Technological changes and
political effects
*Edited by Jens Damm and
Simona Thomas*

**Mobile Media in the
Asia-Pacific**
Gender and the art of being mobile
Larissa Hjorth

Literature and Society

Literature and Society is a series that seeks to demonstrate the ways in which Asian Literature is influenced by the politics, society and culture in which it is produced.

Titles include:

The Body in Postwar Japanese Fiction
Douglas N. Slaymaker

Chinese Women Writers and the Feminist Imagination, 1905–1948*
Haiping Yan

Routledge Studies in Asia's Transformations

Routledge Studies in Asia's Transformations is a forum for innovative new research intended for a high-level specialist readership, and the titles will be available in hardback only.

Titles include:

The American Occupation of Japan and Okinawa*
Literature and memory
Michael Molasky

Koreans in Japan*
Critical voices from the margin
Edited by Sonia Ryang

Internationalizing the Pacific
The United States, Japan and the Institute of Pacific Relations in war and peace, 1919–1945
Tomoko Akami

Imperialism in South East Asia*
'A fleeting, passing phase'
Nicholas Tarling

Chinese Media, Global Contexts*
Edited by Chin-Chuan Lee

Remaking Citizenship in Hong Kong*
Community, nation and the global city
Edited by Agnes S. Ku and Ngai Pun

Japanese Industrial Governance
Protectionism and the licensing state
Yul Sohn

Developmental Dilemmas*
Land reform and institutional change in China
Edited by Peter Ho

Genders, Transgenders and Sexualities in Japan*
Edited by Mark McLelland and Romit Dasgupta

Fertility, Family Planning and Population Policy in China*
Edited by Dudley L. Poston, Che-Fu Lee, Chiung-Fang Chang, Sherry L. McKibben and Carol S. Walther

Japanese Diasporas*
Unsung pasts, conflicting presents and uncertain futures
Edited by Nobuko Adachi

How China Works*
Perspectives on the twentieth-century
industrial workplace
Edited by Jacob Eyferth

**Remolding and Resistance among
Writers of the Chinese Prison Camp**
Disciplined and published
*Edited by Philip F. Williams and
Yenna Wu*

**Popular Culture, Globalization
and Japan***
*Edited by Matthew Allen and
Rumi Sakamoto*

medi@sia*
Global media/tion in and out
of context
*Edited by Todd Joseph Miles Holden
and Timothy J. Scrase*

Vientiane
Transformations of a Lao landscape
*Marc Askew, William S. Logan and
Colin Long*

**State Formation and Radical
Democracy in India**
Manali Desai

Democracy in Occupied Japan
The U.S. occupation and Japanese
politics and society
*Edited by Mark E. Caprio and
Yoneyuki Sugita*

**Globalization, Culture and Society
in Laos**
Boike Rehbein

Transcultural Japan*
At the borderlands of race, gender,
and identity
*Edited by David Blake Willis and
Stephen Murphy-Shigematsu*

**Post-Conflict Heritage, Post-Colonial
Tourism**
Culture, politics and development
at Angkor
Tim Winter

Education and Reform in China*
Emily Hannum and Albert Park

**Writing Okinawa: Narrative Acts of
Identity and Resistance**
Davinder L. Bhowmik

Maid in China
Media, mobility, and a new semiotic
of power
Wanning Sun

**Northern Territories, Asia-Pacific
Regional Conflicts and the
Åland Experience**
Untying the Kurillian knot
*Edited by Kimie Hara and
Geoffrey Jukes*

Reconciling Indonesia
Grassroots agency for peace
Birgit Bräuchler

Singapore in the Malay World
Building and breaching regional
bridges
Lily Zubaidah Rahim

Pirate Modernity
Delhi's media urbanism
Ravi Sundaram

**The World Bank and the post-
Washington Consensus in Vietnam
and Indonesia**
Inheritance of loss
Susan Engel

Critical Asian Scholarship

Critical Asian Scholarship is a series intended to showcase the most important individual contributions to scholarship in Asian Studies. Each of the volumes presents a leading Asian scholar addressing themes that are central to his or her most significant and lasting contribution to Asian studies. The series is committed to the rich variety of research and writing on Asia, and is not restricted to any particular discipline, theoretical approach or geographical expertise.

Southeast Asia*
A testament
George McT. Kahin

Women and the Family in Chinese History*
Patricia Buckley Ebrey

China Unbound*
Evolving perspectives on the Chinese past
Paul A. Cohen

China's Past, China's Future*
Energy, food, environment
Vaclav Smil

The Chinese State in Ming Society*
Timothy Brook

China, East Asia and the Global Economy*
Regional and historical perspectives
Takeshi Hamashita
Edited by Mark Selden and Linda Grove

The Global and Regional in China's Nation-Formation*
Prasenjit Duara

* Available in paperback

Mapping Modernity in Shanghai

Space, gender, and visual culture in the sojourners' city, 1853–98

Samuel Y. Liang

LONDON AND NEW YORK

First published 2010
by Routledge
2 Park Square, Milton Park, Abingdon, Oxon OX14 4RN

Simultaneously published in the USA and Canada
by Routledge
711 Third Avenue, New York, NY 10017

Routledge is an imprint of the Taylor & Francis Group, an informa business

First issued in paperback 2012

Typeset in Times New Roman by Exeter Premedia Services

British Library Cataloguing in Publication Data
A catalogue record for this book is available from the British Library

Library of Congress Cataloging in Publication Data
Liang, Samuel Y.
Mapping modernity in Shanghai : space, gender, and visual culture
in the sojourners' city, 1853-98 / Samuel Y. Liang.
    p. cm. – (Asia's transformations)
Includes bibliographical references and index.
1. Architecture and society–China–Shanghai–History–19th century.
2. Space (Architecture)–Social aspects–China–Shanghai–History–19th
century. 3. Public spaces–Social aspects–China–Shanghai–History–19th
century. 4. Refugees–China–Shanghai–History–19th century.
5. Immigrants–China–Shanghai–History–19th century. 6. Sociology,
Urban–China–Shanghai–History–19th century. I. Title. II. Title: Space,
gender, and visual culture in the sojourners' city, 1853-98.
    NA2543.S6L53 2010
    720.1'03095113209034–dc22
                        2009045807

ISBN13: 978-0-415-56913-2 (hbk)
ISBN13: 978-0-415-63116-7 (pbk)
ISBN13: 978-0-203-85214-9 (ebk)

献给我的父母
For my parents

Contents

List of figures   xv
Acknowledgments   xvii

Introduction   1

A history of "new nature" 2
Gender, architecture, and visual culture 5
The organization of the chapters 7

1   **Fluid tradition, splintered modernity**   11

Space, time, and modernity 13
The problem of modernity in China 16
The neo-Confucian continuum 17
The discontents of Confucianism 20
Toward a splintered modernity 22

2   **The convergence of writing and commerce**   27

Imaginative geography and print culture 28
Hybrid journalism 32
Literature of urban consumption 37
Knowing historical experience 40
Wang Tao and courtesan literature 43
The new literati-journalists 47
Han Bangqing and his novel 49

3   **Ephemeral households, marvelous things**   53
Merchant residences and courtesan houses 53
The "family" business 56
The public boudoir: banquets and tea parties 60
Shifting gender roles 64
Magical and fashionable objects 71

Interior settings 76
Destruction and disillusionment 80

4   The meeting of courtyard and street   84
Changing views of the pleasure quarter 84
Joint production 87
Fluid space 93
Diverse functions 100
Distinct neighborhoods 106

5   Ultimate ingenuity, amorphous crowds   113
The challenge of human ingenuity 113
Marvels on the Bund 118
Flowers of Chessboard Street 121
Streetscapes of Fourth Avenue 125
Spectatorship of street events 131
Markets in the teahouses 136
Shops on First Avenue 140

6   The mingling of magnates and masses   144
Restaurants 144
Opium houses 148
Storytelling houses 151
Theaters 156
Street parades 164
Carriages and rickshaws 171
Gardens 174

Conclusion   181

Glossary of frequently-used Chinese terms   183
List of Chinese characters   185
Notes   192
References   204
Index   213

List of Figures

1.1   Map of Shanghai, ca. 1901   12
1.2   A Chinese building abutted Western-style mansions on the main street
       of the French Concession   13
1.3   A teahouse in the artificial lake of the West Garden of the
       City Temple   23
2.1   Courtesan portraits from *Xinji haishang qinglou tuji* (1895)   39
3.1   Well-dressed courtesans acted like the streetwalkers in Ju'an li   56
3.2   Hoodlums harassed young maids escorting courtesan sedans in
       an alleyway   59
3.3   Illustrations from *Flowers of Shanghai* (1894)   61
3.4   A gambling party held in a courtesan boudoir in Qingyun li   78
4.1   Left: plans of the *li* house; right: site plan of a *li* compound,
       Shanghai   94
4.2   Entrance to Puqing li between shops   96
4.3   A house with modern-style windows in Zhaofu li   98
4.4   Illustrations from *Flowers of Shanghai* (1894)   99
4.5   Illustrations from *Flowers of Shanghai* (1894)   104
4.6   Flower opium houses in Langfang li during a police raid   108
5.1   The Bund in the International Settlement   116
5.2   Customers attempted suicides in Hongshun tang at
       Chessboard Street   122
5.3   Visitors fell from a building that used to be Beauty Water Terrace   125
5.4   The middle section of Fourth Avenue   126
5.5   A carriage accident in front of the teahouse Five-Story Building   128
5.6   Chinese convicts in a road-construction work   131
5.7   Two courtesans in a quarrel in two running carriages   133
5.8   A fire accident and a false fire alarm in teahouses   135
5.9   A brawl between a waiter and a madam in Building Number One   138
5.10   Customers joined the *yeji* for tea in a teahouse   139
5.11   A child hurt in an accident in the shop Quanheng   142
5.12   Illustrations from *Flowers of Shanghai* (1894)   143
6.1   Up One More Story Building and Gathering Harvest Court on
       Fourth Avenue   145

6.2   A leopard displayed in the entrance hall of First-Class Flavor   146
6.3   Two couples with their spouses swapped dined in
      First-Class Flavor   147
6.4   Ranking Jade House detained a customer   155
6.5   An accident in a village temple theater near Shanghai   157
6.6   The entrances of Heavenly Blessing Court and Heaven
      Immortal Court   159
6.7   An interior view of Red Laurel Court   160
6.8   A Hungry Ghost Festival parade at Suzhou   166
6.9   A procession escorting the statue of Tianhou through the
      foreign settlements   167
6.10 A clash between the police and a *saihui* parade on First Avenue   168
6.11 The Cantonese parade in the Jubilee of the International Settlement   170
6.12 A courtesan fell on the street after her rickshaw collided with
      a carriage   172
6.13 Shanghai Garden (Shenyuan) next to Tranquility Temple   176
6.14 A carriage accident in Zhang Garden   178
6.15 A meeting of Western merchants; a meeting of Chinese and
      foreign elite women   179

Acknowledgments

I have accumulated many intellectual debts to mentors, colleagues, and friends in the long process of writing this book. Its final revision in summer 2009 benefited enormously from Mark Selden's penetrating comments on the earlier chapter drafts, which had pushed me to think harder on the broad themes I wish to engage and helped me tighten my narratives. Mark has seen the development of this project since 2006 and I feel deeply indebted to him for his long-time encouragement and prodding. I wish to thank Ronald Knapp (whose work on Chinese vernacular architecture has always been a source of inspiration in my research) and two anonymous reviewers for Routledge for their insightful and critical comments on the earlier versions of the manuscript. I also thank the publisher's editors Stephanie Rogers and Sonja van Leeuwen for their interest in my work and their help in the publication process.

This book has developed from my doctoral dissertation completed in November 2005. I am grateful to my dissertation committee members for their candid advice during my studies at Binghamton University, SUNY. Special thanks to Tom McDonough for introducing me to the literature of nineteenth-century modernity, to Anthony King for teaching me more than just how to research and his attention to my academic endeavor, and to John Chaffee for many cordial and stimulating discussions.

I am greatly indebted to Alexander Des Forges for his meticulous reading of a chapter draft and the Introduction; his insightful and generous comments were extremely helpful in the early and final stages of this project. I appreciate that Dorothy Ko took time to peruse a earlier version of the manuscript; her encouraging and provocative comments helped me better organize the manuscript and identify its weak points.

Since I began my doctoral studies, I have benefited from intellectual exchanges with teachers, colleagues, and friends, including Barbara Abou-El-Haj, Roland Altenburger, Hilary Ballon, Karen Barzman, Kathryn Bernhardt, Morris Bian, Yomi Braester, Charles Burroughs, Sarah Fraser, Gail Hershatter, Amelia Jones, Abidin Kusno, Haiyan Lee, Steven Pierce, Stephen David Ross, and Nancy Um. I am also grateful to Fa-ti Fan, Jeffrey Kinkley, Wanning Sun, and Ruan Xing, who had read my dissertation or an earlier version of the manuscript.

I thank the Department of Art History at Binghamton University for funding my doctoral studies from 2001 to 2005. I had also benefited from the excellent service of Binghamton University Library. The British Academy awarded me a small research grant (SG-46135) for conducting more research related to this project in Shanghai in 2007. I also thank the University of Manchester for providing me with excellent research facilities since I joined the Chinese Cultural Studies program in 2006.

My experience with the city of Shanghai began in the early 1990s and I would like to thank Luo Xiaowei for supervising my Master's study in architectural history in that time. I also thank Chao for hosting my stays in the city in the last three years.

Finally, I thank my parents for their love and unconditional support to my pursuit of a career so far away from them. This book is dedicated to them.

***

Earlier versions of Chapter 3 and Chapter 4 were published as two articles in *Modern China* (33.3: 377–418) and *Journal of the Society of Architectural Historians* (67.4: 482–503). I appreciate that these journals have allowed me to include the published materials in this book.

I have presented materials from the book in a number of conferences and public lectures. Parts of Chapter 4 were presented in the Association for Asian Studies Annual Meeting 2005 and Art History Department, Pennsylvania State University in 2006. Parts of Chapter 5 were presented in Harpur College Dean's Workshop on Visual Culture, Binghamton University in 2005 and the Society of Architectural Historians Annual Meeting 2008. And parts of Chapter 6 were presented in the Association of Chinese and Comparative Literature Biannual Conference 2007, Sinologisches Kolloquium, University of Zurich in 2008, and Department of Art History, Northwestern University in 2009. I thank the organizers and audience of all these events for their comments on my presentations.

I also wish to acknowledge permission to reproduce the following illustrations: Figure 1.1: Author's digital compilation based on 重修上海縣城廂推廣租界地理全圖 (1901); Figure 4.1: Author's digital compilation based on Wang Shaozhou and Chen Zhimin, *Lilong jianzhu* (1987), pp. 9, 39; Figures 3.3, 4.4, 4.5, 5.12: Author's digital compilation based on *Haishanghua liezhuan* (1894); Figures 1.3, 2.1, 5.1, 5.4, 6.13: Courtesy of Shanghai Municipal Library; and Figures 1.2, 3.1, 3.2, 3.4, 4.2, 4.3, 4.6, 5.2, 5.3, 5.5, 5.6, 5.7, 5.8, 5.9, 5.10, 5.11, 6.1, 6.2, 6.3, 6.4, 6.5, 6.7, 6.8, 6.9, 6.10, 6.11, 6.12, 6.14, 6.15: Courtesy of Shanghai Daketang Culture Co., Ltd. (上海大可堂文化有限公司, the producer of *Dianshizhai huabao: Daketang ban*, 2001).

Samuel Y. Liang
Manchester
September 2009

Note: Unless otherwise cited, translations from Chinese sources in this book are my own.

Introduction

This book aims to reconstruct the spatial, visual, and gender modernity of nineteenth-century Shanghai, from the beginning of *huayang zaju* (mixed residence of Chinese [sojourners] and foreigners) during the Small Sword rebellion (1853–55) and the invasion of the Taiping rebels (1860–62) to the years around China's humiliating defeat by Japan (1894–95) and the beginning of the imperial reforms (1898), which initiated the Shanghai-based construction of a modern Chinese national identity. Its central argument is that modernity first arrived in China via a revolutionary concept of space rather than of time. My focus is not on the imagined space of new Chinese nationhood but on the urban spaces of everyday life, which are examined as fluid and dynamic configurations of social and gender relationships.

This focus on the late nineteenth century—especially the last three decades—and the city's everyday spaces reflects a different approach to modernity, in fact a different historicism, than those in the recent scholarship of late Qing Shanghai, which includes in-depth analyses in the fields of Chinese literature (Wang 1997; Huters 2005; Des Forges 2007), cultural studies (Yeh 2006; Meng 2006), and studies of print media and technology (Ye 2003; Mittler 2004; Reed 2004; Wagner 2007a). Theoretically informed and empirically based, these studies chart the development of Chinese modernity in Shanghai—especially of the period 1895–1919—with different emphases on dynamics within Chinese society, imprints of the West, or the native adaptation of the "global." While avoiding linear narratives and presenting nuanced analyses of the complexities and contradictions of the period, the scholarship either rediscovers early roots of a later Chinese modernity that fully flowered after the May Fourth Movement in 1919 or diagnoses alternative forms of modernity in literary production.[1]

The scholarship still embodies a historicism that centers on human activities and productions that evolved along the temporal dimension, though this dimension is often re-qualified negatively as nonlinear; it does not fundamentally challenge the historiography of modern China as a radical break with the imperial past but merely constructs revisionist narratives of *change* with greater sophistication and for the earlier periods. This sophistication and different temporal emphasis notwithstanding, the scholarship underscores the same historicism that late Qing and May Fourth reform thinkers had embraced. Leo Lee writes:

> Modernity in China… was closely associated with a new linear consciousness of time and history, which was itself derived from the Chinese reception of a social Darwinist concept of evolution made popular by the translations of Yan Fu and Liang Qichao at the turn of the century. In this new temporal scheme, present (*jin*) and past (*gu*) became polarized as contrasting values, and a new emphasis was placed on the present moment "as the pivotal point of making a rupture with the past and forming a progressive continuum toward a glorious future."
>
> (Lee 2000: 31, 1999: 43–44)

This consciousness of time signals the rise of humanism above the natural world and legitimates man's conquest of nature and the Western hegemony across the world. It contrasts sharply with the long-established Chinese view of the world in cyclical changes and history as natural obsolescence.

A history of "new nature"

The humanist history heralds the emancipation of mankind from the "dark ages" of religious enslavement, but it nonetheless evolved from the Judeo-Christian notion of sacred history, which had earlier chanted a salvation of mankind from the equally "dark" paganism of natural spirits. Modern theories of evolution and progress, such as social Darwinism, repudiated the notions of Creation and Salvation as well as emulated their linear and encompassing narrative.

China's embrace of the notion of historical progress in the twentieth century contrasted sharply with its resistance to Western missionary efforts that had for centuries sought in vain to bring a Christian "salvation" to the land of pagan "idolatries." The Catholic missionaries since the late Ming produced little if any substantial impact on Chinese society. Whereas missionary experiences, such as Jesuit studies of the Confucian classics, were reported back to Europe and contributed to the secularization of European powers and to the Enlightenment discourse of meritocracy and knowledge, China held on to its heavenly imperial order and the ideal of nature-man harmony in folk cultures rather than succumbing to any mandates that transcended the natural world and imperial territory.

It was later Western capitalist development—guided by the Protestant ethic and more concerned with expanding territory (of markets and resources) than with sacred history—that had more profound impact on Chinese society by positing a larger world of interconnected regions and rivaling imperial powers against the Middle Kingdom that had been imagined as the only civilized land (or empire).[2] Sacred history was now spatialized or secularized into a new civilizing or imperialist mission spreading from European centers to their colonies at the periphery. Derailed by that mission from its long-time imperial course, China was eager to construct its own master narrative of progress, resisting as well as mimicking the Occidental narrative. This resistance and emulation generated a discourse of modernity Lee succinctly summarizes above. It indeed testified to a change in the worldview from the natural obsolescence of human society to the secularized sacred history of a new nation—a change that was driven by the native desire to emulate a new and superior kind of imperialism rather than was imposed by Western players such as the missionaries or colonialists.

This emulation, as scholars have repeatedly shown, was full of reversals and contradictions rather than forming a linear progression. But we still need an interpretive framework for such reversals and contradictions—merely describing them as contradicting a linear historical process is not adequate. As unilinear historicism has been extensively critiqued in all fields, many scholars are influenced by the postmodern and poststructuralist attention to linguistic deconstruction or discourse analysis and to such themes as cultural pluralities, ambiguities, and hybridities, which all enrich our understanding of the complexities and messiness of modern history. But we would like to move beyond these complexities and details toward a generally structured understanding of modern transformation, for which I would suggest the thesis of the dual character of modernity, as summarized by Christine Buci-Glucksmann (1994: 98):

> On the one hand, the modernity of progress, derived from the grand Hegelian synthesis and lodged in evolutionist and historicist interpretations of Marxism, postulates a linear continuum of time, a development of culture and productive forces "without barbarism," an aesthetic of beautiful classical and Romanesque totalities, a vision of history in which a subject, however "alienated," gives it meaning.
>
> On the other hand, for the modernity which Benjamin draws out of the Baudelaire–Nietzsche–Blanqui constellation, the overcoming of the illusion of totality, system, and unicity in history makes it necessary to recognize an inescapable truth of catastrophist utopianism: namely, the central recurrence of barbarism, fragmentation, and destruction as a critical force.

Modernity also entails two contrasting ways of surmounting religious enchantment: one is to reinvent sacred history and apply it to secular space by, for example, replacing the journey to Salvation with a heroic progress toward utopia, and the House of God with a "public sphere"; the other is to critique the rational spatialization of time (which results in a homogeneous time-space that can be mathematically represented) via a return to the unity of nature and human history, and to redeem primordial mysticism as a critical force against pseudoscientific certainty. The latter approach posits natural transience against masculine monumentality; thus, instead of being a narrative of conquering the world according to (Western) man's design, history should merge into nature: "When… history becomes part of the setting, it does so as script. The word 'history' stands written on the countenance of nature in the characters of transience" (Benjamin 1977: 177; see Hanssen 1998). A few moments of reflection on these words would remind us of the ancient Chinese sages' teaching of the harmony of nature and man and the eternal transformation of seas and farming fields.

Inspired by Walter Benjamin's theological dwarf in historical materialism,[3] I intend to redeem a Chinese "traditionalism" in interpreting a hybrid form of Shanghai modernity that predated, and was later suppressed by, the hegemonic discourse of modern progress. Before being repudiated by later advocates of modernization, this "backward" traditionalism lingered in the timeless teaching of the legendary sages, the ancient art of pleasure and entertainment, and the folk beliefs of the local gods and spirits, as recorded in the "minor" writings of the period when a new industrial culture first took shape, but the narrative of national progress was yet to be constructed. This traditionalism entails a historicism that is not tainted with human (or Western) arrogance toward nature and the material world and therefore helps to diagnose industrial culture as a "new nature" that remains ever-the-same in spite of its progressive or fashionable appearances.

While sharing with many scholars the aim to demonstrate continuity between late imperial and modern China, my approach emphasizes how the new industrial culture reproduced the ever same and mythic nature. That said, this book nonetheless charts an unprecedented historical development of the "new nature" in late nineteenth-century Shanghai, which indeed marked a rupture of China's old imperial and local cultures and the beginning of the alienation of the urban communities from the natural and the rural.

In mapping this rupture as a distinct form of Shanghai modernity, I take into full account the impact of capitalist organization and modern technology on the native society, such as the commodification of bodies and things, the new form of open-style architecture, and the rationalization of the urban layout. But this "impact" was more manifested in the natives' active appropriation or domestication of "things modern"—a thesis Frank Dikötter (2007) has applied to the material culture of modern China. In fact, I consider the technological impact as hybrid rather than purely Western: the new technology was always put into practice through the combined effort of the colonial regime and native labor management, especially in the construction of the city's new residential compounds for native sojourners, which is examined in Chapter 4.

The hybrid modernity of which traditionalism is a crucial part has another part that demonstrates the imprints of the colonial powers and modern technology. I do not intend to offset the master narrative of Western hegemony by constructing a Sino-centric history that interprets modernity purely in terms of Chinese internal dynamics. Such a history, I suspect, would construct a new master narrative that merely reproduces the Eurocentric one, albeit in reverse.[4]

An alternative, and in my view more effective, way to resist the master narrative is to excavate what lies beneath it and expose what remains invisible to its totalizing lens—namely the city's everyday space and visual and material culture, as recorded in the contemporaneous travel notes, guidebooks, journalism, and lithographed drawings. Rather than reconstructing an encompassing narrative from these sources, I seek to reveal their hidden, unconscious agendas and the historical experiences that had settled in them like invisible dust.[5] These experiences are seen as mediation between the subjects and the new nature as their material surroundings rather than as "objective" historical accounts, and are fragmentary and contingent rather than complete and absolute. They are put together and reorganized in this book along the city's spatial dimension (from private to public) rather than forming a temporal narrative.

The fragments from the past thus assembled in this book are held together through my own interpretative angle, which on the one hand might shed insight into the period and on the other hand betray that my reading of nineteenth-century Shanghai is conditioned by, and seeks to better understand, the present in which we live. A redemption of the past is always for the sake of the present, as Benjamin (1968: 255) reflects:

> To articulate the past historically doest not mean to recognize it "the way it really was." It means to seize hold of a memory as it flashes up at a moment of danger. Historical materialism wishes to retain that image of the past which unexpectedly appears to man singled out by history at a moment of danger. The danger affects both the contents of the tradition and its receivers.

About a century and a score years separate the subject-matter of this book and the "dangerous" world condition under which it was written. As I am finishing its final revision, the world still struggles to cope with the worst financial crisis in decades; earlier, the research on which this book was based was conducted during the depressing years of Bush's administration.[6] I would consider my sketch of the cultural displacement of Shanghai sojourners to be conditioned by my own sojourn in the United States. If my readers do not keep this in mind, I would feel guilty of writing like an Orientalist who caters to the long-standing Western desire for an eroticized, exotic China, one that is always the other. On the contrary, I hope that my reconstruction of the pleasure and sorrow of the displaced natives in an emerging international metropolis is equally relevant to individuals in contemporary global society.

Gender, architecture, and visual culture

I have said that a Sino-centric history runs the risk of emulating Eurocentric narratives. The scholarly critique of Eurocentric and Orientalized images of China is of course justified, as is the feminist critique of long-established misconceptions of women. Thus historians of China and feminists often share a common task in recovering positive images from neglected historical records. In this project about Chinese modernity and gender, however, I adopt a different approach, being reluctant to give myself over to the baggage of history that might drag me to counter-efforts which I suspect might lapse into a new kind of positivism that is merely an inverted copy of the old bigotry. Therefore, I do not refrain from critiquing Chinese culture simply because it has been Orientalized for so long, or from exposing the everyday selves of men and women alike simply because the latter have long been marginalized. If some wretched images and decadent lives in this book might please the Orientalist or masculine ego, it is because they happen to be the latter's self-portraits, which have been cunningly displaced onto the other in the subject's effort to hide its own inner subjectivity.

For instance, I hope that my critical examination of the male perceptions of gender and sexuality in late Qing Shanghai would supplement the influential studies of Dorothy Ko (1994) and Susan Mann (1997). Ko and Mann show that traditional gentry households, usually considered to rigidly enforce gender division and hierarchy, in fact made possible impressive female achievements in work, writing, and education. They refute the May Fourth victimization of Chinese women by presenting a complex and dynamic picture of gender relations in Ming-Qing Jiangnan societies. To be sure, it is necessary to avoid overemphasizing the impact on society of a few elite gentry women and itinerant female professionals from restricted circles (though these circles extended beyond their families). Neither of these studies shows that these women subverted or challenged the existing Confucian structure. According to Ko (1994: 9), "the most educated members of the female population were inclined more to celebrate their role as guardians of Confucian morality than to repudiate it." She admits that her disagreement with the May Fourth formulations is not so much that they are not "true," but that they obscure the dynamics of Chinese society (Ko 1994: 3–4).

Perhaps a more effective way to refute May Fourth formulations is to locate the dissenting and subversive voices within the Confucian social structure, voices that were plentiful among male writers (though very difficult, if not impossible, to document among Chinese women). The real fault of the May Fourth formulations lies less in their victimization of Chinese women than in their failure to recognize that Chinese men were equally "victims" (as well as "beneficiaries") of the rigid social structure. Focusing on a place and moment that facilitated subversions of this structure but was still closely linked to late Qing Jiangnan, this book portrays not the achievement of the "victim" but the loss, alienation, and decadent pleasure of the "patriarch-turned-sojourner."

While mapping the city's gendered geography of street neighborhoods and public spaces, the second half of this book seeks to broaden our knowledge of the built environment of nineteenth-century Shanghai—its production as well as consumption. The architecture of modern Shanghai has been well documented and studied, but architectural historians mainly focus on iconic buildings designed by Western-trained architects in the early twentieth century and have not paid sufficient attention to late Qing buildings created by merchants, compradors, and construction guilds before the arrival of professional architects.[7] These buildings seemed to have formed a transitional type: on the one hand, they looked similar to vernacular architecture created by local craftsmen; on the other hand, they were the country's first commercial estates whose production reflected the capitalist ways of financing and development. But rather than seeing them as products of an incomplete modernization, I examine them as a distinct spatial type, embodying a Shanghai or Chinese modernity, one full of complexities and hybridities and in sharp contrast to the modern marked by purist designs and functionalist planning.

The late Qing buildings all disappeared from Shanghai when it was relentlessly modernized and rebuilt in the early twentieth century. I merely examine their representations in contemporary visual and textual sources, especially lithographed drawings from the pictorial *Dianshizhai huabao* (1884–98).[8] One might doubt whether these nineteenth-century graphic representations realistically recorded the city's built environment, but they surely reflected and influenced the sojourners' conceptualization of the city and its novel buildings and spaces. Contemporary photographic evidence shows that some lithographs faithfully rendered the buildings (see Yeh 2006: 103). Yet I have not used any photographs of the city in this book, not only because all available photographs from the period lack accurate dates, indexes, and provenances but also because the combination of images and texts in the pictorial allows much richer readings of the visual experience of the urban spaces than photographic records would.[9]

This visual experience was a key component of modernity in Shanghai. In mapping this modernity I construct the visual cognitive maps of the body and its decorations, the interior, the neighborhood, and the main street. The city's new spatial, material, and gender configurations were primarily mediated through the experience of viewing novel displays in the private and public spaces. Marvelous visual attractions seemed to have dominated everyday life in the city and marked a departure from the old lifestyle in which the unity of multisensory pleasures was more important than merely visual gratification. This emerging development toward a modern world of phantasmagoria or "the society of the spectacle" (Debord 1970) was also recorded in folk-style poems, guides, and travelogues.

I also rely on one—and only one—crucial fictional source, namely Han Bangqing's novel *Flowers of Shanghai* (*Haishang hua liezhuan*, 1894), in mapping the cultural and gendered geography of Shanghai. In a way comparable to Balzac's *La Comédie humaine* that cast a kaleidoscopic look at nineteenth-century Paris, the novel functions in this book like a prism through which a multitude of spatially related issues and events surface into view. The novel has been rigorously studied by scholars in Chinese literature (Wang 1997; McMahon 2002; Starr 2007); they have demonstrated the novel's unique contribution to modern Chinese literature and explored some cultural and ethical themes. Alexander Des Forges' (2007) meticulous and insightful examination of the novel in the context of late Qing media production convincingly demonstrates its influences on the emerging Shanghai identity. These scholars all situate the work in the literary tradition from the Ming-Qing courtesan novels to modern urban fiction and the novel is yet to be studied as a document of the social history of everyday life and entertainment culture in fin-de-siècle Shanghai. I hope that my intertextual analyses of materials from this novel as one of nineteenth-century historical documents also contribute the literary scholarship that mainly examines it for its own sake.

The organization of the chapters

This book highlights a hybrid and multifaceted modern development that stands in contrast to the positivist conception of the modern marked by progress and totality. Chapter 1 proposes the theoretical model of the book. Chapter 2 deals with the city's print culture and commercialization of literary production. Chapter 3 discusses the courtesan house as a surrogate home (private space). Chapter 4 examines a new kind of residential neighborhood (semipublic space). Chapters 5 and 6 survey a range of public spaces. These spatially defined chapters together reinter-pret the meanings of modernity by mapping the city's cultural geography that spreads from the body and (domestic) interior to the neighborhood to the street and public spaces.

Chapter 1 theorizes that modernity is embodied in the spatio-temporal strategy of capitalist development, which is marked by fragmentation and contingency rather than (the positivist notions of) totality and progress. In the China context, modernity (or modernization) as a linear historical progression under the impact of the West consisted of discursive ideals and images imposed upon a social framework that had shown remarkable resilience and continuity in the modern times. Nonetheless, this long-established framework, as exemplified by the social continuum of public and private spaces, of sacred and secular realms, and the organic configuration of rural and urban areas, was disrupted and fragmented by the artificial order of modern industrial culture, which first emerged in late nineteenth-century Shanghai via a new consciousness of space and materiality. In this process, many "traditional" elements marginalized by the neo-Confucian ide-ology, such as bohemian literati, itinerant merchants, and their ephemeral lovers (courtesans), played a role that was as important as the Western influences. The fluidity of spaces, identities, and the material existence of these transient people is analyzed in this book as the distinct manifestation of a hybrid modernity.

Chapter 2 examines the historical tradition from which the new urban literature was developed and its transformation after Western-style publishing mechanisms were introduced in Shanghai. Under the increasingly commercialized conditions of literary production, the literati-journalists depicted a city of novel and marvel-ous spectacles that was in sharp contrast to the timeless and natural world taught by the ancient sages. The surmounting of the sages and the commercialization of writing and publishing incurred a sense of isolation and loss among writers who found themselves abandoned into an alienating as well as pleasurable urban envi-ronment. As artificial urban wonders replaced timeless natural imaginaries in the urban literature, it prepared the readers for the city's new order of the machine. In examining this transition, special attention is given to the various genres of courtesan literature in which the courtesan's ambivalent image shifted between the allegory for nostalgia or self-pity and the icon of new commercial culture.

The courtesan house had become the sojourners' surrogate "home," one which inherited and parodied the communal function of the traditional household lost to the sojourners. In Chapter 3, the dynamics of this home are understood through closely reading *Flowers of Shanghai* as well as nineteenth-century guidebooks and travel notes. The male sojourners lacked comfortable, homelike residences and as a result adopted courtesan houses not only as places for romantic liai-sons but also as sites in which they could entertain friends, join broader social networks, and even stay overnight under circumstances that were materially and emotionally more comfortable than their temporary lodgings. The courtesan houses were marked by a different sense of family organization which merely masked their commercial nature, and a different set of gender roles, in which the courtesan could challenge normative understandings of male and female. The new types of relationship between clients and courtesans, and the interior spaces in which they encountered each other, were increasingly structured around material objects. By reinterpreting Freud's idea of the "uncanny" and Marx's concept of commodity fetishism in a different context, the chapter examines the implied connections between social and material realms and between traditional and industrial cultures.

The rise of the courtesan house signified a changing notion of "home," as both a physical and social space, in metropolitan culture. Chapter 4 maps the architectural and urban setting of this new type of home. Most of the courtesans and sojourners resided in the *li* residential compounds built with local materials and technology. The foreign landowners introduced a business model of large-scale production of houses for quick profit, but relied on their Chinese compradors and local builders to carry out specific construction works. Resulting from this hybrid production, the *li* combined vernacular architectural motifs with a rigid row layout, and generated fluid spaces between houses, neighborhoods, and streets, which replaced the traditional walled domains. The *li* was surrounded by busy shops and commercial space extended into the neighborhood, where houses were flexibly adapted for a wide range of residential and business uses. Analyzing textual and visual materials in *Flowers of Shanghai* and nineteenth-century periodicals, this chapter shows how these innovative uses, especially those in the courtesan houses, transformed the traditional spatial order and hierarchy, and how the borderline between the elite and the lower class was redefined as well as transgressed in the inclusive neighborhoods.

Chapter 5 examines social spaces outside the *li* compounds, highlighting the mythic perceptions of industrial marvels, the native adaptations of colonial spatial types, and the pursuits of private pleasure in the public realm, as recorded in the poetic, journalistic, and visual representations of the sojourners' experiences in the city's broad avenues, teahouses, and exotic shops. In the streets and teahouses, the spectacle of the "sea of flowers"—various kinds of courtesans and sex workers—not only testified to the erosion of traditional social order but also subverted the rational spatial order of Western-style mansions and avenues. But new displays and visual experiences generated in these spaces nonetheless trained the street crowds to behave collectively like an urban public. The chapter argues that the idea of the modern public is embodied in the new spatial arrangements and visual economy.

Chapter 6 continues to map the city's other public spaces such as restaurants, opium houses, storytelling houses, theaters, and commercial gardens. Unlike the promiscuous streets and teahouses, these commercial spaces were more exclusive, offering visitors a dream world in which everyone could enjoy the life of the "magnates and kings." The interiority of the traditional palaces and courtyard mansions then seemed to have been reinvented in the city. The city's cosmopolitan glamour so appealing to the masses was in fact for the new privileged, while the change of fortunes in the city made the borderline between the elite and the masses quite permeable. Analyzing luxurious interiors, theatrical spectacles, and artificial landscapes, this chapter demonstrates how the traditional concepts of class, gender, and religion transformed into fragmentary, short-lived, and secular-ized visual sensations. The chapter also discusses emerging developments that anticipated the spatial strategies of modern Chinese political movements.

In sum, by mapping the city's native spaces of leisure and everyday life, this book examines the implied paradoxes between, and the hybrid culture of, colonial modernity and indigenous innovation, the reinvention of traditional ideals and adjustments to the new industrial culture.

1   Fluid tradition, splintered modernity

In the early nineteenth century, Shanghai was already a prosperous market town that had developed beyond its walled urban core and formed a bustling suburb along the Huangpu River. But compared to major urban centers in the Jiangnan (or lower Yangzi) region, such as Suzhou and Yangzhou, it was still merely a frontier county seat. In the wake of the First Opium War, the Treaty of Nanking (1843) designated it an open port, and soon the British Settlement (1845) and the French Concession (1849) were established to the north of the old walled city. In 1863, the British Settlement merged with the American Settlement to form the International Settlement. In the beginning, the residents of the settlements consisted of only a few hundred foreigners and their servants. But during the Small Sword rebellion and the invasion of the Taiping rebels in the 1850s and 1860s, Chinese refugees streamed into the settlements, which became a city of mixed residence (*huayang zaju*). After the Taiping rebels were suppressed, many refugees returned home and the settlements fell into a temporary economic slump. From the 1870s on, however, Shanghai experienced phenomenal economic growth, especially in trade and real estate, and it attracted hundreds of thousands of immigrants and sojourners from the hinterland.

By the early twentieth century, Shanghai had become China's first modern metropolis, epitomized by the glamour of the Bund and Nanking Road. The city was also puzzlingly complex: the old and new Chinese districts adjoined the porous borders of the settlements, and even within the latter spectacular modern mansions in Western architectural styles abutted the dense sprawl of Chinese stores and dwellings. This juxtaposition of Western and Chinese spaces seemed to entail a dichotomy between modernity and tradition. As the unrivaled metropolis of the Far East, Shanghai combined economic growth and moral decadence, and it gained a reputation as "the Paris of the Orient," a modern pleasure land, but also a world of gangs, coolies, and prostitutes. Perhaps it was precisely these contrasts and complexities that constituted Shanghai's modernity.

Today scholars no longer see the rise of modern Shanghai as merely the result of Westernization, but the city's modernity is still mainly understood to reflect the impact of Western ideals, technology, and style. Mapping the cultural geography of early twentieth-century Shanghai, Leo Lee (1999) underscores the city's glittering Western-style façade and its influence on a few Chinese intellectuals who

Figure 1.1 Map of Shanghai, ca. 1901.

lived humbly in the crowded Chinese quarter but also frequented coffeehouses and other public spaces—the modern face of Shanghai. His conception of modernity emphasizes the Western impact on Shanghai and the formation of a new consciousness of time and history among Chinese intellectuals.

By contrast, Hanchao Lu (1999) explores the city's "traditional" side "beyond the neon lights" by focusing on the daily lives of the "little urbanites" in the *lilong* (alleyway) neighborhoods. He considers their lifestyle to represent China's past and tradition—the antithesis of Shanghai modernity that took shape under the influence of the West. But this "past" and the "tenacious traditionalism" of the displaced immigrants were, in fact, new developments in China's long history. Under

Figure 1.2 A Chinese building abutted Western-style mansions on the main street of the French Concession.
Sources: *Dianshizhai huabao,* March 1890; Wu et al. 2001: 7.23.

urban conditions that had never existed before in hinterland towns and villages, these immigrants had left behind their "past" and evolved new hybrid cultural forms, which became crucial marks of the city's multifaceted modernity.

A problem with the notion of a dichotomized Shanghai—modernity imported from the West versus tradition inherited from the past—is that the importation from the West was, in fact, quite unique in the world and the inheritance from the past also took equally new forms. It is precisely this hybridity that should be understood as Chinese modernity.[1] To argue for this uniqueness and the complexity of Shanghai modern culture is not to deny the imprint of the West. It is important to consider both the meaning of modernity in the nineteenth-century West and how it impinged on Shanghai and China then and later.

Space, time, and modernity

The emergence of modernity in the West was intimately associated with capitalist development, a rapid industrialization and urbanization process signaling a radical break with the past. The modern West was a bourgeois world marked by accelerated social changes, as Marx describes in the *Communist Manifesto*:

> Constant revolutionising of production, uninterrupted disturbance of all social conditions, everlasting uncertainty and agitation distinguish the bourgeois epoch from all earlier ones. All fixed, fast-frozen relations, with their train of ancient and venerable prejudices and opinions, are swept away, all new-formed ones become antiquated before they can ossify. All that is solid melts into air, all that is holy is profaned, and man is at last compelled to face with sober senses his real conditions of life, and his relations with his kind.
>
> (Marx and Engels 1976: 487)

Though "all that is solid" was usually a retrospective imaginary, indeed the modern world was marked by faster and fundamental changes. Here Marx mainly refers to the transition from a religious, feudal world to a secular, bourgeois one. This temporal narrative derives from Hegel's teleological and synthetic dialectics: the modernization of the West was driven by contradictions within European society, such as the struggles between religious and secular powers and between the aristocracy and the bourgeoisie; the old was defeated by the new, which in turn would be superseded by a more progressive class. But contrary to Marx's prediction, neither did religion disappear nor was the bourgeoisie defeated by proletarian revolutions; capitalism has constantly revalorized itself and become more powerful than ever, penetrating into every corner of the globe.

Capitalism's success at perpetuating itself is inseparable from its production and consumption of space (Lefebvre 1991; Harvey 1982, 2001). Since its inception, capitalist development has been all about acquiring new resources, capital, and external markets (which proved to be crucial in solving the internal contradictions of European society), as Marx perceptively notes: "The need of a constantly expanding market for its products chases the bourgeoisie over the entire surface of the globe. It must nestle everywhere, settle everywhere, establish connexions everywhere" (Marx and Engels 1976: 487). But Marx is too concerned with the temporal narrative to give due attention to this complex spatial strategy of capitalism. Instead, he oversimplifies the spatial dimension of capitalism in order to fit it into his totalizing historicism. His center–periphery model of capital accumulation suggests that capital first centered in one place (England or Europe) and diffused outwards to encompass the rest of the world (Harvey 2000: 32). Thus space is considered a homogeneous medium dominated by a linear movement, a one-way "civilizing process" from the West to the East and from metropolises to countryside:

> The bourgeoisie, by the rapid improvement of all instruments of production, by the immensely facilitated means of communication, draws all, even the most barbarian, nations into civilisation. The cheap prices of commodities are the heavy artillery with which it batters down all Chinese walls, with which it forces the barbarians' intensely obstinate hatred of foreigners to capitulate.
>
> (Marx and Engels 1976: 488)

Marx is not alone in painting this picture, which is equally attractive to his opponents. Liberals and conservatives, imperialists and nationalists, social Darwinists and fascists all embrace the Hegelian teleology and synthesis and project the transformation of modern material and social space onto a linear scale of total progress, even if this "progress" is directed at a retrogressive ideal.

Yet progress cannot account for the whole of this transformation, which neither leads to the demise of the bourgeois world nor sustains its infinite territorial expansion. The success of capitalism lies in its reproduction of space along a more complex temporal scale: there are constant returns to "barbarism" and fragmentation no less than progress. In the periodic commercial crises, "a great part not only of the existing products, but also of the previously created productive forces, are periodically destroyed" (Marx and Engels 1976: 489). Today the problem of overproduction is less embodied by crises than by isolated places, such as abandoned urban quarters in North American cities and sweatshop factories in costal China. By destroying old technology and consuming products, by creating uneven and patched regional and urban geographies, capitalism escapes the place-bound conflict between the rich and the poor and perpetuates itself with a spatial strategy of constant, contingent, and multidirectional movements (Harvey 2000).

Marx gives us a glimpse of the dark side of modernity when he compares modern bourgeois society "that has conjured up such gigantic means of production and of exchange" to "the sorcerer who is no longer able to control the powers of the nether world whom he has called up by his spells" (Marx and Engels 1976: 489). What the nether world is to the sorcerer is the new material world to modern men and women. The latter, being reduced to "the appendage of machinery," became slaves rather than masters. This crude materialist vision of the modern world contrasts sharply with the sacred humanism of the Renaissance: God is now dead, and man is no longer the favored center and master of the world, but is displaced, uprooted, and "alienated" by the new material nature he helps to create and destroy.

Marx's visionary solution to this spatial displacement and fragmentation, however, entails a return to anthropocentric historicism: though born in the lowest strata of society, Marx's proletariat hero, the collective revolutionary class, acts like the Renaissance man in restoring meaning to modern life and bringing back totality to a splintered world. Whereas this collective hero forges historical progress toward a classless utopia, Walter Benjamin's angel of history fixes his contemplative gaze backward at that fragmented material world:

> His face is turned toward the past. Where we perceive a chain of events, he sees one single catastrophe which keeps piling wreckage upon wreckage and hurls it in front of his feet. The angel would like to stay, awaken the dead, and make whole what has been smashed. But a storm is blowing from Paradise; it has got caught in his wings with such violence that the angel can no longer close them. This storm irresistibly propels him into the future to which his back is turned, while pile of debris grows skyward. This storm is what we call progress.
>
> (1968: 257–58)

This "progress" contrasts sharply with Hegelian progress. In Benjamin's "natural history," man's central stage is replaced with ruins and shards that bear cryptic traces of his creaturely existence. Like Marx, Benjamin considered the nineteenth century the crucial stage of capitalist development, but he saw it from the vantage point of the early twentieth century when the self-destructive power of the capitalist world was full revealed. His unfinished *Arcade Project* intended to draw a critical map of the artificial culture, or "new nature," of industrialization, consisting of dialectical pictures of objects and spaces discarded by that process (Buck-Morss 1989; Benjamin 1999).

If these objects and spaces fully reveal the infernal character of modernity, then they as "the powers of the nether world" can be redeemed as a critical force, not to restore the dream of a total order and thereby duplicate illusion, but to problematize the distinction between dream and reality. The industrial reality, the real, lived experience in the modern city, has become increasingly combined with phantasmagoric spectacles. If we realize that our current life in fact consists of and is conditioned by oneiric, incoherent images, then we may be able to recover from the last nightmare of a splintered world.

The problem of modernity in China

The temporal narrative, the anthropocentric historicism, has mainly informed the interpretation of modernity in early twentieth-century China as a radical break with the stagnant tradition (although this "break" has been pushed back to earlier times by recent scholarship). Assuming that this tradition mainly manifested itself in neo-Confucian values, we are tempted to paint a picture of modern China in which "all that is solid melts into air": those venerable ideals were swept away by a storm of modernization or Westernization. But the neo-Confucian ideology neither constituted a religious doctrine nor was exclusive to an aristocratic class, and as scholars have repeatedly shown, later imperial China was a secular and commercialized world with great social mobility.[2]

When the Hegelian teleology is applied to Chinese contexts, its internal drives are replaced with external impacts and its dialectical dynamics get lost in the one-way "civilizing process." The violent struggles between religious and secular powers and between aristocracy and bourgeoisie that had shaped the modern West are not evident in the making of modern China, where the social upheavals always entailed peasant revolts and internecine conflicts among warlords that can hardly be assimilated into the discourse of modernity. So aside from an industrial and technological revolution, what was *fundamentally* new in modern China?

The modern Chinese nation was based on the old imperial framework. Its leader inherited some privileges of the former emperor, its government officials were similar to the imperial bureaucrats, and even its intelligentsia and bourgeoisie were not new classes emerging from violent struggles in which they defeated their enemies; rather, they had evolved from the literati and merchant classes of the earlier period. Of course these new elites borrowed Western-style ideals and imageries in playing a progressive role. But these appearances merely hid their entrenched traditionalism, which was still best summarized by the tenet of mid-nineteenth-century reformers: "Chinese learning as structure, Western learning as application."

Thus it seemed that the long-established social structure had not melted into air. Because of this lack of revolutionary change from within, modernity in China was often seen merely as the transplantation of Western ideals and technology, coexisting in the same society with a backward tradition. But if the introduction of these ideals and technology did not lead to an internal social revolution similar to the one in the modern West, perhaps our assumptions about their roles in the formation of modern China should be called into question. In fact, modernity considered merely as an import from the West often consisted of superficial images imposed on a social framework that had shown remarkable resilience and historical continuity. This long-established social framework was often considered an essentially backward "Asiatic" tradition that resisted modernization, or simply ignored. But it, in fact, coexisted and functioned well with the capitalist system and absorbed the impact of the West without being drastically reshaped.

The narrow Eurocentric view of Chinese modernity entails a dichotomy between Asiatic tradition and Western modernity and between backwardness and progress that is misleadingly imposed on the fragmented geographies of China and its modern metropolises. As in the West, it is this very fragmentation of space that is paradigmatically modern. By denying this fragmentation and ascribing backwardness or traditionalism to a part of the modern geography, the positivist concept of the modern retains a narrative of total progress devoid of any internal dialectics. To avoid this grotesque distortion of modernity in the Chinese context, we need to reexamine the "traditionalism" that is so resistant to modernization and ask these questions: Did Chinese traditional society have its own internal dialectics containing the seeds of modern secular and commercial society, ones key to the creation of a hybrid, multifaceted modernity, when it came under the influence of the West? And what were the features of China's traditional social space from which the modern spatial fragmentation diverged?

The neo-Confucian continuum

In a sense, a certain medieval "revolution" during the Tang-Song transition had already "modernized" imperial China: an inclusive class of *shidafu* (scholar-officials or literati) replaced a few powerful, exclusive aristocratic clans as the ruling elite and broadly promoted education and meritocracy in Chinese society (Chaffee 1985; Ebrey 1991b: 45–53). Urban centers and regional networks, especially in the Jiangnan region, became noticeably commercialized (Twitchett 1968; Shiba 1970; Skinner 1977b: 23–26). At the core of this transformation, the neo-Confucian revival of classical learning had constructed a hegemonic ideology, which was then imposed upon extremely diverse vernacular cultures.

Neo-Confucianism was, of course, different from ideologies grounded solely in the sacred or public realm. It was not based on any divisions between the sacred and the mundane space, or between the public and the private; it centered around the ideal of an essentially private and secular space, namely the household. The rich documentation of the ritual practices mandated by this ideal suggests an unusual stability of family structure throughout the vast geographical area and time period of late imperial China and immense success of neo-Confucianism at both elite and popular levels (Bray 1997). A typical elite household was always a self-contained space, literally enclosed by high windowless walls; a complex of doorways, courtyards, halls, rooms, and gardens constituted a communal space of the extended family, a "hall shared by five generations" (*wudai tongtang*). Here the liturgical rituals of birth, maturation, marriage, and death were performed, rivaling the ceremonies of any "public" worship.

These rituals were sacred. Originally only the imperial or aristocratic family was entitled to practice them to demonstrate its political strength and noble standing. The decline of such families since the late Tang and the rise of the new elite in the Song called for a revision of the ancient rituals for broader application. Many early Song *shidafu* were often troubled by a sense that their roots were shallow, as they could not trace their ancestry to distinguished genealogical sources, and that their family's standing was insecure, as the fierce competition for limited official positions worsened their descendants' career prospects. In this context, the neo-Confucian scholars revised and reinforced the ancient rituals so that they could elevate their family standing to a level comparable to the former noble families (Ebrey 1991b: 46–47). But this also meant that any family with a good educational background could practice these rituals.

While the ancient rituals were a political expression of the powerful clans, the "modernized" rituals also sought to demonstrate the elite status of a family and endow it with a certain sacred and public nature. If the ancient rituals were a symbol of the state rather than a family, and the sacred rather than the mundane, then the modernized rituals had to negotiate meanings between these opposing realms. Indeed, in the self-contained household space, the public and the private and the sacred and the mundane were unified rather than opposed to each other. This rather ambiguous space centered around a patriarchal order which not only functioned as a "sacred" communal ideal but also organized everyday life in the household. Sima Guang, one of the founders of the neo-Confucian doctrines, laid out these rules:

> As the family head (*jiazhang*), he must carefully observe rituals and laws so as to rule his sons, juniors, and household multitude, divide them into specific jobs (such as in charge of storeroom, stable, kitchen, house property, field, or garden) and assign to them specific duties (including daily routines and unusual tasks), and see to it that they fulfill these responsibilities.
>
> As the subordinate or junior members of a family, for anything they do, large or small, they should not act on their own, but must notify the family head and seek his advice.
>
> Sons and their wives must not accumulate private assets. Their income from salary, field, and house should all be handed over to their parents, uncles, and

aunts; when they have expenses, they shall ask the parents [for permission] to use these resources. They dare not lend or give them [to others] in private.

(Huang 1341; Ebrey 1991a: 25; translation revised)

In such a household, family members had little private space and social relations were not so family-like; comparable to social and economic bonds in a feudal community, these relations were instrumental in maintaining the prosperity of the grand household as a social-economic production unit.

The neo-Confucian ideal of family aimed at a broader social order and was key to the construction of a homogeneous socio-political landscape structured along a continuous scale of hierarchical social institutions, ranging from patriarchal families to government seats at different levels to the imperial court. The concepts of extended family and filial piety were analogically applied in the "public" realms: local mandarin officials who took good care of their subjects were understood to be *fumuguan*, or "parent officials"; even the entire empire was seen as "private" property of the imperial family. Thus these public realms were also self-contained spaces that acquired a certain private nature, and were housed in walled complexes, as was a grand household. This organic spread of traditional social spaces stands in sharp contrast to the separation of public and private spaces and sacred and mundane realms in modern society.

Was this organic geography drastically altered by the onslaught of modernization? And was Chinese modernity manifested in the fragmentation of this unitary socio-political landscape? As we have seen, modernity is embodied in the spatial strategy of capitalist development: on the one hand, it knocks down all "Chinese walls" that impede its movement across national and global surfaces; on the other hand, it produces new geographical imbalances—more fragmented urban, regional, and global spaces—which then give momentum to the contingent flows of capital, labor, raw materials, and products. Along this dimension of modernity, we detect a similar development in modern China: the disruption and fragmentation of the idealized social-political continuum and the breaching of the walls that structured an organic but hierarchical system of self-contained social units.

This disruption also spawned a conflict between the artificial and the natural orders. Central to modern cosmopolitan culture is the ideal of the public sphere, or civil society, which is infinitely extendable (as well as pluralistic and fragmentary) rather than contained within definite bounds.[3] But this public sphere is essentially an artificial realm restrained by reason and law, and distinctly separated from the private realm, in which men and women may return to their natural state. The unity of the private and the public in the Confucian household, however, was based on the ideal of the harmony of nature and man (*tianrenheyi*): the household was a microcosm of the cosmological order; its patriarchal order was legitimated by heavenly laws and was supplemented by feng shui principles in seeking co-existence with the natural surroundings.

Similarly, the homogeneity or continuum of the various social structures and spaces was also organic and natural: the household was like a monadic cell, bearing the blueprint of the entire social organism; it was reproduced and multiplied to form villages, towns, cities, provinces, and the empire. The result was a continuous urban–rural landscape of human settlements (Mote 1977, 1973; Skinner 1977c, 1977d).[4] This organic layout of rural and urban areas would be disrupted by the artificial order of the modern metropolis; thus Shanghai soon became distinct from the rest of China.

If modernity in China can indeed be understood as the disruption of the organic social and physical landscape and the fragmentation of the self-contained spaces, were these transformations solely a result of Western influence? The European capitalist expansion surely played a key role in creating semicolonial enclaves distinct from the hinterland and a new urban order whose legible layout reflected industrial and technological efficiency. But the complexity of Chinese tradition and its modern transformation also entailed other less visible endogenous factors.

The discontents of Confucianism

The success of neo-Confucian ideology belied a cultural syncretism in late imperial China. We all reject the static and monolithic notion of Confucian China as an oversimplification of a complex society, but we should also notice that the abstraction of Confucian ideals from other cultural factors in Chinese society would oversimplify a messy reality. Taoism, Buddhism, and popular cults had distinct manifestations in various regional and local cultures. In the everyday lives of the elite as well as the populace, these diverse cultural elements were always mixed with one another and with Confucian values: behind the ritualistic façade of his palace, the emperor (and his ladies) had no trouble embracing at once a Taoist sect's promise of immortality, a Buddhist school's notion of paradise, and hedonistic pursuits of carnal, profane pleasure; the elite (or their wives) did the same in the inner quarters of their household complex. There was a distinct gender dimension to the dialectic of the Confucian and its alternatives. Usually in a household, a small Buddhist shrine was found in the inner quarter as its counterpart of the ancestral shrine in the reception hall. The latter represented the patriarchal order, while the former marked the mysterious and the feminine.

Though dismissed by the Confucian elite as vulgar, negative, and ephemeral, the alternative cultures profoundly shaped the history of late imperial China and generated regional, historical, class, and gender variations that refute the notion of a monolithic Chinese culture. In contrast to the unitary, organic neo-Confucian landscape, China was fragmented by diverse folk beliefs and dialects, and any local society was in turn fragmented by walls as well as extramural spaces such as streets and waterways, where there were no shared ideals such as Confucian values and no bonds between people like those in a household.

The complexity of Chinese society was also reflected in the discursiveness of neo-Confucian ideology itself, whose rather universal applications took on wide-ranging forms. These flexible applications potentially compromised orthodox Confucian teaching and planted within the hegemonic social structure seeds of rebellion. While the Confucian values had distinct meanings and functions in governments at different levels or households of different classes, they were also applied to societies beyond rulers and families and were sometimes deployed to contest the official realm and patriarchal authority. Three of the Five Relationships (*wulun*) central to the Confucian moral order—between father and son, husband and wife, and older and younger brother—were defined within the household; the fourth was a similar hierarchical relationship between ruler and subject defined in the court; but the last one, that between friends, crossed the household boundary and had to be defined in a fluid community.

The fraternal community of literati scholars also produced some alternative cultural practices. Their learning was driven by a desire to succeed in the impe- rial civil service examination system, which would lead to an honorable official career and gentry status. But the available government positions were so few and the examinations so competitive that most of the candidates suffered utter failure. Many gifted scholars then became disillusioned with the official realm and consid- ered themselves great talents unrecognized by society. Turning away from official- dom, they consoled themselves through a cult of nature—as embodied in aesthetic appreciations of mighty mountains and waters—which embraced Buddhist and Taoist ideals of personal spirituality rather than the moral and political implica- tions of Confucian values. Some chose to live like hermits, staying away from the "evil regime more vicious than a tiger." Such dissenting voices became more articulate in the Yuan, when many scholars in the south were at a disadvantage in competing for official positions and felt obligated to disassociate themselves from the alien Mongol court. In the Ming and Qing, the mainstream literati culture in the south remained independent from the court culture of Peking.

Aside from the cult of natural aesthetics, the literati culture entailed a hedonis- tic lifestyle, characterized by drinking parties in the company of female entertain- ers or courtesans. A young scholar's pursuit of success in the official realm also exposed him to temptations outside patriarchal control. His trip to the triennial examination site in a provincial capital such as Nanking was a chance to breathe different air than that in his austere household, as many pleasure establishments were located right next to the examination facility (Wang 1988: 78–83, 138–44; Ko 1997: 82–86). He might build friendships with other candidates in the pleasure quarter, where they all enjoyed a private life outside their family and self-pitying unsuccessful candidates could be consoled.

The fluid community of literati scholars and their ephemeral lovers was still a male-dominated world where domestic women were prohibited. But with the courtesans considered the men's equivalent, the community transgressed the Confucian gender code through the cult of *qing* (emotional love). As a critique of the lack of emotion and love in the traditional marriage, the concept of *qing* ideal- ized the romantic encounter between a gifted scholar (*caizi*) and a beautiful lady (*jiaren*), or between two scholars. Richly represented in Ming-Qing vernacular literature, such encounters were spontaneous and fleeting moments outside the patriarchal realm. In fact, the *jiaren* became an imaginary character onto which the scholar projected his subconscious protest against that realm. In the real world this imaginary character seemed to be best embodied by the courtesan in the plea- sure quarter, who, as a beauty gifted in music and poetry but fallen from the proper household, was imagined as a mirror image of unrecognized talent. Though the courtesan tradition can be traced back to the female entertainers hired or enslaved by the court and rich families in the Tang and Song, courtesan houses in Ming-Qing Jiangnan were commercial establishments independent of any Confucian structures.[5] These establishments nonetheless borrowed features from the Confucian structures and constructed a "home" away from home for the male patron.[6]

The success of neo-Confucianism was accompanied by increasing commercialization in late imperial China, especially in the Jiangnan region. While the well-to-do landowning gentry in this region always combined Confucian values with material fortune, merchants seemed to be too commercial-minded to be given a respectable position in the Confucian social hierarchy. Respect eluded the latter because they were detached from the land and agricultural heritage. They sojourned in various market towns connected by a system of waterways, and their floating world lay beyond the Confucian walls, consisting of canals, streets, boats, and stores.[7] Yet wherever they sojourned they carried with them the heritage of their ancestral land; their commercial network connecting market towns overlapped with the imperial system of administrative seats (Skinner 1977d). Thus, they also became closely associated with Confucian institutions, with which their guilds (*huiguan* or *gongsuo*) shared similar organizing principles; their guild houses were, in fact, built to resemble clan temples. These guilds emerged as a new power that negotiated with the local Confucian ruler (Golas 1977; Johnson 1995: 122–54), and wealthy merchants would eventually buy land and become assimilated into the gentry class.[8]

The merchants probably led more licentious lives in the pleasure quarter than did the literati. Whereas the latter always relived their romantic pursuits in composing poems and essays, the merchants were silent about their private life. Yet the elite merchants-turned-gentry would party with their literati friends in the courtesan houses. Though the courtesan was always romanticized as a female talent and a peer of the literati, in reality she closely followed the merchant's example in running her business.

In the fluid communities of self-pitying literati, itinerant merchants, and their ephemeral lovers, Confucian tenets were contested and parodied rather than observed. These communities and their spatial settings, such as seductive tour boats, bustling streets, and courtesan boudoirs, constituted subversive warps within the smooth socio-political and rural–urban landscape constructed by the neo-Confucians. The modern transformation of this landscape can be seen as resulting from an internal mutation that originated from the "warps" no less than from an imposed transformation under the impact of the West. In fact, it was the combination of these endogenous and exogenous factors that made possible the drastic transformation toward a hybrid and multifaceted modern urban culture.

Toward a splintered modernity

There was already a prosperous community of sojourners in early nineteenth-century Shanghai, consisting of merchants from Guangdong, Fujian, and other coastal areas, who established at least twenty-six trade associations before the

Opium War (Du 1983: 146; Goodman 1995: 49). As economic activities flourished beyond the walled county seat, a sprawling commercial suburb took shape in contrast to the orderly "Confucian urban core" (Johnson 1995: 96–97). But there was no clear borderline between commercial and Confucian spaces. Even the City Temple at the heart of the walled city became a marketplace of antiques and artworks, and the neighboring West Garden (Xiyuan or Yuyuan) that exemplified the traditional gentry culture was sold in 1760 by the Pan family (which was in decline) to the transport merchants, who later donated the garden to the temple and made it a meeting place of their guild (Chi [1893] 1989: 162; Figure 1.3). Around this time, Shanghai "courtesans" moved their businesses from boats on the Huangpu River into the walled city.[9] In the early 1850s, a range of different sex establishments was found at the heart of the walled city, in suburban hovels, and on the boats in the Huangpu (Wang [1860] 1992a: 5641–43). Thus was "Confucian" Shanghai transformed by those sojourner communities. Yet, until the arrival of the Western powers, this transformation had been gradual and within the control of the local authority.

The establishment of the foreign settlements not only raised Shanghai's prosperity to a new level but also created for the Chinese sojourners a "foreign place" (*yichang*) mostly beyond the jurisdiction of mandarin rulers as well as a safe haven from the later civil wars. In this *yichang*, where commercial ethos eclipsed

Figure 1.3 A teahouse in the artificial lake of the West Garden of the City Temple.
Source: Meihua 1894: 1.6.

Confucian values, the merchants did not have to purchase gentry status to gain social recognition. Instead, they emulated the foreign traders and Chinese compradors to expand their businesses and power bases; many started humbly but quickly became nouveaux riches. Within half a century, the first generation of Chinese industrialists and bourgeoisie was born in this treaty port.

Business opportunities in the settlements also attracted other immigrants from agricultural hinterlands, who took up a wide range of urban occupations, from the storekeeper to the rickshaw puller. Among them were a few literati who were unsuccessful in the imperial examinations and had become salaried writers, usually employed by foreigners. These men of letters were among the first to learn Western ideals; they were the predecessors of a later generation of Chinese intellectuals who promoted "democracy" and "science" in the early twentieth century.

In the settlements, entertainment businesses also developed with great sophistication, revolving around the exquisite houses of elite courtesans. These female entertainers marketed a homelike space to the male sojourners and became, as Catherine Yeh (2006) shows, the city's cultural icons. Their iconic image signified the decline of the old Confucian order and could be considered a harbinger of Shanghai modernity. But a couple of decades later, this harbinger became an antithesis of modernity as the ideology of national and public progress replaced Confucian values as the new hegemonic narrative. Thus, unlike the merchants and literati who evolved into the key players in modern Chinese society, the courtesans fell "from a throne of glory to a seat of ignominy" (Lemière 1923; Henriot 1996). In the new modernization discourse they were equated with common prostitutes, a social vice to be regulated or eliminated (Hershatter 1997). Because of this later discourse, the role of the nineteen-century courtesan economy in eroding the Confucian social order and thereby paving the way for modern positivist ideals has never been fully acknowledged, despite the fact that the earliest reformists and revolutionaries often held meetings in courtesan houses (Yeh 1997).

The courtesan business is usually considered an archaic, elite form of prostitution. When Christian Henriot (1996: 156) writes that "Chinese courtesans belonged to a cultural tradition and a social structure that could not survive the onslaught of modernity," he does not realize that this "tradition" was an alternative to the hegemonic one and that its rise was in fact a crucial component of the modern transformation. Elsewhere he seems to realize the complexity of the courtesan culture:

> It would be futile to try to force this phenomenon into a framework of tradition or modernity. It was but a straw in the wind, an ephemeral and nostalgic movement corresponding to a final unconscious and involuntary burst of energy on the part of an elite that was already profoundly destructured and had reached the threshold of a more radical and even more brutal transformation.
>
> (Henriot 2001: 72)

But this problematic phenomenon clearly refutes the reductive understanding of tradition and modernity as mutually exclusive. Henriot dismisses the "unconscious and involuntary burst of energy" too quickly.

Influenced by poststructuralist theories of discursive practice, Gail Hershatter (1997) presents the narrative histories of Shanghai prostitution as seen by literati, reformers, regulators, and revolutionaries. Her study, which focuses on the twentieth century, tracks the place of prostitution in ongoing debates about the shape that Chinese modernity should take and considers prostitution "key" to modern Shanghai (Hershatter 1989: 464, 1996: 168). But prostitution appears in her study merely as a foil to the positivist discourse of modernization, and her tracking of the transformation of the discourses and practices of prostitution conforms to a teleological process of modernization, which was to eliminate or regulate prostitution as it turned from a luxury market in courtesans to mass prostitution. The courtesans in her work were therefore simply expensive prostitutes, whose image in the eyes of Republican writers often evoked a nostalgia for the courtesans' "golden age" in the late nineteenth century. These writers often recycled earlier literature rather than presenting original observations. This problem in Hershatter's twentieth-century sources indicates that the earlier period was a crucial moment in the history of Shanghai prostitution.

The rather unique courtesan culture of late nineteenth-century Shanghai merits a more sophisticated treatment. There was always a full-fledged sex market—whether in the prosperous urban centers of Ming-Qing Jiangnan or in late Qing Shanghai—in which the courtesans were involved with the elite. But their social role was extremely complex: they were icons of beauty and glamour as well as women for sale, and their establishments were both exotic and homelike, real and dreamlike. The courtesan provided a comprehensive set of services that ranged from singing and conversation to companionship and sex, and seemed to combine the roles of diva, mistress, and upscale call girl in modern society. Thus she represented the male sojourners' integrated leisure lifestyle, which was soon to be replaced by the fragmentation of modern life that separated cultural icons from sex workers, and dream images from physical pleasures.

Although the courtesan gradually entered the market of mass prostitution, her iconic image evolved into the modern spectacle of the star. This theme was explored in Yeh's (2006) study of entertainment culture in late Qing Shanghai. Yeh argues that this entertainment culture played an "unwitting role" in the city's modernization at large and highlights the courtesan's positive impact in "modeling the modern." This imaginary construct of the courtesan as a "heroic" modernizing agent is mainly based on brash tabloid representations (produced by men) and falls short of noticing the fact that many Shanghai courtesans were virtual slaves in the business establishments (i.e. courtesan houses). Yeh also compares the "new" craved by the courtesans with the "new" promoted by the later reformers such as Liang Qichao (Yeh 2006: 341). But she does not sufficiently recognize that the "new" craved by the courtesans was all about everyday life, and that the "new" promoted by the later reformers was an ideological construct. While the adoption of "Western-style" material culture by the late Qing courtesans and their patrons might have anticipated some "progressive" movements in the following decades, these later movements could not have changed the decadent nature of the preceding period. Just before the aftermath of China's humiliating defeat by

Japan, that period was quite unique: Shanghai's "decadent" lifestyle was not disguised by any ideological narrative or troubled by any sense of national crisis.

In their rediscovery of this period as a crucial stage of Chinese modernization, revisionist histories of Shanghai—which have been produced by the city to glorify or legitimate its current reglobalization, and to a lesser extent by Western scholars—have reiterated the positivist ideal of progress. These new histories of the rise of colonial Shanghai from the late nineteenth to the early twentieth centuries are more celebratory than critical. They examine the emergence of a new urban culture under the impact of commercialization and Western ideology as well as the modern regulation and policing of prostitutes, gangs, and the unruly masses. They largely see nineteenth-century modernity as incomplete, repressed, or merely preparatory for a fully flowered modernity in the next century.

In contrast, I view nineteenth-century modernity as another form of modernity rather than a premature version of the positivist notion of the modern. This other modernity was a hybrid, and the Chinese sojourners did not just play a passive role in its formation under the impact of the West. Instead, these traditionally marginalized people, such as bohemian literati, itinerant merchants, and courtesans, actively appropriated Western-style material culture and reinvented (or domesticated) it as a distinct new Shanghai culture.[10] The formation of this urban culture involved a process of decay and disintegration. Within a couple of decades, this ongoing process was repressed under the newly constructed narrative of national progress. I aim to redeem this process as a critical force against that narrative.

Nineteenth-century Shanghai witnessed a rupture of the organic spread of traditional walled domains from private families to the empire and a disruption of the seamless landscape of villages, cities, and the capital. Displaced from their homeland and reduced to alienated labor, the Chinese sojourners led a decadent lifestyle in the pleasure houses and on the streets. Their feeling of alienation was balanced by physical pleasure rather than disguised by the imagination of total progress. Whereas the notion of total progress was an ideological construct superseding and reinventing the former Confucian ideals, the decadence reveals a lack of existential meaning in the modern world and the fortuitousness of capitalist production.

Rather than interpreting modernity purely along the temporal dialectic of progress and decline, this book maps the spatial and material existence of those transient people. This spatial modernity is manifested in the sojourners' new conceptual configuration of home, city, and beyond—an imaginative geography drawing on their empirical experience of the new material conditions.

2 The convergence of writing and commerce

As outlined in the last chapter, the organic system and layout of neo-Confucian spaces, including households, villages, and towns in late imperial China, was above all an imaginative geography, which after layer-by-layer charting, writing, and building solidified as truth. It drew on the teachings of the ancient sages, such as Confucius, whose worldly wisdom was transmitted variably but timelessly, often via stories and parables told and retold and eventually collected in the classics.

As Benjamin (1968: 83–109) points out, the age of the storyteller and the sage waned upon the rise of information and the novel as the dominant forms of communication in the modern age. As the timeless narratives modeled after nature died out along with the legendary sages and storytellers, modern urban literature and information created new narratives that referred to, and were verifiable in, specific moments and places in the shared space-time of the capitalist world. The new narratives prepared the readers for that world, one dominated by the machines, or the "new nature."

A similar development can be detected in modern China: the advent of modernity incurred ruptures of the sages' imaginative geography, which manifested as textual reconstructs no less than physical remappings. Indeed, literary modernity since the May Fourth Movement has been considered to be a cultural enlightenment that repudiated the established notion of learning rooted in the classics. Yet well before that moment, and even before Liang Qichao's new novel movement at the turn of the twentieth century, the commercialization of literary production in late nineteenth-century Shanghai already entailed a gradual distancing from the sages' space-time as well as continuity with Ming-Qing print culture. Jointly created by native men of letters and foreign merchants with newly introduced technology, a new media-based literary culture posited an urban geography of marvelous and seductive spectacles against the timeless imaginaries of the Middle Land, and let the historically marginalized literary genres of travel notes, urban guides, casual verse, and vernacular fiction evolve into the dominant styles of urban expression.

Below I first sketch a condensed picture of the timeless space of the Middle Land as imagined in the late imperial print culture, and then contrast it with new developments in the Shanghai print media. I do not mean to suggest that the concrete social spaces perceived by different people in late imperial China were all unchanging like the abstract spatial concepts in the classics. Rather, I intend to show that the dominant spatial imagery in literary production went through a drastic transformation in the works of the writers who had been trained in the classical tradition but were displaced into a new urban and commercial environment.

Imaginative geography and print culture

Neo-Confucian learning was quite different from the esoteric teachings of Buddhist and Taoist schools. It was concerned with defining proper conduct, or orthopraxy, in the secular realm rather than with the orthodoxy of a sacred origin or transcendental world.[1] The classics did not envision a (sacred) historical process but merely offered timeless and worldly guidance, which basically ignored distinctions between past and present. Yet China's long history was certainly not of a static tradition living in the past, as obsessions with the past in Chinese society (such as with the ancestral cult) in fact served to ensure the well-being and continuation of the present. There were no futuristic visions of either teleological progress or cataclysmic change in the classics. The sages' wisdom reduced this immense continent of constant transformations into an unchanging "heavenly creation," equating ever-changing with ever-the-same and interpreting social upheavals as natural obsolescence.[2] Thus, the classics never prophesied an inevitable destiny of humankind but envisioned an ahistorical world that was both social and natural.[3]

Nor was there a concept of otherworldly paradise in the classics, which instead envisioned an earthly "paradise"—none other than the Middle Land (*zhongtu*), the only civilized, worthwhile country amidst barbarous territories. In promoting proper moral and political conduct in this idealized world, the classics ignored the particularity of any location within it: any social spaces of either family or polity were conceived to be analogous to one another, as the opening chapter of *The Great Learning* (*Daxue*) stipulated: "The ancients who wished to illustrate illustrious virtue throughout the kingdom [*tianxia*, or all under the heaven], first ordered well their own states. Wishing to order well their states, they first regulated their families" (Legge 1966: 310). This analogy conceived social spaces of different sizes and sites in the idealized model of the self-contained unit: a collection of such units formed a larger but similar unit. The spatial embodiment of this model was the walled courtyard, which as the basic unit of houses, palaces, and temples accommodated diverse social functions. Thus households, public institutions, and even cities became similarly structured spaces, of which the courtyards were centers and the extramural spaces were peripheries.

The courtyard not only represented the artificial code of family and state but also reflected the cosmological order, which was also manifested in the nature of human existence and material things. The classics reproduced the family-state analogy in the relation between person, mind, and things:

> Wishing to regulate their families, they first cultivated their persons. Wishing to cultivate their persons, they first rectified their hearts. Wishing to rectify

their hearts, they first sought to be sincere in their thoughts. Wishing to be sincere in their thoughts, they first extended to the utmost of their knowledge. Such extension of knowledge lay in the investigation of things.

(Legge 1966: 310–12)

Thus an encompassing analogical relation between things and beings was constructed, which on the one hand linked the *shen* (person/body) to the family and state, and on the other linked the mind to external things of nature. Indeed, the analogy between small/inner and large/outer space was based on the idea of nature, which either a huge mountain range or a tiny tree leaf could embody. The courtyard was then built as a miniaturized universe, a complete "natural" realm in which mountain, water, and plants were re-created. Thus nature as a realm outside the manmade space was also its prototype. This inherent naturalism was combined with the rational social order mandated by the classics and framed by the walls to form a harmony between nature and man (*tianrenheyi*).

With this syncretism of the social and natural orders and of history and nature, the sages' teaching attained an enduring and universal standing without invoking a transcendental origin or an inevitable destiny. Their authority lay in nature rather than in any supranatural ideals, leading to a discursive rather than an absolute concept of authorship in Chinese literary production. Confucianism became influential mainly through the dissemination of the classical texts, which were recomposed from the memory of Han scholars (after the originals were destroyed in the Qin) and continued to pass through the hands of later editors such as the neo-Confucian scholars of the Song. The authorship of these texts became rather legendary as their formations and transformations reflected a collective work through the ages. Layers of experience were piled up in them and in the wisdom of the legendary sage, who came to his readers from the totality of an immeasurable scope of space and time rather than from a specific site and moment in history. Indeed, the sages' terse words were comparable to dry seeds that contained rich genetic codes; when drenched in the experiences of their interpreters, they sprouted anew and lived an afterlife as practical wisdom.

The sages' teaching mandated an orthopraxy of household rituals that created an illustrious family legacy. The rules for these rituals were stipulated in the ancient classics *Liji* (Records of ritual) and *Yili* (Etiquette and ritual), the most authoritative texts in establishing the names and sequences of the steps that constituted Confucian family rituals. But the rules in these archaic texts could not be mechanically put into practice, so new texts were written to supplement them, most notably imperial ritual codes and private etiquette books (Ebrey 1991b: 44). In the Song, the rise of the scholar-official class led to a major revision of these rituals originally designed for exclusive aristocratic clans. As a result, Zhu Xi's *Family Rituals* (*Jiali*) became the standard text for guiding ritual practices in gentry households of the late imperial period (Ebrey 1991b: 145–66). This neo-Confucian text also went through later revisions and adaptations. In the Ming, writers (or editors) reshaped it to suit their readership. They responded to the demand of book buyers by adapting the original text to include Ming rules, adding numerous subheadings and illustrations and incorporating ideas and practices from outside the orthodox Confucian tradition. Their work shaped how people talked about, performed, and experienced the rituals (Ebrey 1991b: 167–68).

Thus was the afterlife of the ancient rituals and classics. These later editors were to the classics what the storyteller was to the tales he heard from others. As an artisan form of communication, storytelling "sinks the [tale] into the life of the storyteller, in order to bring it out of him again" (Benjamin 1968: 91–92). Similarly, the revision of the classics sank the sages' wisdom into the lives of the modern interpreters, in which it led an afterlife that grew out of them again.

The demand for up-to-date interpretation and adaptation of the classical texts was accompanied by a sophisticated print culture. The neo-Confucian promotion of learning in every sector of Chinese society was supported by a continuous development of the publishing business, which reached a new stage in the late Ming when economic growth stimulated demands for luxury goods such as books (Clunas 1997).[4] Ebrey's study (1991b: 231–34) lists forty-eight Ming editions of *Family Rituals*—thirty-one from the late Ming—testifying to this publishing boom. As guides to the formal organization of the elite household, these "modern" editions provided detailed directions on various rituals and daily etiquette. There were also other kinds of guidebooks or manuals on the hobbies and tastes of the refined gentry, such as tea tasting, incense burning, and collection of rocks and antiques (Ko 1994: 45). There were guidebooks on the interpretation of dreams, divination, fortune-telling, geomancy, medicine, jokes, and verbal games as well (Shang 2003: 190). Broadening the scope of elite culture, these guides pretended to spread the sages' wisdom in offering readers useful counsel. But compared to the revised ritual manuals, the guides were more ephemeral in nature and were often anthologized into a kind of daily life encyclopedia. Compiled in haste for quick profits, these guides borrowed contents from one another and became books of miscellaneous information, which in a way anticipated modern print culture.

The authors of these commercial publications were often anonymous. The editor's name, rather than the author's, featured prominently on the cover or title page (Shang 2003: 190). The editors of the new editions of *Family Rituals* played the important role of interpreting and revising original sources; Ebrey (1991b) considers them authors. Such productions still reflected a syncretism of the collective experience of a broad scope of time and space rather than being individual works grounded in specific moments and sites. Some remnants of the sage or storyteller remained in them.

Such remnants were also visible in vernacular romances and dramas that flourished in the Ming and Qing as "lowbrow" genres outside the classical canon. A romance usually opens with a mythic scene in which the narrator acquires the story from an immortal or sage as the personification of countless storytellers whose craft and experience through the ages have accumulated in the narrative. It usually has a specific historical setting, but merely as a convenient starting point from which the storyteller spins timeless or anachronistic tales. Different from such pseudo-historical narratives, Cao Xueqin's masterpiece *Dream of the Red Chamber* (*Honglou meng*) employs an ageless setting:

> If you say no dynasty or date can be ascertained in my story, you may falsely borrow a date from the Han or Tang dynasty. How easy is that!. . .Since I only want to tease out patterns of things and reasons of sentiments, why shall I be limited to a dynasty and period?
>
> (Cao and Gao 1971: 3; trans. Cao 1968–70)

Here Cao emulates the sage or storyteller in order to transmit timeless wisdom. While avoiding a false dynasty, his novel is set in a real city, the imperial capital Nanking, which foregrounds the prestige and wealth of two grand households. Everyday life in these houses, however, is separated from the city by their high windowless walls. This lack of spatial interconnectedness with the city mirrors the ageless picture of the households, whose rise and fall resemble natural obsolescence.

What *Family Rituals* left untouched beyond the formalities of the Confucian household is portrayed in detail in *Dream of the Red Chamber*: the former promoted and guided orthopraxy in the courtyard-hall as the patriarch's central stage; the latter constructs a courtyard garden as the playground of a few "extraordinary women" (*yiyang nüzi*) and then lets it fall apart. Cao is a homebound storyteller spinning tales out of his own experience. Though depicting everyday life in the elite households, Cao's novel is filled with marvelous (*qi*) content that appeals to the ordinary folks, who "do not like to read the [sages'] wisdom of moral and governing, but like fun and impertinent words" (Cao and Gao 1971: 1). Both Cao and the romance authors celebrated the strange and extraordinary in critiquing the Confucian normative, drawing on the timeless and placeless imaginaries of the homebound storyteller rather than the traveler. Just as landed gentry and peasants humbled itinerant merchants and artisans, the homebound storyteller overshadowed his rival who gathers tales from travel.

Nevertheless, late imperial China had a very mobile population and its natural sceneries and urban centers attracted many travelers, including business sojourners and sightseeing literati. The latter would write *biji* (notes or short essays) to record natural wonders, cultural activities, and anecdotes in specific periods and localities. Often published under titles that ended with (*za*)*ji* or *lu*, these travel notes were quite different from both the classics and vernacular fiction. Their authors were not storytellers but scholars trained in the classical language, and their miscellaneous contents included accounts of personal experiences as well as factual information about the localities. Some notes were similar to records of local history and customs (*difangzhi* or *fengtuzhi*), such as Li Dou's *Yangzhou huafang lu* (Record of Yangzhou tour boats, 1795). Local cultural customs were also recorded in informal short verses known as "bamboo poems" (*zhuzhici*) that were collected into volumes. While the ritual manuals and daily life encyclopedias directed household affairs, the travel notes and local literature could be read as guides for pleasurable trips to various urban or suburban locales, which were much more transient and fluid than the space framed by the classics or household manuals.

The travel notes often depicted the *huafang*, or ornate tour boats, often with courtesans aboard, on scenic waterways at major urban centers such as Nanking and Suzhou. In the neo-Confucian geography there were no places for such water-ways or streets, because they were the locales of transient people such as mer-chants and courtesans and constituted a problematic realm between the walled courtyard and pristine nature. Located within or nearby a city structured in the Confucian order, the streets and waterways were the other space of both society and nature; marginal or placeless as they were, they formed pleasurable and sub-versive warps within that idealized geography. The literature about them formed a genre outside the mainstream tradition: Yu Huai's *Banqiao zaji* (Miscellaneous notes of Banqiao, 1654) on the pleasure quarters in late Ming Nanking had become a "classic" of this genre and inspired such later imitations as *Xu Banqiao zaji* (Sequel to the miscellaneous notes of Banqiao, 1784) and *Qinhuai huafang lu* (Record of Qinhuai tour boats, 1817). These works invoked a sense of nostalgia for the transitory spaces and people they recorded; this nostalgia to a great extent retained the timeless nature of the classics, making their writings much less specific in time than in space.

Hybrid journalism

The imaginative geography of the natural and cosmological order, as constructed in the Middle Land's classical and "lowbrow" literature, gradually lost its ideo-logical standing in the nineteenth-century treaty ports in the face of the advances of Western powers and modern technology.

Since the late Ming, the Jesuit missions had sought in vain to introduce to Chinese society a supranatural order. Early nineteenth-century Protestant mission-aries were a little more successful, especially with the help of modern print media; they published the first modern Chinese periodicals from their bases at Malacca, Canton, and Macao (Britton 1933: 16–29). Bolstered by advanced printing and communication technology, such media could be effectively deployed in religious missions that aimed to convert the unruly Chinese masses into an organized soci-ety under the vision of a common destiny. Similarly, the modern secular media educated the masses in the form of free political discourse in a disinterested and unbounded public sphere. The missionaries traveled in the boats of European trad-ers, whose capitalist development shared with the former's evangelical mission many interests and strategies. It was ultimately the territorial expansion of capital-ism that breached the "Chinese walls." Commodities and gunpowder surely con-tributed much to this process, but the introduction of modern print media probably played the most crucial role in breaking down the wall in the collective mind of Chinese society and thereby transforming its established conceptions of space and time.

Before the advent of modern presses in China, local news and stories were circulated mainly through spoken words. In major cities there were some popular illustrated newsprints known as *xinwenzhi* (newssheets) spontaneously printed and hawked on streets whenever eventful news occurred; they dramatized real events like folktales.[5] The imperial court also had a system to distribute its edicts and memoranda to various official posts through the *Peking Gazette* (*Jingbao*), whose terse texts were similar to official chronicles and needed to be interpreted by experienced readers (Mittler 2004: 173–242).[6] These news items were rather different from the edited and explained information in the modern press. While the latter sought to "educate" the reading public and inform them of a progressive world, the former merely chronicled events in the empire.

The development of capitalism required that up-to-date information of local societies in different regions be gathered for traders whose business connected these areas separated by great distances. Both Chinese and Western merchants in Shanghai needed to be well informed of government policies and local customs. It was in this commercial milieu that Western-style newspapers were introduced: *The North China Herald* (1850), *The North China Daily News* (1864), and its Chinese edition, *Shanghai xinbao* (Shanghai new paper, 1864), were among the first modern newspapers published in China. They were all founded by Henry Shearman, an auctioneer and business agent; three missionaries, Marquis L. Wood, John Fryer, and Yong J. Allen, served as the editor of *Shanghai xinbao* (Britton 1933: 49–50).

The London Missionary Society Press at Shanghai also sought to reach the Chinese readership by employing native scholars. Wang Tao helped Walter Henry Medhurst and his colleagues translate the Bible and later assisted James Legge in translating the Confucian classics. Though Wang did the writing, his foreign employers closely supervised his work and so "butchered the Chinese language" that "even Confucius, if resurrected, would [have found] it impossible to correct their composition" (Wang 1880: 2.2; Cohen 1974: 13). The Chinese employees of *Shanghai xinbao* were in a similar situation. Its foreign editors did not compose the articles but gave the substance to their Chinese aides, who did the phrasing. The contents included excerpts from the *Peking Gazette* and the new Chinese newspapers in Hong Kong and condensed translations of news and advertisements from *North China Daily News* (Britton 1933: 50). There was also considerable religious content, which might have hindered the paper's growth (Xu and Xu 1988: 86). Overall it was an alien press that claimed to bring enlightenment to the backward Chinese. This patronizing attitude had limited appeal to literati readers, and in 1872 *Shanghai xinbao* met a formidable rival.

The brothers Ernest and Frederick Major arrived in Shanghai from Britain in the early 1860s as venture businessmen and enjoyed some initial success in the tea trade and chemical manufacture. Following the advice of his comprador Chen Xingeng, who noticed the robust sales of *Shanghai xinbao*, Ernest Major decided to establish a Chinese newspaper. The first issue of *Shenbao* (Shanghai daily) was published on April 30, 1872 (Britton 1933: 66). A pragmatic businessman probably more connected to Chinese merchants and literati than to foreign diplomats and missionaries, Major foresaw a potentially immense native reading market and made the *Shenbao* a paper for the Chinese, by the Chinese.[7] With literati as its editors and contributors, the paper gained considerable appeal among local readers, and consequently *Shanghai xinbao* went out of business eight months after the launch of the *Shenbao*.[8]

A crucial factor in the success of the *Shenbao* was that it first introduced editorials as an integral part of newspaper content (Mittler 2004: 55). In these editorials, Major's mercantile pragmatism lay underneath the sublime rhetoric of his literati employees. Unlike the awkward relationship between the missionary editors and their Chinese aides, Major and the literati collaborated closely, which also contributed to the paper's success. And their joint product more effectively challenged the established ideology than did the missionary presses.

The editorial of the inaugural issue compares the paper with "abundant works by chroniclers and sages (*shiji baijia*) and minutely detailed writings of mountain and plain," but criticizes their ancient content and archaic style (*wenyan gaogu*), which limited the scope of their readership. The editorial then praises legends and romances (*baiguan xiaoshuo*) as elegant literature. This reevaluation of the classical texts and lowbrow literature challenged the established literary hierarchy and demonstrated the paper's intention of reaching a broad readership:

> When we cast about for something which records and narrates modern events in a style simple but not vulgar, and which reports current affairs concisely yet in sufficient detail so that scholars and officials as well as farmers, artisans, traders and merchants all can understand, we find nothing so suitable as the newspaper.
>
> (Quoted in Britton 1933: 64)

Yet unlike the legends and romances whose contents were beyond proof (*wuji zhitan*), the newspaper was "to convey only confirmable news without misrepresentation and make the news understandable"; it should refrain from "indulging in shallow and exaggerated talk or absurd and preposterous content." The paper was to cover the "politics of the state, changing customs, important developments in foreign relations, prosperity and depression in commerce, and all that evokes surprise, astonishment, and delights (*kejing ke'e kexi*) or refreshes the public ear." The inaugural editorial attempts to draw a line between news and marvelous tales, which had never been clearly defined in the Chinese literary tradition. In practice, the paper's "astonishing and delightful" stories were often exaggerated and preposterous.[9]

As the modern newspaper sought to win a broad readership by satisfying its desire for sensational stories, this profit-driven practice was legitimated via a new spatio-temporal conception. Unlike a fabulous tale which borrows its authority from the miraculous, from its sheer distance from real space-time, a news item must sound verifiable in a specific time and place. This verifiability was a new device by which modern journalism captured its audience, and was potentially more misleading than the miraculous by which the storyteller amazes his (Benjamin 1968: 89). Whereas the storyteller's tale is for no particular audience and lives an afterlife in any place it is retold, a modern news item is often written for specific readers and can only survive in a specific time and place. Once a story is verifiable, it lives only as long as its limited usefulness permits. This usefulness lies precisely in the commercial or political value of the story. In practice, the distinction between news and fiction is much less important than a news item's salability to, or influence over, the reading public.

The *Shenbao* not only posited the novel and strange against the established normative order, and the popular against the elite, but also intended to introduce astonishing stories from the outer world into China, as the editorial concludes:

> Since the emergence of newspapers, all the world's affairs which are worthy of record are in fact disseminated throughout the world. Since the rise of news press every person may know the whole world without crossing his own doorstep. Is not this excellent?
>
> (Quoted in Britton 1933: 65)

Affairs from remote "barbaric" areas became worth knowing to the elite and the populace alike and were instrumental in constructing a new imaginative geography of the interconnected world, in which the Middle Land would lose its central position to the peripheries.

However, as most previous efforts by the missionaries to appeal to the Chinese elite with ideas and things from the West had not been particularly successful, the *Shenbao* had to primarily focus on what happened within China. A week later, Major made this announcement:

> For the last centuries, European countries have published newspapers so that the world's famous mountains and great rivers, strange hearings and marvelous scenes, become widely known (for either their people or their things). . .I consider that China, the greatest country of the world, has many talented and skilled people, as well as *strange and marvelous things*, different each day and year, and that there have been many famous relics since the ancient times. Among these are many detailed records and insightful comments to be reported. But it is a pity that what are heard in the imperial court are not heard among the folks, and what are known here are not known there. Though there is news, it cannot be disseminated across the world. It is even stranger that the *Peking Gazette* publishes the emperor's edicts and official reports representing people's interests but *none of the people's affairs was transmitted to the court*. Thus, as to the saying "ruling above produces effects below," what is the intention of such effects? Today I have made with Chinese literati an agreement that we do not spare small expenses for the world's great benefit, with a hope of collecting ideas and disseminating merits. Our method is efficient and our cost low. If this effort can last long without great losses, it will be multiplied, my intention will be fulfilled, and my concerns will be consoled.
>
> (*Shenbao*, May 6, 1872; in Xu and Xu 1988: 5; my emphasis)

This joint effort was to disseminate marvelous stories that had been neglected in Chinese society and thereby open a channel of transmitting news from the bottom up.[10] When the top-down and center–periphery hierarchy was challenged from within the Middle Land, it would eventually be displaced from its imaginary center of the world.

Thus the paper's front-page editorials always focused on local issues that affected the city's inhabitants and that often lay beyond the scope of traditional discourses.[11] Though they quoted from the classics and were structured in traditional formats, these articles deliberated on pragmatic issues rather than claiming to pass along timeless wisdom. Local and other domestic news followed the front page, while excerpts from the *Peking Gazette* were reprinted on the fifth or sixth pages. The last two pages were for commercial advertisements.

The paper also included some "lowbrow" content and solicited submissions from its readers: "If there are scholars inclined to romances and rhymes, who may wish to favor us with contributions, short or long, such as the bamboo poems of each region, or long narrative poems, we shall publish them without charge" (*Shenbao*, April 30, 1872; quoted in Britton 1933: 66). Four-line informal verses or bamboo poems (*zhuzhici*) were regularly published in the paper, admiring, mystifying, or caricaturing the city's novel sceneries. Thus, while adopting the Western-style newspaper format, the paper filled it with native contents and let the "strange and marvelous" that had previously been repressed or neglected surface into view.

Its miscellaneous contents notwithstanding, the *Shenbao* was still a paper of the elite. But Major's business plan did not end with it. In 1876, the *Shenbao* press published the vernacular newspaper *Minbao*, which, according to an advertisement in the *Shenbao*, intended to serve readers from the lower strata of society (Mittler 2004: 250). The press also published three short-lived periodicals: *Yinghuan suoji* (Global notes, 1872–74) and *Siming suoji* (Remote worlds notes, 1874–76) included literati contributions and reports on the world's different regions, such as news of an earthquake, theories of the sun, stars, earth, and moon, and notes of overseas travels in the first issue of *Yinghuan suoji* (Xu and Xu 1988). The third periodical, *Huanying huabao* (Global pictorial, 1877–80), according to Rudolf Wagner (2007b: 111–21), was Major's first attempt to introduce to China a Western-style illustrated periodical. It only published five issues, featuring copper prints by Western artists of world wonders that included Windsor Castle as well as China's Great Wall and Temple of Heaven.

Supplementing news and stories with visual images was surely a more effective way to reach common people than unillustrated news. But Major was yet to create a pictorial by Chinese artists primarily of Chinese content. Then, in April and May of 1884, the *Shenbao* advertised a new pictorial titled *Dianshizhai huabao* (Point-stone-studio pictorial):

> We have specially invited famous artists to choose items from the daily news to surprise and entertain you, and provide illustrations and commentaries.... The sketches are done with meticulous care and the calligraphy is the finest. They

are traditional Chinese realistic paintings characterized by fine brushwork and close attention to detail.

(Quoted in Ye 2003: 5)

Major employed a team of freelance Chinese illustrators, who worked mainly in the style of professional painting traditionally considered a lower category than (amateur) literati painting. Their artistic style was also influenced by Western prints shown to them by Major: hatching surfaces and perspective rendering of buildings were often seen in their illustrations. The meticulous depiction of figures and urban scenes by the leading illustrator, Wu Youru, greatly appealed to the public and probably shaped its visualization of an exotic Shanghai.[12]

Combining modern journalism with marvelous tales, and lithographic printing with traditional ink drawings, the pictorial was a great success. It was published three times a month from 1884 to 1898 and produced over 4,000 illustrated reports; many were about Shanghai and nearby locations, and quite a few were about foreign countries and Sino-Western relations (see Kim 2007). The pictorial also included stories of the supernatural or grotesque side by side with everyday scenes of Shanghai urban life, and sensational stories of the city's elite courtesans, who had become highly visible in the city's public space.[13]

The success of the *Shenbao* and *Dianshizhai huabao* signaled a larger publishing boom in late Qing Shanghai, for which Major had set a widely-emulated model through his in-depth understanding of Chinese culture and close collaboration with native literati and artists.[14]

Literature of urban consumption

During this publishing boom, a new urban literature of marvelous spectacles and entertainment culture flourished to meet the demands of travelers and sojourners in the city. However unprecedented, this literature also evolved from traditional travel writings.

As noted, literati travel notes published since the late Ming, such as *Banqiao zaji* and *Yangzhou huafang lu*, became the standard references for later urban literature. Wang Tao's *Haizou yeyou lu* (Record of visits to the distant corner at the sea, preface 1860), drawing on his experience with the city's native courtesans, served as an important link between traditional courtesan literature and the new literature of Shanghai marvels. Later, in exile, Wang wrote two sequels ([1878] 1992b, [1878] 1992c) and a new work, *Huaguo jutan* (Dramatized talk on the flower country ([1878] 1992d)), based on stories he collected through friends in Shanghai. Though considered "classics" of Shanghai courtesan literature, these works became out of date in the next two decades, when the courtesan business developed with great sophistication. More up-to-date accounts were found in Huang Shiquan's *Songnan mengying lu* (Record of dream images of Shanghai, preface 1883) and Chi Zhicheng's *Huyou mengying* (Dream images of touring Shanghai, 1893).[15] Such literati poets as Yuan Zuzhi ([1876] 1996) and Chen

Qiao ([1887] 1996) composed or edited volumes of bamboo poems of new urban scenes and courtesan houses.

In the meantime, more pragmatic urban literature appeared. Yang Jingting's *Dumen jilüe* (Brief records of the capital, 1864) was a "best seller" written in plain language for business travelers to Peking. Ge Yuanxu acknowledged that he followed Yang's model in compiling the first guidebook to Shanghai's foreign settlements, *Huyou zaji* (Miscellaneous notes on visiting Shanghai, 1876), which assembled 157 notes on a wide array of new urban phenomena, a great number of bamboo poems, and long lists of shops, foreign companies, and guild houses. The notes, or one-paragraph essays, were titled using the urban neologisms they sought to explain for quick reference. As noted in the preface, "the guide was to provide useful information for visitors so that they would not get lost in the city and, even if they got lost, would not need to ask passersby for help" (Ge [1876] 2003: 8). It set a model for later guidebooks, which not only followed the format but also reprinted the essays with little or no revision.

In 1884 the eponymous studio that published *Dianshizhai huabao* produced a pictorial guide to Shanghai, *Shenjiang shengjing tu* (Illustrated grand views of Shanghai), featuring Wu Youru's sixty-two lithographed drawings of the city's new wonders.[16] The guide presented the city as consisting of distinctly manifested spaces, from traditional gardens to Western-style mansions, new factories to broad avenues, and theaters and opium dens to courtesan boudoirs (see Figures 5.1, 5.4, 6.13). Each of the drawings was accompanied by a fine verse in exquisite calligraphic rendering, which supplemented the realistic visualization with the sublime poetics that had traditionally been reserved for natural wonders. The marvelous images of the city's artificial wonders in this guide were reprinted or imitated in the guides of the next decade.

Most of these later guides were anonymously produced during the publishing boom that followed the introduction of lithographic printing. Their authors or editors presented themselves as the owners of private studios that presumably published the guides. The way these guides freely assembled materials from other contemporary sources was not so different from how late Ming commercial publications were compiled. The guides combined three styles of writing, namely long introductory essays on the city's marvels, plain explanatory notes of urban phenomena, and bamboo poems, and were often illustrated with images that copied or imitated Wu Youru's depictions of courtesans and urban scenes. Their texts often reprinted excerpts from *Huyou zaji* and *Huyou mengying*. Some guides also included up-to-date information about the city's courtesan houses.

There were also guides that specialized in introducing the city's pleasure quarters. They included explanatory essays about rules and terms in the courtesan houses and biographies and portraits of famous courtesans. The biographies of selected courtesans seemed to have evolved from the "flower list" (*huabang*), to which literati authors had regularly elected the city's best courtesans since the 1870s (Wang [1878] 1992b: 5753–63). *Jingying xiaosheng chuji* (Mirror images and flute sounds, the first collection, 1887) featured fifty courtesan portraits by a Japanese artist, each with a brief biography on the opposite page (Yeh 2007: 152–53).

The success of this publication was acknowledged in the preface of *Haishan qinglou tuji* (Illustrated record of Shanghai courtesan houses, 1892), which presented in the same format an expanded collection, not only reprinting the original fifty por-traits but also borrowing images from Wu Youru's work (some in truncated form). Three years later a new edition (Huayu 1895) included 116 courtesan portraits and biographies (Figure 2.1), dedicatory poems and letters to some courtesans by their patrons, an appendix of terms and rules in the business, and some essays from *Huyou zaji*. Such eclectic composition did not prevent the guides from being "best sellers," as the traditional-style renderings of idealized beauties were as much devoid of individualized features as the succinct courtesan biographies. Thus, the guides presented the anomalous and transitory as normative and timeless, and helped create the courtesan's iconic image in the settlements. These courtesan guides were produced in what later authors called the "golden age" of the courte-san culture, and they in turn became crucial sources for new guides compiled in the early twentieth century. As these guides became increasingly popular, the courtesan business ironically declined from its golden age.

There also appeared new novels that were set in the city's pleasure quarters and other spaces and which provided vivid scenes of everyday life in or around the courtesan houses. They mostly followed Han Bangqing's masterpiece *Flowers of Shanghai* (1894), which signaled a break with traditional courtesan literature (Lu Xun 1981; Wang 1997). Like the guides, these novels, as Alexander Des Forges

Figure 2.1 Courtesan portraits from *Xinji haishang qinglou tuji*. Left: A courtesan with children and servants in a domestic setting. Right: A courtesan in a traditional-style interior.
Source: Huayu 1895: 2.21–22.

(2007: 8) argues, explained and presented the city, but in more subtle and contagious ways. Such lowbrow literary works were first published as installments "one page at a time" in local tabloids, or *xiaobao* (Des Forges 2003), which appeared in great numbers around the turn of the century. Coexisting with the progressive and nationalist narratives advocated by Liang Qichao and other reformists in the mainstream media, such entertainment papers as *Youxi bao* (Playing game paper), *Shijie fanhua bao* (World prosperity paper), *Tuhua ribao* (Pictorial daily), and *Crystal* (*Jingbao*) devoted much of their content to gossip about famous courtesans and popular fiction that was later known as the Mandarin Duck and Butterfly school.

Knowing historical experience

What can historians learn from these commercial publications that freely recycled earlier materials? Were they historical documents or literary representations? These questions have been the subject of recent scholarly debate. In writing the social history of Shanghai courtesan culture, scholars have drawn widely on such publications of the late Qing and early Republican periods. The *Shenbao* is frequently referenced in Hershatter's comprehensive study of twentieth-century Shanghai prostitution, though she points out that the paper had more coverage of common prostitutes than of courtesans in the twentieth century.[17] Her study of the courtesans relies on reports from the tabloids, such as *Crystal*, and the guidebooks to the pleasure quarters of the Republican period. Catherine Yeh's (1998, 2006) recent studies of nineteenth-century courtesan culture also rely on guidebooks and periodicals in presenting a narrative of "rituals," "proper conduct," and "stars" in the courtesan culture.

Henriot (2001, 1996: 133) cautions that these materials constitute discourses rather than evidence of historical practices, and are of little use in unbiased reconstructions of reality. But he acknowledges that historians have to make do with what is available, and he himself relies heavily on Wang Tao's work in analyzing the nineteenth-century courtesan economy, without making much distinction between Wang's accounts of his own experience and the anecdotes he heard from others. Hershatter (1997: 3) is also acutely aware of the discursive nature of these materials when she states that her study is "both less and more than an imaginative reconstruction of the lives of Shanghai prostitutes." As the authors of these materials had their own agendas, which were very different from those of the historians, she advocates a more nuanced evaluation of them. She also seeks a relationship between the text and the craft behind it, with neither the hope of re-creating the categories of meaning as exactly understood in them nor the desire to relinquish her own agenda (Hershatter 1996: 164, 1997: 13). Therefore her study presents the narrative histories of Shanghai prostitution as seen by literati, reformers, regulators, ⸱⸱ ⸱ revolutionaries.

⸱y reconstruction of the past, including of the history that courtesans did
⸱te themselves, involves a risk of putting words into the mouths of silent
⸱d of unduly filling various gaps and lapses to make a continuous narrative.

How else could this narrative of courtesan culture be reconstructed when it must rely on the literati's random notes and the guidebooks' fragmentary information? If historians' agendas are so different from those of guidebook authors, how can they achieve their goals by using the latter's products? What is the limit to recounting undocumented historical practices and reconstructing continuous narratives of them? And how can such reconstructions be free from subjective bias if the anonymous or obscure nature of their sources betrays their own bias? Henriot (2001: 14) surely has these questions in mind when he dismisses those "Chinese sources" or the "representations as a set of discourses"; he therefore seeks to develop a "social history" of the courtesan economy based on archival records of its financial and spatial aspects—one that is more "objective" than Hershatter's "study in representations." But it is not clear how objective the police and League of Nations records that Henriot used were, since their ways of counting and recording were also subject to the interests of specific parties and many invisible factors. Why should these materials be treated with less care? Thus, his rejection of the "Chinese sources" in favor of others seems no more objective than other historians' choices.[18]

Probably more important than the selection of sources are the objectives and methods of study. If reconstructing a narrative of the past from such "representations" is indeed limited, history might best be approached from a different perspective, by deploying an alternative "infinitesimal" method, which is to deconstruct the representations and learn the whole from fragments, and to discover the permanent from the contingent. By relinquishing the agenda of reconstructing an all-encompassing narrative, we can move from "nuanced evaluation" to a vigorous excavation of these materials so as to lay bare their hidden, unconscious agendas, and to a critical, intertextual examination of them in order to reveal some genuine historical experiences that had settled in them like invisible dust. According to Benjamin (1968: 163), experience (*Erfahrung*) is the long-lasting fracture left by the inscription of historical stimuli onto the subject's (unconscious) memory without the screening of the consciousness. It is the mediation between the subject and the social and material surroundings from which such stimuli originated rather than an "objective" historical fact, and is fragmentary and contingent rather than complete and absolute. As fragments from the past, those representations may contain particles of genuine experience and the collective (un)consciousness of the age; or they may just consist of piles of dry information resulting from the atrophy of experience. It would be futile to reassemble the fragments as if they were part of a jigsaw puzzle. There are no predesigned pictures of history. The historian's task is not to put a period to rest by revealing the complete, objective picture of it, which often results simply in piling up historical information, but to interpret some genuine experience which is transmittable to our own age, and which can have an afterlife.

The emphasis on reconstructing historical narrative from a vast amount of diverse sources may have prevented historians from conducting detailed case studies and critical analyses of transmittable experiences in a few representative texts. The anonymous production of Shanghai courtesan literature and urban reportage may also discourage such in-depth analyses. Therefore a danger exists that these materials are treated too literally, and their hidden agendas remain undisclosed. There is a case of a fabricated news item in the 1894 novel *Flowers of Shanghai*: a newspaper reports that the courtesan Yao Wenjun has disappeared and is nowhere to be found, while a customer is searching for her to exact revenge after a brawl with her in a restaurant the previous night. A merchant reads the news and worries about Yao until his friend tells him that the news was made up to mislead the thug Lai Touyuan, from whom she had gotten away using an excuse (45.518–19).[19] As the novel's author, Han Bangqing, was a contributor to the *Shenbao*, this episode reveals the potentially fabricated nature of courtesan reportage, the subtexts of which may hide forever from historians. However fictional such materials may be, their covert agenda can be revealed from beneath their texts through an "archeology" of Shanghai modernity.

For instance, what was the agenda of the guidebooks? To what extent were they practically used in patronizing the courtesans or in regulating behavior in the courtesan houses? The later guides seemed to be heavily indebted to earlier ones in terms of style, content, and illustration. Though there were few changes in their content for more than half a century, one wonders whether the business practices of the courtesans were really so stable. Yeh (1998: 29–30) asserts that the "rituals" of the courtesan houses were very stable. But while some nineteenth-century features might indeed have survived into the twentieth century, it would be ahistorical to consider them the same as before. Hershatter (1997: 20–22) attributes the continuity in the guidebooks to the reproduction of the contents of old guides verbatim by new ones and to the authors' nostalgia for the golden age of courtesan culture. But the writings in the golden age were also full of nostalgia. She argues that the imaginations and nostalgia of male authors were not only reflective of the thinking of the period but also formative in the discourse of urban masculinity. But this view hardly takes into account the fact, which she admits earlier, that such imaginations and nostalgia were derivative rather than original. Was the nostalgia in the guidebooks truly reflective of the authors' experience, or was it simply taken from earlier sources? To answer this question requires an intertextual reading of the guidebooks and their sources.

Henriot (1996: 158) also directs our attention to plagiarism in these guidebooks. But why plagiarism? And why nostalgia? After all, Shanghai sojourners did not read these guidebooks about exotic courtesans as we read automobile manuals today; they might read them for an imaginary dream world. Thus old fantasies could be repackaged to meet the public's demand for novelty or nostalgia. The nostalgia repackaged from the earlier works in later guides became a commodity sold to the public rather than evidence of contemporary experience. Just as realistic reports and marvelous tales were juxtaposed in the newspapers and periodicals to win broad readership, these guides too had mixed contents, and were of both practical and imaginary value. As commodities, they were presumably inexpensive and accessible to those readers who could not afford to visit the courtesan houses.[20] Though the addresses of elite courtesans and some terms in the guides were quite useful for the clients of the courtesans, the guidebooks had multiple agendas and their original function was often superseded by new ones. More important than the function of luring the public into the courtesan houses, they promoted a seductive image of Shanghai as a pleasureland full of exotic and strange experiences; in so doing they became commodities themselves whose shifting meanings were produced more by their consumers than by their authors.

These publications resulted from a development that gradually antiquated the literati culture. The transition from literati to journalists or salaried writers had by the end of the nineteenth century brought a relentless commercialization of writing. This change was paradoxically embodied in the lack of change in the content of the guidebooks, whose recycling of such traditional motifs as literati nostalgia and timeless beauty for public consumption in fact radically altered their original meanings. This transition can be illustrated by comparing Wang Tao's *Haizou yeyou lu* (preface 1860) with the guide *Xinji haishang qinglou tuji* (1895): in the former, Wang, based on his own experience, "not only recorded news of flowers and moons but also supplemented talk of water and sky [during the Taiping war]" (Huang [1883] 1989: 126); in the latter, the anonymous editor compiled information and anecdotes that would be useful for readers in imagining or finding their dream courtesans. Wang's memoir was published long after it was written and its narratives hardly had any practical value; the guide was hastily compiled, and contained up-to-date information, such as the addresses, ages, skills, and personae of famous courtesans. However traditional the guide's content and style appeared, it had become a modern commodity.

These later commercial publications tell us more about their authors and readers than the courtesans, and should be examined to show the transformation not only of the courtesan houses but also of the male elite and urban consumers in general. Thus the courtesan was always an allegory, a reflection of the male author, and the transformation of the literati was fully embodied in the change of rhetoric through which they celebrated, scorned, or lamented the courtesan: from a protest against the official Confucian realm to a representation of the new commercial culture, from an allegory for ephemeral life and love to a commodified literary trope devoid of genuine meaning. If the earlier self-pitying literatus portrayed a mirror image of himself in the beautiful and talented but mistreated courtesan, modern commercial writers, in turning their labor into commodities, also resembled the courtesans, who were falling into the category of common prostitutes at the same time.

Wang Tao and courtesan literature

Both Major and the missionaries relied on Chinese literati in carrying out their cultural projects in China. These traditionally trained scholars were unsuccessful in the imperial examinations; their new profession as salaried workers employed by the foreigners clashed with their traditional manner and prestige (Yeh 1997; Ye 2003: 13–20). But the foreign settlements allowed them to express alternative views and to enjoy and advocate a new, marvelous, if decadent, urban culture. If they became in the eyes of the traditional elite a kind of bohemians, then their unconventional lifestyle reflected a cultural displacement in the new urban milieu.

Wang Tao was among the earliest of these displaced literati. His experience with the London Missionary Society (LMS) in Shanghai in the 1850s was indispensable to his becoming one of China's first reformist thinkers, but the conflict between the literati tradition and Christianity deeply affected his private life. Evidence from his diary and LMS records shows that as of 1854 he had become a practicing Christian, but he never mentioned this in his published works, in which he consistently pointed to Confucius as a historical figure whose wisdom came closest to perfection (Cohen 1974: 20–23). Moreover, his licentious lifestyle of patronizing the city's courtesans seemed to diverge greatly from the proper conduct of either a pious Christian or a Confucian patriarch. These conflicting elements engendered in him a sharp sense of cultural displacement. He wrote about his LMS job in a letter: "In name, I am an editor, but in fact I am the one who is given orders. [My work] is so irrelevant and outside of true scholarship.... I idle away day after day wasting the best years of my life. Nothing I do here is meaningful" (Wang 1880; quoted in Yeh 1997: 431). His anguish resulted from the huge gap between his life and the literati ideal: he felt he had been reduced to an artisan providing services to the foreign employer. Indeed, it was purely because of financial concerns that he continued to work for LMS (Cohen 1974: 14).

Wang's anguish was caused by a sense of impotence in pursuing a manly ambition, which according to the sages' teaching was "to regulate the family, to rule the state, and to pacify all under heaven" (*qijia, zhiguo, pingtianxia*; Legge 1966: 310–15). He had to be separated from his family in the hinterland in order to support them, and that was not regulating his family well; nor had he had much success in the imperial examinations which would have given him a chance to help rule the state. Yet when the Taiping rebels and the British and French troops ravaged the Qing Empire around 1860, he thought that he might have a chance to realize his biggest ambition and that his experience with Westerners might be quite valuable in offering advice to Qing rulers and generals and even the rebels. He then plied them with proposals, being quite an opportunist, ready to serve whoever might pay attention to his ideas (Cohen 1974: 26–31, 35–44). But his proposals were all neglected and the capture by the imperial troops of a letter of his to the rebels eventually caused his long exile in Hong Kong.

During this series of failures in his endeavors, Wang balanced his frustration with an unconventional lifestyle. He and two friends were known in the local community as "the three odd men" (*san yimin*) (Huang [1883] 1989: 130). They regularly got together for drinking and visiting courtesans in the walled city, as no other entertainment activities were available in the settlements, which were then still "deserted graveyards." After the walled city was ravaged by the Small Sword rebels and a new type of prosperous city flourished in the settlements, Wang seemed to have strong nostalgia for his early experience in the still-idyllic town setting. He recorded it in his first work on Shanghai courtesans, *Haizou yeyou lu*. Its preface, written in 1860, reflected on how the work was originally written:

> In the winter of [1853–54], I stayed home recuperating from an illness and, remembering my earlier visits [to courtesan houses in the walled city], grabbed a brush to record them. At that time, the red [Taiping] rebels were striking forth and Nanking was lost, where pearl curtains and jade tiles turned into flying dust and dancing sleeves and singing skirts were trodden over. Here [in Shanghai] smoke also rose and rains fell; the moon was blemished and flowers were ruined; people were gone and time was not; much was the sorrow and little was the delight. After the [Small Sword] rebels were gone and the empty city was recovered, spring is back and sparrows arrive again; but their nests have already changed and my sweet dreams cannot be found again. Enjoy the non-moment between life and death, and sigh about the nowhere of my wandering. Desolate and lost, smoke and moon, who knows this sorrow? With redecorated pools and terraces, the beautiful grottoes open again. Since a time unknown, the [walled] city has recovered its former prosperity, while outside it there are many new pleasure houses near the Racecourse. But the good old time has gone, and the former beauty is not. The time and circumstance are bleak and news and stories are tasteless. Passing the old place, I see old nails and timber stains still there, crows perching on fragrant trees and flies crawling on painted silks. While the deserted land and neglected tombs have changed into new houses of pink shadows and rouge scents, the former homes of red lanterns and green wine have turned into ruins.
>
> (Wang [1860] 1992a: 5638–39)

This stark scene of decay and death not only implied Wang's frustration over pursuing a traditional career but also showed his vision of a new world in which the sage or hero was dead or appeared as Death. When the preface was written, the city was a safe haven from the ravagings of the Taiping troops, and the flood of refugees from the wealthy Jiangnan region brought a morbid prosperity to the settlements, where new types of courtesan houses flourished. Wang was rather critical of the new courtesans and related their lack of elegance to the age when the heroes were dead:

> Today in this city of a bucket size, yet with airs from four seas, there are neither reputable courtesans nor righteous heroes. Those wearing colorful make-up are of a changed nature and those who have dropped weapons and sought shelter here are clever slaves competing against each other. I have not heard of any beauty in a golden boudoir who can sing a new melody of the jade terrace; I can neither draw a blade to kill the villains in order to honor a chaste lady nor wear a sacred cloak to consult Buddha's spirit for evidence of my immortal standing. Because of this [impotence], silk dresses have lost color and powders and rouges have become demonic.
>
> (Wang [1860] 1992a: 5637)

Abandoned to this "distant corner of the sea," Wang felt so powerless that he could only "record the fragrant love forever passed and chase the beautiful traces already fading." Though it was impossible to fully retrieve these traces, he could revisit the flame that had devoured them so as to rekindle his own shivering life, which lacked the energy of a manly pursuit. In this unusual wartime prosperity, he felt that "the good old time" was gone—that of the sage and the righteous hero; and gone with it were the courtesans who had entertained him. Their disappearance became an allegory for the sage's death. The benevolent sage of boundless wisdom was a legendary figure embodying certain mythical elements that made him appear as a maternal male.[21] This maternal sage had died out in the life of a scholar who had not succeeded in his career of ruling the state or pacifying all under the heaven. As in a dream, Wang alleviated his mourning of that death by reenacting it in a distorted fashion, namely mourning the ephemeral life and beauty of the courtesan, who had been displaced from the inner quarter of a household and "abandoned" in the brutal world of men. Thus, in his memory of the lost courtesans, Wang secretly kept alive the ghost of the benevolent sage, the fading flames of the righteous man.[22]

He also adhered to the traditional ideal of writing as self-expression rather than as a means to earn a living. He did not consider for his work specific readers who might share his thoughts, let alone those his book might be sold to. The preface notes that readers who looked for enchanting beauties in his work did not understand the author's idea, and that he would hear from them if they regarded the work as worthless and deviating from the sage's teaching (Wang [1860] 1992a: 5639–40).

In exile in Hong Kong, Wang collected new stories of Shanghai courtesans into two sequels to *Haizou yeyou lu* and a new work, *Huaguo jutan*. They were all, in turn, collected into *Yanshi congchao* (Anthology of courtesan history), which he edited. These new works consisted of more or less fictionalized anecdotes of courtesans, which would, according to the preface of *Huaguo jutan*, "add more prosperity to southern flowers, represent the riotousness of northern heroes, and disseminate their astonishing affairs and their deplorable fates throughout the world" (Wang [1878] 1992d: 5247). Unlike the 1860 preface, this one did not show any personal anguish. Wang assertively defended his work against the traditional criticism of courtesan literature: "The prosperity of pleasure houses also has an original spirit and the courtesans are heavenly created too; did the famous Tang officials also write about historical courtesans?" He even justified his appropriation of stories from other sources by citing ancient precedence and argued that his improvement of these sources was different from stealing. He also had his readers in mind in composing the new courtesan stories; he urged them to "take the dramatized talk of the flower land as a navigation through the sea of pain, as a raft in the city of sorrows" (Wang [1878] 1992d: 5249).

Thus Wang seemed to behave like a sage in offering counsel to his readers, but he was now in fact a successful journalist and would also get involved in commercial publishing. At this time he had for five years successfully run the first modern Chinese newspaper, *Xunhuan ribao* (Cyclic daily), in Hong Kong to promote reform in China, and he began to be considered a rebel or reformist (Cohen 1974). Now, in writing about the courtesans, he relished his successful but reformist journalistic career, and the spirit of the sage or hero was found alive again in his life, which had been enriched by travels to Europe and Japan. He kept his faith in the sage's imaginative space-time by applying the concept of cyclic (*xunhuan*) history to the whole world, in which Chinese domination would eventually arrive.

The new literati-journalists

Soon after Major launched the *Shenbao* in early 1872, he sent Qian Xinbo to Hong Kong to learn how Wang Tao managed his newspaper. Wang had entrusted his daughter to Qian's family before he fled Shanghai, and Qian later married her (Xu and Xu 1988: 24). It might be mainly through Qian that Wang gathered the sources of his later works on Shanghai courtesans. Two years later, in 1874, Qian returned to Shanghai and served as the *Shenbao*'s new chief editor.

Around this time "the city of sorrows" that Wang had depicted earlier had already been transformed into a prosperous metropolis, where a new generation of literati associated with the *Shenbao* press were more adapted to commercial publishing and modern journalism and had little or none of Wang's frustration over working for the missionary. But they had not given up traditional ideals. One of the *Shenbao*'s first editors, Jiang Zhixiang, was still pursuing a traditional scholar-official career during his twelve-year tenure and left the press when he achieved a metropolitan degree (*jinshi*) in the imperial examination (Xu and Xu 1988: 24). Other important editors included He Guisheng and Huang Shiquan (also known as Huang Xiexun). Huang was considered to have been responsible for most of the paper's editorial articles and the paper's conservative position against the reformists when he became the chief editor in 1896–1905.

Probably because of such conservative stances, these earlier journalists have been considered by historians to have been obscure figures sandwiched between the prominent reformist thinkers Wang Tao and Liang Qichao. But their new profession was, in fact, unacceptable in the eyes of contemporary officials and elites. Like Wang Tao three decades earlier, they were also considered "odd men" by local conservatives (Lei [1922] 1987: 27; Gentz 2007: 49–50). Notwithstanding their problematic status, either in the late Qing historiography or in the contemporary society, their work arguably paved the way for later reformist journalism, and their new lifestyle entailed nostalgic longings as well as adjustments to the city's emerging industrial culture.

The editors of the *Shenbao* press and their friends formed a sizable circle of educated elites, who often wrote prefaces for each other's books and quoted excerpts from each other's poems and essays. There was once a poetry club established by Yuan Zuzhi in his own residence in the western section of Fourth Avenue (Simalu or Fuzhou Road), which he called Yangliu loutai (Willow Terrace), and to which "many pearls and jades all submit poems, as many as thousands" (Huang [1883] 1989: 122; Sun 1995: 31). The bamboo-poem anthology *Haishang yin* edited by Yuan might have been born out of such literary activities he hosted. As a son of the renowned poet Yuan Mei and a retired official, Yuan appeared to have broad social connections (Yeh 2006: 197), and his penname, Cangshan jiuzhu, was frequently mentioned in contemporary writings. In the preface he wrote for *Huyou zaji*, he expressed a wish to write a similar work but lamented that he was too busy to accomplish it (Ge [1876] 2003: 4). His busy social life might have included contacts with many men of letters, officials, and merchants who had chosen to sojourn (*yuju*) in this increasingly attractive city.

Influenced by Wang Tao's early work, Huang Shiquan's *Songnan mengying lu* celebrated the city's marvelous spectacles and depicted a broad array of entertainment spaces. He Guisheng wrote a preface for that work: "It takes non-dream as dream, and non-shadow as shadow. . .Consider them as dreams, their affairs are real and leave traces; consider them as real, their impressions are dazzling and illusory" (Huang [1883] 1989: 96). By considering life (or visual experience) and dreams interchangeable—an idea taught by the ancient sage Zhuangzi—these literati-journalists avoided the kind of anguish Wang suffered earlier and enjoyed the new urban spectacles. Their everyday life became colorful and dreamlike, as they benefited from a wide range of leisure attractions available in the city as well as such material intoxications as opium smoking.

In this new commercial milieu, the spirit of the sage or "righteous hero" was more dead than in Wang Tao's Shanghai, while the new type of reformist "heroes" were yet to arrive. But unlike Wang, the new literati-journalists did not mourn that death; their life and dreams now embodied the city's new ethos and they were more or less content with their identity as salaried professionals. Though increasingly distanced from traditional literati ideals, they nonetheless relished their decadent lifestyle with nostalgic imageries, especially the idealized courtesan as the *jiaoshu* or *cishi* (book emendator or lyric scholar). The courtesans in these literati-journalists were still comparable to those in Wang Tao in filling up the emptiness left by the sage's death, although the former were highly visible in the city rather than being recalled as "beautiful traces already fading." Like Wang, most men of letters were enthusiastic patrons of the courtesan houses (see Yeh 2006: 178–98).

Meanwhile, the city's merchants demanded expressions of their newly gained elite status. In this treaty port they did not have to purchase a gentry identity to gain respect; instead, they became well-mannered "gentlemen" by stealing from the literati the role of "flower protector." Thus, the declining literati and the emerging capitalists often partied together and befriended each other in the courtesan house. Defending their traditional cultural privilege, the literati often expressed outrage at the decline of the courtesans' talent and skill in serving the vulgar merchants—as did Wang Tao just before his exile—and at the various forms of the lower-class sex trade. Their contempt at the new types of courtesans was perhaps due to the latter's inaccessibility: the new literati-journalists now had to accept the fact that their dream girl in the real world would leave them for richer clients. The courtesan house as a commercial establishment was not to cater to the literati's nostalgic longing but rather to sustain itself by generating profits.

In fact, the literati's poetic terms for the courtesan, such as *jiaoshu*, *cishi*, *jiaofang* (music department), and *wushi* (music teacher), were never used in the courtesan houses, which instead invented a set of vernacular terms for their new business practices. The terms *changsan* (double three) and *yao'er* (one-two) for two types of courtesans were borrowed from gambling jargon to indicate how much the courtesans charged their clients; there also appeared many terms such as *jiaoju* (make a call) and *dachawei* (tea party) that referred to the houses' new business activities. Such neologisms sometimes puzzled guidebook authors, who had to speculate on their origins. Unlike the literati's poetic essays, the guidebooks methodically explained myriad terms invented in the commercial world, and in so doing they probably helped standardize the business practices of the courtesan houses. The anonymity of such publications could hardly conceal the involvement of the literati-journalists in commercial literary production in a vernacular and colloquial language. Ge Yuanxu's plain-style notes in *Huyou zaji* were in fact not so far from that language.

The contrasting language and ideals in self-expressive essays and commercial publications demonstrated a conflict between traditional literati values and the commercialization of writing. The literati-journalists had to sell their writing in the commercial market for a broad readership in order to earn a living (*yuwen weisheng*). Thus, they became rather similar to the new types of courtesans in catering to the desires of the urban public, which was increasingly dominated by wealthy merchants.

Han Bangqing and his novel

Among these literati-journalists, one unconventional mind seemed to be more perspicacious than any other in exposing dreams in the courtesan house as "non-dreams," in contrast to Huang Shiquan's celebration of non-dreams as dreams. From October 1887 to June 1890, there appeared in the *Shenbao* quite a number of articles signed by Dayishanren or Taixianhanqi; they ranged from poems dedicated to courtesans to essays on topics as varied as quitting opium-smoking, making friends, and current events. These articles are now attributed to Han Bangqing (Fang 2002). In early 1892, Dayishanren advertised his own journal in the same newspaper:

> *Haishang qishu* (Book of Shanghai marvels): two issues per month, ten cents a copy, sold via the *Shenbao* press. It has three major components and is published immediately after the author finishes composition in order to ensure the fastest readership. The most marvelous (*qi*) component, *Flowers of Shanghai*, written in the *yanyi* (romance novel) style, uses the Wu dialect to narrate affairs and loves in Shanghai's courtesan houses. Its vivid depiction comes from [the author's] ten-year personal experience. Drawing on what he has seen and heard, the author presents truth through a real-life presentation (*xianshen shuofa*) and composes this book to warn pleasure seekers; it is without any obscene content. The other two components are "Taixian's Rambling Drafts," which makes new stories from the old in a unique fashion totally different from the *Liaozhai* model, and the "Reclining Travel Anthology,"

which collects exciting and fascinating stories from various novels for leisurely reading.

(*Shenbao*, February 22, 1892)

Han continued to advertise the journal until it went out of business after fourteen (or
fifteen) issues, which contained the first twenty-eight chapters of *Flowers of Shanghai*.
Now considered the first of its kind in literary history (Chen and Yuan 1993: 241), the
journal was obviously established mainly to publish the novel. Its other components
basically served to fill the remaining pages left after the installments of the novel.
A sixty-four-chapter version of the novel was published as a book and sold via the
Shenbao press in 1894. Han died in the same year at the age of thirty-nine.[23]

The character *qi* in Han's journal title indicated an approach similar to Major's
pursuit of "all that evokes surprise, astonishment, and delight." As noted above,
some sensational stories in the *Shenbao* and *Dianshizhai huabao* were fiction
rather than news. The *Shenbao* press also reprinted a huge number of vernacular novels and advertised them in the paper. But among the *Shenbao* editors and
contributors, no one would deign to write vernacular fiction—a lowbrow literary
genre in their eyes. Only at the margins of this "elite" circle, which itself was
already marginalized by the traditional elite, might such a person as Han attempt
to present the marvels of Shanghai through fiction in a plain style.

As the advertisement shows, the novel's "real-life presentation" is embodied
in Han's choice of writing all conversations—its most important component, as
many stories are told in long dialogues—in the Wu dialect, which faithfully reveals
the characters' emotional nuances (see Des Forges 2007: 29–55). Moreover, the
novel presents much less idealized images of the pleasure quarters than the mainstream courtesan literature discussed above, and adopts a realistic urban setting,
which stands in contrast to the timeless setting of secluded boudoirs in traditional
courtesan novels.[24] Lacking a central plotline and key characters, the novel devel-
ops more than a dozen parallel and intermingling plots, portrays dozens more
characters, and relates their complicated affairs and emotions. It demands unusual
patience from the reader to plough through its convoluted narrative lines, which
are revealed, or hidden rather, in lengthy conversations and minute accounts of
everyday details in the courtesan houses. By this stark realistic depiction (which
is distinct from the positive realism of the May Fourth fiction), Han reveals the
city's most "marvelous" space rather differently than in a sensational newspaper
story, a nostalgic anecdote, or a guidebook entry.

The novel begins with a cautionary note to readers, typical of how a storyteller
passes on a story as his own experience:

> Since Shanghai became a trading port, the flowers in the south have flour-
> ished. Many who visit these flowers indulge in obscene and improper con-
> ducts. Fathers and brothers cannot forbid them; mentors and friends cannot
> dissuade them. Their stubborn minds cannot be enlightened, because they do
> not have a *guolairen* (person who has experienced such things) to give them
> a real-life presentation. . .If the reader searches for footsteps from traces, he

will understand the meanings; sees in the front what is more attractive than [the legendary beauty] Xizi, will know in the back what is more ferocious than yakshas; sees what is sweeter than a loving spouse in these days, will foresee what is more poisonous than a snake or scorpion in other years.

(1.279)

This reads as typical of Confucian moral didactics, which are also found in the guidebooks to the pleasure quarter.[25] But the novel is far from simply a condemnation of the courtesan house.[26] Instead the novel fully captures the complexity of the emerging urban culture, in which the marvelous was homelike as well as uncanny, and dreams and life were indistinguishable from one another:

> [The author] Huayeliannong is indeed a host of the Dark and Sweet Country, living everyday in dreams. But he refuses to consider his life as a dream but believes it to be real in writing this book. Thus he makes up this book within a dream and then wakes up [those indulging in] the dream in the books. Reader, do not just dream there; do read this book, which does no harm!

(1.279)

What is "the dream in the books"? Could it be the pursuit of an official career as mandated by the classics; or the longing for the talented beauties as represented in the boudoir fiction; or the seeking of novel pleasures as depicted in the guidebooks? By revealing real lives in the courtesan house, Han seeks to smash all those dream pictures constructed around it.

Han's own life seemed to be one of oneiric disillusionment. He grew up in Louxian, Songjiang Prefecture (near Shanghai), adept at learning the classics at a very early age. In spite of his literary talent and early travels to Peking with his father, an official with a *juren* degree, he failed the imperial examinations and did not succeed in pursuing an official career. Leaving his wife, who was a couple of years older, behind in his hometown, he settled in Shanghai, becoming an opium-addict and a generous spender despite his poverty. He also befriended *Shenbao* editors such as Qian Xinbo and He Guisheng and other distinguished scholars, and became a contributor to the newspaper. An unruly character, he composed a few essays but could never commit himself to tedious editorial work. His most intimate relationship was with a courtesan and he often hid himself in her boudoir, where "he would pick up leftover pieces of paper and a blunt brush to write tens of thousands of words when an inspiration seized him. It must be assumed that [*Flowers of Shanghai*] was written in this time."[27]

Seeking shelter in the unique urban environment of Shanghai rather than on a remote mountainside or in a secluded garden, Han led a life different from that of the former literati disillusioned with officialdom, as he wrote in the essay "Le shuo" (On happiness):

> As for the sky, it does not have to be fine, clear, breezy, and mild to bring happiness, even a bleak and desolate one does not hurt; as for the land, it does

not have to have flourishing trees, elegant bamboos, and clear streams, even a damp, narrow, noisy, and dusty one does not hurt; as for people, they do not have to be a virtuous group of the young and old, even despicable, petty, and dirty ones do not hurt.[28]

(*Shenbao*, June 20, 1888; Fang 2002: 231)

This is indeed a summary of his world: the alienating city, the noisy courtesan room as his hideout, and his friends of diverse backgrounds. He wrote in the essay "Lun jiao wenda" (On making friends): "For the past three or five years, those who wanted to be my friends and whose names I can recall have amounted to more than five hundred people" (*Shenbao*, November 20, 1889; Fang 2002: 236). Apparently these many friends of his, besides a few literati, mainly consisted of the "despicable, petty. . .ones" sojourning in "narrow, noisy, and dusty" places. He might have befriended them in courtesan houses, just as his fictional characters, mainly merchants and officials, have gotten to know one another in such settings. If the novel was indeed based on his ten years' experience, this experience was one shared with local merchants rather than with the small circle of *Shenbao* literati.

By closely reading this novel in the next chapter, I reveal a picture of the courtesan house quite different from those in the literati essays and guidebooks.

3 Ephemeral households, marvelous things

The foreign settlements contributed to an economic boom in Shanghai and also created for the Chinese sojourners a "foreign place" (*yichang*), free from the administration of mandarin rulers. After the 1860s, many business-minded sojourners arrived and played crucial roles in the development of the settlements. Aside from trading, cultural exchanges between the Chinese and Western communities were relatively rare in the nineteenth century but the Chinese sojourners actively appropriated and domesticated "things modern" as well as reinvent old ideals. Like the *Shenbao* literati, these sojourners were intoxicated by marvels in the *yichang*, which eased their sense of displacement from home; their ultimate dream life was also found in the city's courtesan houses, which conceptually and practically became their surrogate "home"—one that parodied as well as subverted the traditional ideal of the household.

As discussed in Chapter 1, in the self-contained gentry household the public and private, the sacred and mundane, were unified rather than opposed. Space was organized in line with a patriarchal order, under which relations within the family were comparable to the social and economic bonds in the community of the feudal lord and his subjects. This preindustrial production of space was to ensure the perpetuation of the family clan as a socio-economic power rather than to guarantee individuals' private pleasure. In the settlements of Shanghai there were few such grand households but many sojourners who left their families behind in the hinterland. Because of the high cost of living, many a sojourner rented only a tiny space—a temporary lodging of a commercial nature that could hardly be considered a home.

Merchant residences and courtesan houses

In *Flowers of Shanghai*, many merchants and shop owners have no real home in the city though they spend much time and money in courtesan houses. Hong Shanqing, the owner of Yongchang Ginseng Store, apparently does not even rent an apartment in Shanghai; sometimes he spends a night with Zhou Shuangzhu, the courtesan he regularly visits, sometimes he sleeps in his store, but most of his leisure time is spent socializing with friends in various courtesan houses. Another shop owner, Chen Xiaoyun, has only a bedroom on the second floor of his lottery store (11.328). For such small entrepreneurs, the shop was both the workplace and a temporary abode, where money could be made and saved for a future permanent home. There were also many occasional visitors, like itinerant merchants, who traveled regularly between Shanghai and the hinterland. In the novel, the merchants Li Shifu and Li Heting live in a hostel (*kezhan*) and are eager to patronize courtesans or sex workers. Visiting Shanghai for the first time to find a job, Zhao Puzhai and Zhang Xiaocun also live in a hostel, Yuelai kezhan on Baoshan Street.

In the novel a few wealthy merchants or officials such as Wang Liansheng, Yao Jichun, and Qian Zigang maintain quite decent residences in the settlements. But such a residence was called *gongguan*, literally a "public house," and a sign with its owner's surname (e.g., "Wang Gongguan") was posted on the entrance. Thus it acquired a public rather than homelike character. Its combination of residential and business functions was quite similar to that found in the traditional household. But merchants in Shanghai were very different from the old-style gentry, and their *gongguan* were usually much smaller and more commercialized than the typical gentry house. Since their residences functioned like offices, they had to find a more private "home"; even the presence of their wives in these houses did not deter them from seeking more homelike and exotic places such as a courtesan's boudoir.

The novel's two literati characters, Gao Yabai and Yin Chiyuan, live as guests in a rich merchant's residence. But in reality, a literatus-journalist like Han Bangqing would live more humbly than merchants or shop owners:

> At that time, the buildings of the news presses were all simple and old. The room for living and office space was no more than ten square meters (*xunzhang*) and had little light. The sleeping quarter was also the dining room and bathroom, and was chilly in winter and hot in summer. The worst was that many smelly bugs, breeding and crawling in the room, often startled them and disturbed their sleep. No food was offered in the building. They ate in small food stores or had meals purchased and brought back…. The highest salary was forty yuan and the lowest a little more than ten yuan. That amount would cover all living expenses, including food, tea, laundry, haircuts, and office supplies.
>
> (Lei [1922] 1987: 28)

Their best escape from this squalid living situation would be the courtesan house, and it was no surprise that they became the most enthusiastic promoters and connoisseurs of the courtesan culture, which is known today mainly through their writings.

None of these various lodgings was called home (*jia*): shops were too commercial, hostels too temporary, and *gongguan* too official. Above all, these male-dominated spaces were different from homes hosted by women. In contrast, the novel's narrator and male characters often call the courtesan houses *jia*. A long-term client considers the boudoir of his courtesan host to be a *jia* of *hers*, while she also wants him to make it his *jia* as well. When he is leaving her, she often asks where he is going to or urges him to come back soon as if her boudoir were also his home.[1] He would also visit and stay in her boudoir more than anywhere else, just like the courtesan room Han used as a hideout, as noted above. When friends or messengers look for him, they would first go to his courtesan's place rather than his own residence or store, as is also true of Ge Zhongying and Hong Shanqing (5.306, 17.367). The courtesan house seemed to be a substitute for, as well as an escape from, the sojourners' hinterland home—usually a communal space with a strong sense of belonging but no much scope for private pleasure. Displaced into this strange city under foreign administration, the courtesan and her client jointly created a temporary *jia*, a dream house of pleasure and sociability. It was at once their private boudoir and their communal space.

Like the shophouse and *gongguan*, the courtesan house also combined residence and small business functions and had the courtesans' signs posted on its entrance. The sign of a first-class courtesan, *shuyu*, had her name followed by *shuyu*, while that of a *changsan* had her name followed simply by *yu* (Huayu 1895; Chen [1887] 1996: 89). Later in the century these two categories became indistinguishable from one another and were called *changsan shuyu*. Whereas the merchant's residence was called (*gong*)*guan*, the courtesan house was called (*shu*)*yu*; the former means an official residence, while the latter means a temporary lodging. Thus the *yu* became comparable to the *gongguan*. Like a private home, the *yu* was small and did not entertain strangers, who had to be introduced by one of its regular clients.

The *tang* was a much larger establishment with up to thirty or even fifty *yao'er* girls.[2] Above its entrance was hung a lantern, on which was written the name of the establishment rather than those of the courtesans. *Tang* literally means a hall or public space in a house or official mansion, but here it defines a pleasure space open to the public, where strangers could enter and pick one from the many courtesans who eagerly showed up in front of them after the servant announced their arrival. The *tang* was less a homelike space than a straightforward brothel, but the *yao'er* were still considered courtesans (*guanren*), though of a class lower than the *changsan*. There were also many small establishments more obscure than the *yu*, but more homelike than the *tang*, called *zhujia* (residence). The *zhujia* could be very similar to the *yu* and usually had only one or two courtesans running their own business (without a madam). A less expensive *zhujia* would charge its clients the *yao'er* standard, and was called *yao'er zhujia* (Huayu 1895: 6.3; Wang [1878] 1992b: 5689; Figure 3.1).[3] Quite different from the collective *tang*, the *yu* or *zhujia* offered its clients intimate spaces with the feel of a private home.

If the *yu*, *zhujia*, or even *tang* was the sojourners' surrogate home, then the concept of home had indeed changed in nineteenth-century Shanghai. The former grand household as a self-contained socio-economic entity was replaced by many fragmented, provisional spaces, such as shops, *gongguan*, and *yu*, scattered in an exotic urban landscape, in which spaces of work, rest, and entertainment were being torn apart. In this displacement, the courtesan house marked a further fragmentation of life as well as a nostalgic reconstruction of the hinterland home—a strange and novel as well as homelike space.

Figure 3.1 Well-dressed courtesans acted like the streetwalkers in Ju'an li. The report reads: "Recently officials and merchants in a difficult situation are no longer spendthrifts and the courtesan businesses are in decline. Many a courtesan rents a room, calls it *zhujia*, and in the evening walks on the street to look for a customer rather than waiting for him to be led into her room."

Sources: *Dianshizhai huabao*, March 1887; Wu et al. 2001: 3.299.

The "family" business

To construct this provisional home, the courtesan house borrowed many ideas from the family-centered Confucian tradition. Many terms for business and social relations in the courtesan house were taken from the domestic realm. If the house was run by a madam (*laobao*), she would organize the business as if it were her own family affair. She, her courtesans, and their servants addressed each other as if they were in a family: the courtesans called the madam "Mother" and were considered to be her adopted daughters, or *taoren*. A newly purchased *taoren* lost her previous family name (if she had one at all) and took the madam's; she was also given a new professional name, which, consisting of two characters, would share a character with the names of other courtesans in the house to indicate their sister-like relationship.[4] And just as the madam and her *taoren* formed a matrilineal descent, the female servants became their close relatives. The latter's roles in the house were described in familial terms: *niangyi* (aunt) was used for senior married servants and *dajie* (sister) for junior servants. Although these women came from diverse backgrounds, they tried to run their business like a unified family.

In this "family" the traditional social hierarchy seemed to be reproduced in the order of the *laobao, taoren, niangyi,* and *dajie.*[5] But this new hierarchy was defined in business terms rather than being based on kinship, age, or gender. The madam purchased the *taoren* in order to profit. A *niangyi* who had shares of investment (*daidang*) in the house also expected to benefit from the *taoren*'s work. Thus these familial titles were employed to conceal naked financial interests which in fact made the hierarchy much less rigid: a shrewd courtesan successful in her business could challenge her madam; on the other hand, those who failed to bring income to the house were in a more deplorable situation than the servants. Indeed, the *taoren*'s position in the hierarchy was quite problematic: she was the ultimate representative of glamour, a central member of the "family," but was at the same time a virtual slave, a mere gambit for business profit, and would eventually be sold into a marriage just as she had been purchased.

The novel provides two examples of this type of family. Huang Erjie, a cunning and selfish madam, has three *taoren*, Cuifeng, Jinfeng, and Zhufeng. Cuifeng is the most successful in business and her strong and shrewd persona makes her more powerful than Erjie. In fact she often censures the latter's relation with a secret lover (*pintou*): "You should count how many years you have lived. Still want to have a love affair! Do you have shame?" (21.393). In contrast, Zhufeng hardly has any clients and is often scolded and sometimes beaten by Cuifeng and Erjie for her incompetence and laziness (8.324). Jinfeng's situation is between that of Zhufeng and of Cuifeng, and she behaves like Cuifeng's subordinate.

The house of Zhou Lan also has three courtesans: Shuangzhu, Shuangbao, and Shuangyu. Shuangbao has the least business and has to give up her room upstairs to the newcomer Shuangyu (3.394–95). The latter turns out to be quite successful and often fights for privileges with Shuangbao who in turn highly resents her. Shuangzhu, the senior sister in the house and Zhou Lan's biological daughter, also has a successful business and holds a respectable position in the house. Unlike the shrewd Huangs, she and Zhou Lan are rarely in conflict and often consult each other. This family seems to have more homelike sentiments, but naked commercial interest still rules. When Shuangyu is about to entertain her first client, Zhou Lan helps her with her grooming and tells her:

> "You need to have your own ambition and work hard on your business, you know? In my eyes, there is no difference between real and adopted daughters. If you can do as well as your sister Shuangzhu, you can have any piece of the jewelry or clothes left by the first and second courtesans [who were already married]; but if your business is like that of Shuangbao, I wouldn't be happy even though you were my real daughter."

(10.331)

In neither house does the madam have absolute power; she is often counterbalanced, and occasionally challenged, by the most successful courtesan, and a courtesan's position in the house is closely related to her business achievements as well as her persona. Thus, the business side of the house seriously compromises the simulated mother–daughter relationship between the madam and courtesan. Indeed, how successfully could the concepts of kinship be deployed to define business relationships? This irony was deeply embedded in the nature of the courtesan business that marketed an illusory home to male clients.

Sometimes a *taoren* could buy her freedom from the madam, as when Cuifeng negotiates such a deal with Erjie and starts her own courtesan business (49.540–44). In other cases, free women began the business on their own; for instance, Zhao Erbao becomes a courtesan when she and her family want to stay in Shanghai but lack other means to sustain their living (35.464). More than half of the novel's elite courtesans are such free women. In their houses, the *niangyi* are crucial business partners, who usually have shares (*daidang*) in the business. When Erbao starts a business without her own money, she relies on *daidang* money from the landlord, who provides 300 yuan, and from her *niangyi* and male servant, who each provides 200 yuan (35.464).

The madam, courtesans, and female servants formed the "family" core, but in order to make it a complete household they still had to have at least one male servant who announced the arrivals of clients and performed some manual duties. He was generally treated as an outsider to this family: unlike *niangyi* and *dajie*, his title, *xiangbang* ("mutual help," used in the *yu*) or *waichang* ("outside place," used in the *tang*), was not a familial term. His living quarter, always in an obscure room downstairs, also reflected his odd position in the house. But in many cases he was a *niangyi*'s husband and his traditional gender superiority conflicted with his low social and economic status in the house.

This conflict is vividly illustrated in the struggle between Ajin and her husband Adebao, the *niangyi* and *xiangbang* of Zhou Lan's house. In the house Adebao holds the lowest position, but as a husband he is powerful. While Ajin has a secret affair with a merchant's servant, Zhang Shou, and some of her money disappears without a trace, the suspicious Adebao often beats her and wreaks havoc in the house (3.293). When this happens, even Zhou Lan and the courtesans cannot stop him; instead, they often help Ajin to cover up her affair (12.344–45). Frequently the courtesans' upstairs rooms become Ajin's sanctuary, but as soon as she returns downstairs, she risks being beaten again.

Not all *xiangbang* were in the lowest positions: some had investments in the houses and were in a position similar to that of the *daidang niangyi*. If the husband of the madam or the brother of a free courtesan also worked in the house (as does Zhao Puzhai in his sister Erbao's house), he was called *benjia*. Like the female members of the house, the male also played a varied role and was closely tied to his financial situation. Outside the house, he was a more contemptible figure than the other members and acquired an infamous title: *guinu* (tortoise slave). Contemporary literature often caricatured him as either a cuckold in the house, like Adebao, or a thug in the alleyway, where he often harassed *dajie* from other houses (Figure 3.2). Similarly the *niangyi*, notorious for having amorous affairs, was portrayed in bamboo poems as a sluttish *dajiao* (big foot) (Gu 1996: 19, 58,

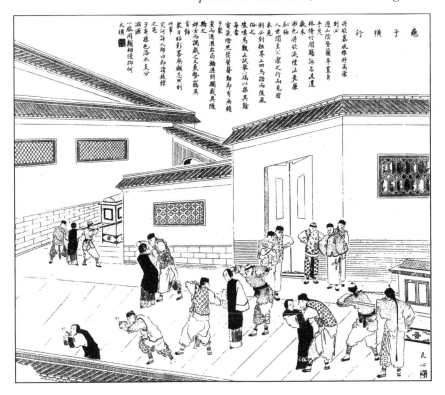

Figure 3.2 Hoodlums, usually workers in courtesan houses, harassed young maids escorting
　　　　　　courtesan sedans in an alleyway.
Sources: *Dianshizhai huabao*, May 1887; Wu et al. 2001: 4.32.

65, 78), her natural feet now a foil to her mistress's more exclusive and erotic
appendages. Thus these servants became scapegoats, blamed for moral decline in
the settlements. The courtesan house was indeed a decadent family loosely held
together by business ties. Its less rigid hierarchy gave the servants plenty of space
to pursue their own pleasure.

　　The male servant's problematic position was a symptom of the uprooting monetary economy rather than an indication of the courtesan house's challenge to traditional male authority. In fact, by catering to its male clients' vanity the house
bolstered the long-established patriarchal order. Addressed as *laoye* (master), the
client seemingly played the role of patriarch in the house, as a team of women—the
courtesan, madam, *niangyi*, and *dajie*—worked together to win his favor and money.
Whenever there was a crisis in his relationship with the courtesan, the madam or
niangyi always tried to resolve it. Here, as in a rich household, the powerful male
figure was balanced by the collective force of these women.[6] Yet the client was
not the patriarchal host but a guest in this house hosted by the women—guest and

client are the same word, *keren*. Thus, the relations in the courtesan house parodied that between the patriarch and his female subjects. Whereas the traditional household accommodated the bride (or concubine) as a guest, the courtesan house offered a provisional home to the male guest. And insofar as the marriage arranged by the parents was merely a business deal, the commercial nature of the courtesan house evoked a strangely familiar sentiment. In both cases, the female was more or less reduced to a commodity: while the traditional household "purchased" the bride (or concubine) to sustain itself, the displaced sojourner bought a temporary homelike space as compensation for his "homelessness." The relationship between the host and guest could be either businesslike or homelike; in the courtesan house, it became more obscure and uncertain.

However ephemeral this house was, the courtesan usually had a long-term relationship with at least one of her clients and eventually pursued a marriage/concubinage with a client as her ideal exit from the courtesan house (see Hershatter 1997: 119–26; Henriot 2001: 59–61). As if this relationship really were a marriage, the courtesans in the same house called each other's clients *jiefu* (brother-in-law). The client was also seeking a long-term lover, or *xianghao*. Whereas the *xianghao* relationship simulated that between a husband and a wife/concubine, it was very different from the arranged marriage, as the parties were free to choose their partners according to their romantic as well as financial interests. It was indeed more uncertain than the bonds in the traditional household, as Hong Shanqing in the novel puts it: "Truly said, a courtesan does not rely on one client and a client does not patronize just one courtesan; [if he is] happy, [he will] visit [her] more; unhappy, visit less. No further complications" (10.334).[7]

The public boudoir: banquets and tea parties

Organized like a private family, the courtesan house was after all a business open to the public, but there was not much conflict between domesticity and business in Chinese society. While the gentry household and merchant residence always accommodated many business functions, the courtesan house was also a social space for certain circles of merchant or literati clients to enjoy their leisure and build their social network. Indeed, the pseudo-familial structure of the courtesan house helped to consolidate the ties between these sojourners from diverse backgrounds, who chose to socialize in this exotic as well as homelike space and in so doing gave their business relationships a familial flavor. This function was epitomized by banquet parties (*jiuju*) held in the courtesan house.

Usually held in a courtesan's private room, a banquet party brought honor and prestige to that courtesan. The novel has many scenes of such parties. A moment after Hong Shanqing introduces his nephew Zhao Puzhai to the *yao'er* courtesan Lu Xiubao, she asks Puzhai to host a banquet for her (2.291). For a new client, hosting a banquet was an initial step toward pursuing a *xianghao* relationship with a courtesan, and he would continue to host many banquets for her—especially on important occasions, such as seasonal festivals or when she moved to a new location. He would invite his friends to fill up a table or sometimes two tables put together (*chi shuangtai*) (Figure 3.3, top left). His friends enjoyed free food and

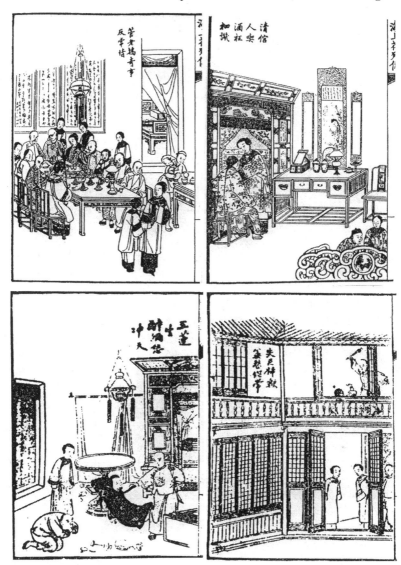

Figure 3.3 Illustrations from *Flowers of Shanghai* (1894). Top left: Wang Liansheng hosts a banquet party in Zhang Huizhen's new residence (Ch. 6). Top right: Zhao Puzhai and Zhang Xiaocun have a casual visit in Lu Xiubao's room (Ch. 2). Bottom left: Liansheng destroys Shen Xiaohong's boudoir after finding out her affaire with an actor (Ch. 33). Bottom right: Liansheng beats his wife Huizhen for her affair with his nephew (Ch. 54).

drink but were obligated to call more courtesans to the party. Sometimes a host could request that each of his guests call multiple courtesans in order to make the party more spectacular and fun.[8] Most courtesans were called to the party from other houses and were to be paid for their services, a practice called *chuju*. Though being present at her own party was not considered *chuju*, the hosting courtesan gained more prestige (*mianzi*) before her potential clients and professional rivals. In the novel, when Shen Xiaohong knows that her only patron Wang Liansheng has started a new relationship with Zhang Huizhen, she is so upset that she picks up a fight with Huizhen in a public garden (9.327); but in the end she only requests that Liansheng hosted a banquet in her house, inviting the same guests who have attended the one he hosted for Huizhen two nights earlier (11. 335–36; 12.341–42). She thereby gets back her *mianzi* and he can still visit Huizhen.[9]

A banquet party could bring many benefits to the courtesan house: in addition to drawing many potential clients, it demonstrated the house's success—music and noise from this late-night party proudly announced the business's prosperity to the entire neighborhood; the hosting client paid for the meal and gave generous tips (*xiajiao yangqian*) to the house.[10] In return, the party improved his relationship with the courtesan and made him feel at home in her boudoir; moreover, on this occasion he could display his wealth and generosity and strengthen his business ties with friends and partners. It was important that friendship and business connections between the merchants and literati be forged in the presence of the courtesans, whose own combination of domesticity and business helped to make these fluid connections more like solid familial bonds, and who became an indispensable part of the homelike setting of the merchants' leisure and business activities.[11]

Fitting into such male-dominated banquet parties, a courtesan resembled her clients in certain ways: like the merchants, she regarded her profession as doing business (*zuo shengyi*); and her two professional titles, *guanren* (official person) and *xiansheng* (teacher/master), also echoed those of her other clients, namely officials and literati. A guidebook remarked on the term *guanren*: "It is not known where its meaning comes from. Is it not because it means 'a public thing'? It surely inherits the meaning of the *guanji* (official entertainer) in the music instruction department (*jiaofang*) of the Yuan and Ming courts" (Huayu 1895: 6.4). It was a term used in conversation to refer to a courtesan in the third person, while *xiansheng* was a more respectable title used to address a courtesan directly. Formerly, only people with unusual skills, such as teachers, doctors, and geomancers, deserved that title.

The first-class courtesans, known as *shuyu* since the 1850s, were the *xiansheng* of storytelling. Their original reputation as professional storytellers with no ties to the sex trade was lost toward the end of the century, when the (*shu*)*yu* title was also appropriated by the *changsan*, who were less skilled in singing but more accessible sexually. But the *shuyu* indeed set a professional standard for the *changsan* and *yao'er*. Previously only male storytellers were called *xiansheng*, but the storytelling art evolved in the settlements. To attract larger audiences, the storytelling houses (*shuchang*) hired female assistants to sing prelude songs (*kaipian*) before stories, and these female singers soon became the prominent figures in the houses (Chi [1893] 1989: 157).

The earliest *shuyu* were such female singers who could perform in their private residences or could be called out (*chuju*) to sing at private parties. The *chuju* also became the routine professional activity of the *changsan* and *yao'er*. But for them, it usually entailed paid attendance at a banquet or gambling party. Because each client could call one or more courtesans, such a party was usually quite crowded; many courtesans did not have to perform, and only the best were asked to sing a few *kaipian*. Here the courtesans were not so much respectable artists as decorative escorts catering to the male banqueters' vanity. Nonetheless, the professional character of their service remained: while they were not exactly storytellers or singers, they were still the *xiansheng* specializing in attending parties; the frequency of being called out to these parties was a direct indication of their professional achievement.

The *chuju* was the most stable and basic income source of the courtesan house. As economic development led to currency and many business activities becoming standardized in the settlements,[12] the courtesan house also developed conventional rules and practices.[13] To invite a courtesan of his acquaintance, a client had to write a ticket (*jupiao*), which was then sent to a house for this courtesan. The ticket had a standard value (1–3 yuan; see Henriot 2001: 252), to be paid by the client at the end of a business season.[14] A successful courtesan usually had multiple *chuju* duties in one night and could earn up to 2,000 yuan or more in a season. Her professional duty required her to answer any call unless she had an excuse such as illness. She could also attend a party briefly if she had another *chuju* to serve. Her movement from one party to another was called *zhuanju*. A busy courtesan would sing a *kaipian* quickly at a party and hurry to another one.

In the novel, Sun Sulan arrives at a party and asks the courtesan Yuan Sanbao if she has performed. Knowing that Sulan has to leave soon, Sanbao's *niangyi* tells her to sing first. Sulan then tunes up her instrument (*pipa*) and sings a *kaipian* and a Peking Opera song. Having finished singing, she drinks two cups of wine for her client and then tells him that she has to go to another party (3.296). Sometimes a courtesan used the *zhuanju* as an excuse to cut short attendance at an unpleasant party, as Yao Wenjun does to get away from the thug Lai Touyuan (44.514). Some might also use this excuse for their late arrival at a party.

The courtesan's duty in such a party was rather simple: sitting behind her client, who was busy with drinking games, she did not touch any food, but she could be asked to drink for him if he lost the games; sometimes her accompanying *niangyi* or *dajie* could drink for the client. As soon as the drinking was over and rice was to be served near the end of the banquet, all the attending courtesans would start to depart. Much as they had arrived at the party after it had already begun, so they also left it early. The client and courtesan would never join and leave a party together, though they might have a date in her house right after it. Thus the courtesan's romantic relationship was clearly separated from her professional duties (*chuju*). This separation also gave the client freedom: though he usually called his *xianghao* to parties, he could also call any other courtesan or even multiple courtesans at once to show off.

Although the courtesan house functioned like a nightclub during the late-night banquets, it was more like a private home on other occasions. It was the resting place for the courtesans, and sometimes their clients as well, in the early morning hours. The courtesans usually got up around noon. In the afternoon, social activities in the house were less formal and more homelike: the courtesan's client, alone or along with one or two friends, might casually visit her room. Such a visit was called *dachawei* or *kaichawan* (tea party), at which watermelon seeds and fruits were usually served. The novel has many scenes of such informal visits in the afternoon or after a banquet party at night (Figure 3.3, top right). If a *xianghao* relationship was established between a courtesan and her client, he would visit and stay in her boudoir more often than anywhere else. These casual visits became his "home stay," during which he would enjoy some private times with his *xianghao*. A more intimate relationship could be built on these private occasions when they played the roles of husband and wife, quite different than their roles in the banquet parties. In private they had long intimate conversations, discussing not only their own affairs but matters pertaining to those around them. Most of the narratives and plots in *Flowers of Shanghai* are revealed through such conversations.

Yet however homelike these private social activities seemed to be, they were never free of financial concerns. Many important business decisions were made during these private times, and the courtesan also sought to use these occasions to solicit gifts—usually jewels (*toumian*) and clothing—from her client. Even when the *xianghao* relationship was developing toward a prospective marriage/ concubinage, that new association was no less a business deal.

Shifting gender roles

Combining intimate privacy and public sociability, the courtesan house blatantly transgressed the Confucian code of man as public (*wai*) and woman as private (*nei*). The courtesan seemed to have acquired an ambiguous gender status that was constantly shifting rather than fixed: in banquets, tea parties, and intimate tête-à-têtes of varying degrees of privacy, she played different gender roles. This perfor-mance in fact reflected a unique understanding of sex and gender as embodied in the Chinese language and the yin-yang theory, which idealizes the balance of yin (female) and yang (male) essences in the body of either man or woman. Rather than being viewed as mutually exclusive, the sexes are considered as external, secondary, shifting qualities temporally associated with a rather neutral subject. This sex model produces a homologous body that varies along a continuous scale of different blends of yin and yang (Liang 2003; see Furth 1999). So in Chinese tradition the borderline between male and female has been quite fluid.

During the *chuju*, the courtesan was the *xiansheng* or *guanren* of masculine standing and was addressed as *a'ge* (brother) by other courtesans (from differ-ent houses),[15] while in the private with her client she played the role of domes-tic woman (*renjiaren*) and was addressed as a sister by courtesans of the same house. But this does not necessarily mean that she was more powerful in public and weaker in private: whereas in public she was subservient to her client, in private she became more powerful in making various demands on him; in public she appeared merely as a decorative possession of her client and her masculine mask was but a foil to his patriarchal vanity, while in private she took the role of the master of the inner chamber to "penetrate" his weak side; in public she was merely a commodity offered by the courtesan house, but in private she fought for her own interests. Her *chuju* duties brought in only a basic income for the house; her real business success depended more on her performance on private occasions, in which her shrewdness and power to manipulate her client could bring greater financial rewards and secure her own survival in this ruthlessly commercialized world.

Both naïve and experienced courtesans knew the importance of dealing with their clients in private. Wu Xuexiang, a courtesan truly in love with Ge Zhongying, urges him to go home with her right after a casual lunch with his friend in a courtesan house next door to her own:

> Zhongying said: "Just wait for a while." Xuexiang said: "Why wait? I don't want to." Zhongying said: "If you don't want to, you go home first." Xuexiang stared at him and said: "Is it that you are not going home [with me]?" Zhongying smiled but did not move. Getting upset, Xuexiang got up and pointed her finger at him: "When you come back later, be careful!"
>
> (5.309)

On this rather private occasion, Xuexiang behaves as if she were in her own boudoir. But in the presence of a friend and his *xianghao*, Zhongying's masculine mask, however fragile, has to be kept intact, and she does not succeed in commanding him to go home with her. When he goes back to her house shortly thereafter, she is still very upset and urges him to obey her commands all the time (6.310). This episode vividly portrays the childlike character of Xuexiang, who is indeed a girl rather than a woman. In her naïveté, she betrays every courtesan's hidden desire that her client be obedient and loyal to her as if he were her filial son.[16] But the pursuit of this desire only makes her behave like a daughter nagging a fatherly figure—a stance that in fact more realistically reflects the age difference between the couple: it is indeed her youth that gives her charm and power over her client. Because most courtesans looked to marry and retire by the end of their teens, they were young girls rather than fully-grown women and their courtesanhood was often a prelude to marriage/concubinage, which would make them real (domestic) women. This unique stage before womanhood gave them freedom to take on different gender roles on various occasions.

In contrast to Xuexiang, Huang Cuifeng is an experienced courtesan, who is strong and shrewd. When Luo Zifu starts to call her out to banquet parties, she often arrives late, leaves early, and while there has a defiant attitude. Though not so pleased with that, Zifu becomes fascinated by a story told by a friend at a party about Cuifeng's strong character in fighting her madam. After this party, he goes to Cuifeng's house, as she has earlier suggested he do, but she is still on another *chuju* duty; her madam makes him wait for her and persuades him to have a long-term relationship with Cuifeng. When she returns, she demands that Zifu end the relationship with his current *xianghao* and not call any other courtesan. He readily agrees and then spends his first night in her bed (6.312–8.322). Fond of drinking, Zifu is portrayed as unruly and tough at the banquet tables; yet after this night he becomes very obedient to Cuifeng. He seems to have found satisfaction in his subservience to this dominating female figure.[17] Nonetheless, he once complains to her: "You are unreasonable; think about this yourself: as a courtesan you can have many clients, but you prohibit your client from having one more courtesan" (9.329). She retorts that to keep her business going she has to have many clients; otherwise, he alone would have to pay for all her business expenses. She apparently has no love for him and considers this relationship as purely a business arrangement. Yet she also has a soft side: she is very devoted to her secret relationship with Qian Zigang, in whose company she behaves like a caring wife. Many other courtesans in the novel, such as Zhou Shuangzhu and Zhang Huizhen, are amiable characters playing the role of domestic women for their clients.

These courtesans not only played different gender roles on different occasions but also displayed a range of personae, from naïve girl to caring domestic woman to bossy shrew. Each would be desired by a client at certain times: the courtesans' ambiguous gender status and diverse social roles reflected the inconstancy of male desire, which seemed to be gratified only by the (re)finding of something elusive. The wealthy sojourners of Shanghai were indeed looking for real love in a home-like space. If "love is homesickness," according to the old saying once quoted by Freud (1953: 245), then this "sickness" is a longing for an elusive "home" lost in the past, which can be retrieved only imaginatively. It was therefore quite natural that the literati's representations of the ideal courtesan, always a bygone or ephemeral figure, were full of nostalgia, as if their visits to courtesan houses were nothing more than incessant searches for this lost ideal. Their nostalgia was merely a symptom of the homesickness of the male subject.

According to Freud, a man's "home" can ultimately be traced back to the fertile body that had once nourished him, to his first perceptions of sexuality embodied in a certain mature woman in his distant childhood.[18] These "primordial scenes" were then repressed but not totally forgotten; they are eventually re-found in new forms that confront the male subject with exoticism, uncanny yet familiar, strange yet homelike (Freud 1953). By this time the firm, fertile body that produced the memory is gone: even if its image can be frozen in his (unconscious) mind, in the physical world it is always ephemeral and needs to be "reincarnated" in a new (bodily) form. But the mind changes faster than the physical being—passion evaporates more quickly than the sweat of the body. Before a fertile body turns sterile, love at first sight often mutates to unbearable ennui, disloyalty, or even hatred. Therefore the man is constantly searching for a new "incarnation" of the fragmented and repressed image buried in his inconstant mind. What happens to the body also happens to the physical home, as the latter is but the former's spatial extension. As time transforms any home, its resident's desire migrates to what is beyond it, to an exotic substitute that recalls the old one—lost in time but *partially* preserved in memory.

The Chinese traditional marriage practice denied this search for a new substitute for the lost "home." It was the bride who was sent to a new home, which had been the groom's "prison" since childhood. Changed by time, it was no longer his childhood home and became further transformed when he suddenly "possessed" this bride, a total stranger brought by a deal arranged by his and her parents, a sexual partner given rather than found. Indeed, as this bride gradually changed his mother's household into her own private domain, he felt more and more alienated in this transformed residence. Producing more children by having concubines was often an excuse to escape from this alienating relationship with his first wife, especially when she became older—that is, when her body was also transformed by time. But the arrivals of new concubines often simply repeated the experience with his first wife and made the home more alienating; he eventually became a vagabond wandering between his women's boudoirs, none of which he could claim as his own home. The richer and bigger his household was and the more women he had, the lonelier this male master tended to be.[19] Though every newly married woman might have brought him a sense of freshness similar to the first perception of the forbidden fruit, this fresh experience would soon fade away and he was always seeking a new cure for his chronic homesickness.

More often than not, this restless male subject ended up in the pleasure quarter, be it an ornate tour boat (*huafang*) in Nanking or a courtesan house in Shanghai. Here he found an ephemeral pleasure which, like that in his distant memory, had disappeared from his own household. But he was definitely seeking more than just sexual gratification, as various forms of direct sex trade were always available (and were especially well developed in nineteenth-century Shanghai). The sojourner in Shanghai was seeking a new "home" different from his hinterland home, which he wanted to escape from as well as return to; those with their wives in the city also frequently visited the courtesan houses, as do Qian Zigang and Yao Jichun in the novel. The attraction of this home was precisely its reversal of the traditional marriage practice: in his temporary union with the courtesan, the sojourner became a guest in her house and the courtesan played a twofold role, at once a "groom" waiting for an unknown "bride" and a "wife" waiting for her wandering "husband" to return.

Yao Jichun maintains a residence in Shanghai and the novel portrays him as a character afraid of his wife. Nevertheless, he is an enthusiastic patron of courtesans. Though his wife cannot forbid such patronage, she seems to have tight control over his activities. In the novel, she is a domineering *jiazhupo* (housewife), while his regular courtesan host Wei Xiaxian is a shrewd courtesan. A clash between them vividly illustrates the rivalry between the two different "homes." One day Jichun has been missing from both his home and Xiaxian's house for two days. Reckoning that he has spent too much time with the courtesan, his wife comes to Xiaxian's house looking for him and behaves as if she were the "ruler" there (see McMahon 2002: 15–16). Xiaxian retorts:

"To look for your master (*zhugong*), you shall go back to your own house. Since what time have you given him to me so that you can now come here to find him? Our *tangzi* [courtesan house] has not come to your house (*fushang*) to solicit clients, whereas you first came to our *tangzi* to look for your master. Is that ridiculous? We open this *tangzi* to do business and whoever visits here becomes our client. Who cares if he is the master of some family? Is it that you do not allow me to do your master's business? Tell you the truth: he is your master in your house, but in this *tangzi* he is our client. If you are powerful, you should keep him in your house; why have you let him play in the *tangzi*? If he has been in this *tangzi* and you want to take him back, you should ask whether the foreign settlements of Shanghai have such a rule. Not to mention that he has not been here; even if he were here, don't you dare to yell at or beat him! If you abuse your master, I don't care; but if you mess with my client, be careful! While he is afraid of you, I don't know who you are at all."

(23.402)

Xiaxian thus sharply delineates a borderline between the two distinct "homes" that is not to be crossed by their respective hostesses. She plays with the Confucian values that keep domestic women within the inner quarter and reverses the normal picture: now Yao's wife becomes a transgressor, whereas Xiaxian like a "chaste" woman stays within her quarter, which has the advantage of being more fluid than Yao's house. Xiaxian continues to humiliate her: "Is it that you are tired of being a housewife, and want to have fun in our *tangzi*…. If there is a client here, I will let him rape you. Then will you have face going home? Even if you sue us in the new court, this kind of things is not unusual in *tangzi*" (23.402). But beneath these cruel words is the same sorrow that has made Yao's wife visit this *tangzi*. After the latter is gone, Xiaxian laments: "If Master Yao really visits our house everyday, we could have just said that, but my madam told the truth that he has not been here for a long time, as if we were afraid of [Yao's wife]" (23.403). In fact, both women are in similar situations, and Xiaxian's ridicule echoes her own failure in finding a loyal client among those given free rein in the *yichang*.

While the courtesan played various roles on different occasions, the client did the same in his two "homes": whereas his position seemed to fall from being the master at home to a guest in the courtesan house, he in fact might feel he was treated more like a master in the latter place and a prisoner in the former. The magic of capital had turned this dislocated guest into a real master, able to enjoy many novel pleasures in the homelike space away from home.

The courtesan's enigmatic charm was also derived from this reversal, from her inverted—and also multifaceted—gender role. Adopting the masculine titles *xiansheng* and *guanren*, she transgressed traditional gender lines and became the host of a quite public space. In a sense, she was both the (feminine) object of male desire and the (masculine) mirror image of the male subject. A man's sexual desire covers a hidden wish to appreciate his own mirrored image in the desired object, as the lost home is to be retrieved nowhere else but in his own double. Even before the first perceptions of sexuality, the primal understanding of the ego is filled with unbounded self-love, as the ego identifies with many external beings/things so as to create many doubles that might fulfill its wish for immortality. "But when this stage has been surmounted, the 'double' reverses its aspect. From having been an assurance of immortality, it becomes the uncanny harbinger of death" (Freud 1953: 235). The courtesan's masculine titles betrayed a new form of the male subject's displaced narcissism. To evoke the ideal of *mingshi cainü* (renowned scholar and talented lady), the literati client called her *jiaoshu* (book emendator), an image onto which he projected his self-pity. The *jiaoshu* was always an ephemeral, tragic figure, not a symbol of fertility but a beauty linked to death and decay, about which authors like Wang Tao could only "chase the beautiful traces already fading."

For a more mundane client, the ideal of the double was reflected in the pairing of his title, *laoye*, with hers, *xiansheng*. As a merchant, he preferred to view her as a businessperson of his own kind, and their relationship revolved more around business concerns than traditional gender roles. Thus the heterosexual and "familial" relationship between the courtesan and her client was ironically represented in the masculine terms *laoye* and *xiansheng* or the business terms *keren* and *guanren*. In both cases, the relationship is cast as asexual, sterile, and unfamilial. Indeed, as a double of the client's ego, a sign of the return of his pristine self-love, the courtesan was desexualized, deprived of female reproductive power; she became a new symbol of commercial (re)productivity, which is nothing other than multiplication of dead objects, of sterile pleasures.

Thus, in the courtesan house sexual desire and romantic love are apparently subordinated to business ties and friendship. Often the (business) relationship between the courtesan and her *niangyi* (or madam) and that between male friends were more solid than the *xianghao* relationship. When the latter was in crisis, friends and the *niangyi* always helped in the negotiations. The novel tells of the intimate friendship between such merchants as Wang Liansheng and Hong Shanqing, or Luo Zifu and Tang Xiao'an. Wang and Luo, who are richer, often commission Hong and Tang to do some business, such as purchasing gifts for their *xianghao*. Hong also has a close friend, Chen Xiaoyun, who like Hong is a shop owner; sometimes they walk together in the alleys "aligning their shoulders and holding their arms together" (*bijian jiaobi*) (25.411). There is no sign that these intimate relations go beyond friendship, but they are often more reliable than the *xianghao* relationship that is in fact sexual.

Such intimate relations could also be found among the literati, who sometimes compared—if not very seriously—their friendships with their romances. A poem by Han Bangqing was inspired by his unusually close friendship with a man:

> Mr. Shi Quan says that [in the next life he] would like to be an ultimate beauty to serve [me] like an inkpad towel. I then quote Zhang Chuanshan's poem: "Everyone wants to be a concubine of the sage; the heaven instructs us to create many next-life romances." What kind of person am I who deserves such flattery? I compose this poem to joke about it: "Take a rest, sir (*xiansheng*)! How many lives do I have to endure to attain that fortune? Disliking all those [thick] beards and eyebrows, only to want those delicate hairdos. The indistinguishable females and males of various colors become united by forgetting their forms. With devotion like this, why bother to have the *yuan* and the *yang* (female and male mandarin ducks) upside down?.... Upon the turning of waves, [I am] suddenly alerted by the painted eyebrows, by the aged person."[20]

> (*Shenbao*, December 17, 1887; Fang 2002: 230)

This enigmatic verse problematizes the conventional borderlines between friendship and love, male and female: if love is essentially the finding of a double of one's ego rather than sexual consummation, then the various forms of male and female should be disregarded. Indeed, however successfully the courtesan played her inverted gender role, she was always outperformed by her client's male friend as his double.[21] The latter relationship was more enduring—the consummation with it was eternally deferred to the "next life." Thus death, the twin of love, was bracketed as sexual love was replaced with a sterile, artificial kind of doubling.

While the literatus projected his self-pity onto the image of the courtesan and the merchant saw her as an entrepreneur of his own kind, she usually found real love not with either of them but with a person closer to her own kind, such as the male entertainers so despised by the traditional elite. Erotic liaisons between courtesans and opera actors (*youling*) were widely reported in contemporary media. In *Flowers of Shanghai*, Shen Xiaohong has a secret relationship with Xiaoliu'er, an actor on whom she seems to have spent much of the money she earns from Wang Liansheng. Such a relationship was often pictured as obscene and immoral. In August 1897, *Dianshizhai huabao* reported that a Sikh policeman arrested a courtesan and an actor because of their lewd conduct in a carriage; a year later, it reported on the affair of an actor and an ex-courtesan discovered by the latter's husband (Wu et al. 2001: 14.205, 15.196).

In all these cases, the actors' attraction was related to their theatrical role of *wusheng* (young warrior). If they were indeed the courtesans' soul mates or doubles, they could also be "harbingers of death": Xiaoliu'er's irresistible charm, derives from his stage character Shi Xiu—who has the shrewish, adulterous woman Pan Qiaoyun killed by her husband in the play *Cui ping shan* (30.437)—eventually brings about Xiaohong's self-destruction (33.456–57; see below). With a sense of the entanglement of love and death, it was often commented that emotional involvement with an actor or *enke* (loved client) was detrimental to a courtesan's business. Similarly, as a merchant in the novel says, too much affection in a *xianghao* relationship would bring a client many troubles (42.502). It was probably a preventive measure against real emotional involvement that the terms *laoye* and *xiansheng*, or *keren* and *guanren*, were used to describe the *xianghao* relationship. They helped to create a certain distance between the client and courtesan and reduced a sexual relationship to an asexual friendship or business partnership and thereby deferred or bracketed love and death.

The hedonistic lifestyle in the courtesan houses was not only a rebellion against the traditional ideals of family and familial reproduction that ensured patrilineal descent but also a subversion of sex and gender norms. Once the reproductive function of sex was subverted, the sexes also became harbingers of death: the male and the female are reduced to transitory displays that can reproduce themselves not biologically but materially (or optically). These self-reproducible spectacles betray a sterilization of sex, an eclipse of maternal love by self-love. Such self-love, fully unleashed in the capitalist world, can be transferred to masculinized images of women; to androgynous, sterile bodies; to persons of the same sex; and ultimately to (displays of) material items. Thus, the asexual or masculine terms adopted in the courtesan houses defined relations based on capitalist rather than sexual (re)productivity, reflecting a general development in which sex became increasingly separated from the family and mingled with commerce to the extent that female sexuality was redefined in masculine, sterile, and material terms, and the love of material abundance eclipsed biological drives. In short, as love and sex were mediated by material wealth, the latter became the ultimate object of desire. The courtesan houses were simply (*un*)*heimlich* homes where love and betrayal were exchanged for one another with the speed of circulating money.

Magical and fashionable objects

As commercial development displaced the sojourners from self-contained households into a sprawling web of fluid social and gender relations, fluctuating in accord with its uncertain cycle, certainty was more likely to be found in relations with material items. While the newly married bride needed considerable social skills and personal resilience to secure a respectable position in the new household that was initially quite "hostile" to this intruder (Mann 1997: 60), the courtesan had to have an extraordinary business capacity to survive in the commercial milieu of the settlements. But whereas the bride would eventually become the hostess of the less changing household, the courtesan's fate was more uncertain; she had to hold on to things less ephemeral, found not in the social but in the material realm. If male desire was so inconstant and her clients so unreliable, she could at least try to eke out from him things that might last. Indeed, the only compensation for the unfaithfulness of living beings was a love of inanimate things. A naïve courtesan like Zhao Erbao, pursuing a "true love" with her client, met with ultimate failure; a successful one like Huang Cuifeng took every chance to solicit or blackmail goods and money from her clients.

Gifts from successful *xianghao* relationships usually carried greater value than the regular income from *chuju* duties. Their traditional precedent would be the *dingqingwu* (the object that cements a relationship), which could be a fan, napkin, or simple decorative item exchanged between the *caizi* (talent) and the *jiaren* (beauty). But for the courtesan, they had to be valuable objects like jewels (*toumian*); in return, she would make her homelike boudoir and sexuality available to the clients. This exchange was still different from the sex trade, however: unlike money, which was soon spent on something else, these gifts were preserved as her treasure and became a decorative extension of her body, an enhancement of her charm, and an elevation of her social and professional status. These decorative objects in fact aided in holding her client longer than her sexuality could, as his desire (or self-love) also shifted to the material realm. He could also imagine that he had transformed her into an extension of his self, as his gifts to her had now become part of her body or physical environment. Thus these objects became the point where their mutually extended selves intersected, where ever-changing human relations could be fixed and signified.

The courtesan wore these decorative items on public occasions such as *chuju* or carriage rides so that she could attract attention and become a public spectacle.

Indicating her professional role, the gorgeous jewels and embroidered outfits in vivid colors functioned like an actor's theatrical costume or a magistrate's ostentatious headwear and gown. In fact she and the actor were more visible than the magistrate in the settlements. Her conspicuous public image could also help to elevate that of her client who, as a member of the nouveau riche, desperately needed some public manifestation of his improved social status. But at home the courtesan often dressed more casually, as does Jiang Yueqin in the novel when she is hosting a banquet at her house without wearing any makeup or fancy dress (15.360). These alternating dress codes reflected the courtesan's shifting gender roles, as discussed above: whereas the ornate dresses and jewels worn in public mirrored her client's masculine vanity, at home her plain clothes revealed the homelike charm of her feminine side. But it was the former that constituted the dominant image of the courtesan.

That her charm was increasingly represented in these material items betrayed a general transference of sexual desire to the realm of inanimate things—that is, to material wealth. Signifying her business success rather than her biological fertility, these objects indeed resulted from her professional activities and played a more important role than sex in her relationship with her client. As this relation assumed, "in their eyes, the fantastic form of a relation between things," it is indeed similar to what Marx (1983: 447) calls commodity fetishism. But these objects were not yet quite modern commodities; they were more like the traditional objects believed to possess a magical power, such as the magistrate's gown. Their durability made them distinct from ephemeral commodities, but they were nevertheless purchased from the market rather than acquired (as was the magistrate's gown) from a more legitimate source. The sojourners' obsession with these objects seemed to be somewhere between the fetishism of magical objects and that of modern commodities. Such an ambivalent position would also explain the twofold status of the courtesan who was at once celebrated as a cultural icon and despised as an entertainer and a sexual commodity.

Yet the courtesan's decorations represented more than a stage in the linear transition from cult objects to modern commodities. In traditional literature, human sexuality was often represented allegorically via images of nature—such as clouds and rain, flowers and butterflies—symbolizing life's creation. Feminine beauty was often compared to vegetal forms of fertility, such as flowers, which were then artificially reproduced in the design of clothes and jewels. In the writings of literati authors like Wang Tao, courtesans were still wrapped in such natural metaphors and their decorations were depicted in greater detail than their bodies. In studying these materials, Henriot (2001: 29) seems to be frustrated by the impossibility of visualizing the courtesans:

> Their physical appearance is always described in conventional language, with little variation on the same theme: "She was as beautiful as morning dew, her skin glistened like the almond, her bones were light and her body could be held in one hand, her gait was like a willow tree in the wind."

Such metaphors evoked a timeless image of the courtesan, as if she were part of (un)changing nature. This image was also an allegory for the ephemerality of life—a fleeting beauty captured in fragile vegetal forms, which were inanimate but still living and fertile. While the literati's desire to freeze feminine beauty appeared to be a fascination with those primordial forms of life, such enthrall-ment, or its visual aspect, was easily transformed into an impulse to fetishize commodities, inanimate things endowed with life. Only a thin line separated the traditional natural metaphors and the "allegorical" images of modern com-modities. The changing images of the courtesan testified to this continuity: as the objects around her body became less natural and more commodified, more fragmented visual displays than integrated forms of life, she herself increasingly became a symbol of commercial culture, or the "new nature"—one that was more ephemeral but still ever-the-same.[22]

As one of the first generation of writers who made adjustment to modern com-mercial publication, Han Bangqing portrayed no poetic or timeless images of the courtesans in his vernacular novel, which instead presents their vivid personae through convoluted narratives of their conversation and conduct. Only occasion-ally does the novel provide brief descriptions, still in conventional language, of their clothes and headwear. For instance, Lu Xiulin, a *yao'er* courtesan, wears "a silver filigree butterfly in her hair, a cotton blouse in the color of dawn's first light, a sleeveless jacket of satin-trimmed black crinkled crepe and pastel pink crinkled crepe trousers trimmed with the palest turquoise satin and three bands of re-embroidered lace" (1.284; trans. in Han [1894] 1984: 100–101). Another example: preparing for a carriage ride, Huang Cuifeng picks out from the closet "a coat made of *hangning* silk, upon which is embroidered golden dots, peony bonsai, and green bamboo roots, and a pair of pastel pink crinkled crepe trousers trimmed with pale turquoise satin and re-embroidered lace; both are very colorful as well as simple and elegant" (8.324–25). These words helped to freeze the courtesan's charm in the material items fashioned after natural forms, but the novel uses such descriptions sparingly, whereas its narrative on the uncertain fates and relations in and around courtesan houses is exhaustive. But eventually this uncertainty in the social realm also affected the material items, which turned out to be just as unreli-able in the modern city.

The courtesans were indeed very particular about the fancy clothes and jew-elry acquired from their clients, as if the value of one were compensation for the unfaithfulness of the other, and they often compared each other's possessions. In a banquet party, while their clients are busy with drinking games, three courtesans have a chat about their hairpins:

> Huang Cuifeng saw Zhang Huizhen's glistening jewels, reckoned that they were newly purchased, took her hand to have a close look at her ring, and said: "This ring with your name on it is of the old [classy] style!" Huizhen saw Cuifeng wore a pair of jade hairpins and wanted to have a close look at it, too. Cuifeng took one off and handed it to Huizhen and the latter said: "A green pin, it is quite alright." As Ge Zhongying [and Wu Xuexiang] was sitting next to Wang Liansheng [and Huizhen], Xuexiang heard Huizhen's admiring com-ments and turned her head to have a look and asked Cuifeng: "How much did it cost?" Cuifeng said: "Eight yuan." Xuexiang took off one of her own pair

to compare it with Cuifeng's. Huizhen saw it was also green and said: "It is quite alright as well." Xuexiang was annoyed: "Alright? This pair costs forty yuan; is that just alright?" Cuifeng heard this, took the piece from Xuexiang for a careful look, and asked her: "Did you buy them yourself?" Xuexiang said: "A client of mine bought them from the City Temple Tea Market, where you can find such a good price; no jewelry shop would sell them at this price." Huizhen said: "But I can't see that; compared with hers, perhaps a bit better." Xuexiang said: "It is difficult to know a jade item well and a slightly better quality is hard to see. No other item is better than mine; forty yuan, this is what it looks like." Cuifeng smiled and returned it to her without saying anything, while Huizhen also returned the other hairpin to Cuifeng. Zhongying was busy with the drinking game and did not hear Xuexiang clearly. After a round of the game, he asked Xuexiang: "What cost forty yuan?" She then handed the piece to him. He said: "You were fooled [by that client]! How can this cost forty yuan! No more than ten yuan can buy this." She said: "What do you know! You don't know any thing. You buy this for me for ten yuan!"

(22.397–98)

Later in private, Xuexiang complains to Zhongying: "When you bought me that bronze bracelet with a watch inserted, you said it cost more than thirty yuan, but [when you] say about my own items none is fancy. Is it that you think I am an awkward courtesan who cannot afford to buy a forty-yuan piece and can only wear that foreign-style bronze bracelet as if it were a gold one?" (22.398).

Besides portraying the vivid characters of naïve Xuexiang, shrewd Cuifeng, and reserved Huizhen, this episode reveals an inherent problem in the attempt to cement human relationships, or social meanings, in material items. In a modern economy, this attempt is reduced to affixing monetary values to commodities. The courtesans' obsession with the values of their belongings can be seen in their heated conversation, in which their admiration for and jealousy of one another are transferred into a comparison of their hairpins, and their professional and personal successes are reduced to the hairpins' exchange values. Though these objects can not be unfaithful, their values and meanings are open to debate and speculation. The inconstancy of human desire also affects the social meanings of dead objects, which then appear "as independent beings endowed with life, and entering into relation both with one another and with the human race" (Marx 1983: 447). Thus these dead objects seem to take on a new life and become as "unfaithful" as living beings, since new or inauthentic meanings and values can be arbitrarily applied to them. Xuexiang is upset when the high value of her piece is placed in doubt. If her former client did lie to her about the item's price, she chooses to accept that false value and defend it as a symbol of her own social status.

When Cuifeng is buying her freedom from her madam, they dispute its price until she agrees to give up all her belongings (48.533–34). As she is soon to start her own courtesan business, she wants to have all new clothes and jewels. The magical objects that are symbols of her earlier success can be jettisoned as her situation changes. Although such objects had been employed to fix social meanings, uncertain fortune and desire in the commercial world eventually made them ephemeral as well. Consequently, neither the client nor the courtesan could really be "faithful" to them. Just like her male client, the courtesan also had constantly craved things novel and marvelous—in her case, not a temporary home but fashionable things filling up that home.

So it is no surprise that the courtesan was a pioneer of modern fashion in Shanghai, vigilant about her own standards and her image in public. In the 1850s, Wang Tao ([1860] 1992a: 5649) observed:

> Clothes [in Shanghai] are made after what is fashionable in the courtesan houses. As the city's courtesans are all from Suzhou, their dresses are mostly in the style of that region. The dresses purchased for them by their clients are all from Color-Cloth Street (Caiyi jie), where [a great variety of dresses of] superb finish and elegant tailoring are for them to choose. Now many courtesans call tailors to their houses, instruct them with new styles, and provide them with fabrics. This is extremely luxurious and wasteful.

In addition, jewelry peddlers regularly visited the neighborhoods of courtesan houses, their cases brimming with expensive hairpins of jadeite, gold, pearl, and coral in the shape of jasmine flowers.[23]

Constructing her image via novel objects and styles, the courtesan tried to be ultrafashionable and was gradually reduced to a commodity item. Thus, those who became very successful and famous were known as *shimao guanren* (chic courtesans).[24] In the novel Tu Mingzhu is such a courtesan who, at a quite advanced age, still retains a degree of fame that others envy. When Zhu Airen and his friends are going to co-host a banquet in her house, his *xianghao* Lin Sufen is jealous and says:

> "Being a courtesan is [good] only [when] being chic. When you are chic, many clients will come to boost your fame. The client is really annoying: for the same one thousand yuan, is it better to patronize some courtesans whose businesses aren't so good? Spend it on the chic courtesan, and she does not feel any gratitude. But he always patronizes the chic courtesan and squanders his money to win her favor." Airen said: "Don't you say the client is annoying; so is the courtesan. When her business isn't good, she is nice to everyone; when her business is getting a bit better, she is interested only in having an opera actor as her lover (*enke*). Later she always ends up with nothing."
>
> (18.377)

Sufen then considers that the courtesan should try to get married before she is out of fashion, while Airen thinks that it is difficult for a courtesan to find a good client to marry.

This conversation clearly underscores the uncertain desires and fortunes of the courtesan and the client. Tu Mingzhu is already in the twilight of her career and is popular only in the eyes of old and nostalgic clients such as Li Zhuanhong. Younger clients often laugh at the idea of calling on her. A client's servant, Kuang'er, comments on her appearance: "Hair on her forehead all gone, not many teeth left in her mouth, which almost swallowed her own face. When she was talking with Master Li, she laughed and became really ugly, her face being stretched like a pond full of wrinkles" (15.359). If she is indeed so ugly, her attraction to clients lies in her fame and wealth. The last was the most reliable feature of this topsy-turvy world that made the ugly beautiful and the cheap expensive (McMahon 2002: 11). Should a courtesan like Mingzhu succeed in lengthening her career through a productive pursuit of valuable and fashionable objects, then her charm would be reduced to a hollow mask of wealth and she herself equated to those dead objects. Both her charm and the objects would finally be washed away by the tide of fashion. In the end, her pursuit of material wealth could not prolong her charm; it only sped up this cycle.

Interior settings

The objectification of social relations and pursuit of fashionable items were not limited to decoration on the courtesan's body but were found as well in the interior setting of her boudoir. Traveling to Shanghai in 1891 from Hangzhou, Chi Zhicheng marveled at the luxuries in courtesan houses:

> Their rooms are furnished like those of kings and magnates: beds, night tables, and wardrobes were made of marble or hardwood; aside from silk curtains, there are also dressing mirrors, calligraphy-painting lanterns, small round pedestal tables, flowers with glass covers, paintings [in colors] of coral and jade, pearl-lined clocks, long-legged plates, and silver opium pipes, all flickering in the light of red lamps, making one feel intoxicated.
> (Chi [1893] 1989: 162; trans. revised from Hershatter 1997: 86)

In this representation, the courtesan's boudoir looked like a luxurious dream house. Both the body and the boudoir were portrayed as displays of gorgeous jewelry and decorative novelties, but was the sojourners' dream for a homelike space so concerned with these marvelous items? Had their "homesickness" already been superseded by a fetishism of modern commodities?

Other sources provide more traditional views of the courtesan house. Huang Shiquan ([1883] 1989: 107) wrote of a famous courtesan who had generously donated 300 yuan to help victims of famine in the hinterland:

> Li Peilan, the hostess of Charm Scent Chamber, elegant and beautiful like a jade, is always demure with few words to say. Graceful and pure is her personality, which brings no undistinguished guests to her house. Entering her chamber, [you] feel the fragrance of tea and the scent of incense and see every item tidily arranged: bright windows and clean tables without any dust.

Like the conventional language in describing a courtesan's physical appearance, these words reveal few details about the courtesan boudoir. Similar words are found in Wang Tao's notes about the courtesan houses in the early years of the settlements. These writers were more interested in presenting the ideal of the timeless secluded boudoir as the mirror image of their own utopia. This utopian boudoir, like the vegetal forms of beauty, allegorized both transient life and timeless nature.

These contrasting images of the courtesan's boudoir—one depicting the visual profusion of fashionable objects, and the other stressing the timeless experience of fragrance and visual simplicity—reflected the diverging ideals of modern consumer culture and literati nostalgia, of the new and the old "nature," which paradoxically converged in this problematic space. Both ideals were also embodied in nineteenth-century visual representations of the courtesan houses. A guidebook (Huayu 1895) included 116 "portraits" of famous courtesans—all rendered in the traditional style and strongly resembling one another. Compiled from a range of sources, including works about legendary beauties, most of the figures were set in idealized gardens or domestic interiors filled with such motifs as flowers, rockeries, balconies, pavilions, vases, bonsai, chess or embroidery tables, and plump children; in these old-style settings the courtesans looked similar to gentry women or "talented ladies"; and the images sold very well (see Figure 2.1). At the same time, the guidebooks and *Dianshizhai huabao* recorded the interior views of some courtesan houses (Figure 3.4; see Meihua 1894: 2.12). Such fabulous images closely matched Chi's description, quoted above. In contrast to the nostalgic vision of the courtesan boudoir, they reflected the new ideal of commercial and urban culture.[25]

The courtesan boudoirs in *Flowers of Shanghai* neither evoke any nostalgia nor appear particularly fabulous. Most of its 128 illustrations, also produced by the *Dianshizhai* studio, are reductive, if also realistic, renderings of the courtesan boudoirs (see Figures 3.3, 4.4, 4.5). Similarly, the novel has few terse descriptions of the physical settings of the boudoirs. The rooms of the two *yao'er* courtesans, Lu Xiulin and Lu Xiubao, are similarly furnished with mirrors, clocks, calligraphy hanging-scrolls, colorful paintings, and silk lanterns (1.285). Visiting Huizhen's new room for the first time, Wang Liansheng sees that she has a totally new look, very different from earlier, and that her room is tidily furnished; the only detail he notices is that a few calligraphy and painting scrolls purchased from the market are not so elegant (5.306). In the house of the famous courtesan Tu Mingzhu, the Western-style dining room has "white walls and draperies, an iron bed and glass mirrors, like a crystal palace," and the room that hold waiting clients is decorated as a traditional-style study (19.378). When Zhao Erbao starts her courtesan business, she "goes to Dingfeng li to rent a house and brings back 300 yuan as [the landlord's] share of investment.... [She then] rents a whole set of red-wood furniture, first sets it up, and equips it with some necessities" (35.464). These descriptions support Henriot's financial analysis of the courtesan house as an entrepreneurial business that required little capital; rooms, furniture, jewelries, and even courtesans were rented (Henriot 1999: 446–48; Hershatter 1997: 82). In the novel the courtesan houses are not as fantastic and luxurious as their representations in other media.

A critical reading of Chi Zhicheng's hyperbolic description quoted above reveals that the fancy objects were in fact such daily necessities as beds, lamps,

Figure 3.4 A gambling party held in a courtesan boudoir in Qingyun li.
Sources: *Dianshizhai huabao,* September 1884; Wu et al. 2001: 1.117.

tables, mirrors, and clocks in novel styles, which had become quite affordable in this prosperous trading port. The ornate paintings were often purchased from the market; only the "silver pipes"—precious opium-smoking tools—demonstrated the owner's wealth.[26]

In the novel, dream lives inside the courtesan houses are neither simply about visual fantasies nor about literati nostalgia; instead they focus on the integrated living experiences—intimate conversations, banquet parties, and expectations of possible marriages. In reinventing the lost home, the courtesan house did not necessarily display luxuries, which might have been exaggerated by provincial travelers or overemphasized by the media in promoting tourism. By linking the courtesan house to the developing consumer culture and to the traditional utopia of a timeless pleasureland, the new urban literature reveals the ambiguity of this problematic space that embodied both old and new nature. But as the modern economy increasingly reduced everything to a fragmented and seductive image, the courtesan was increasingly represented through the objects around her, and the dream for the lost home was soon to be superseded by the wish-images of modern commodities.

Capturing the early stages of this transition, the novel mentions many new industrial products that played important roles in the sojourners' daily lives, such as *zimingzhong* (clocks that ring by themselves) for the standard time, *baoxian-deng* (gas lamps; literally, "insured lamps") always at the center of a room, and dressing mirrors. These items were daily necessities rather than exotic consumables, and as artificial substitutes for natural time, light, and self-image, they were all crucial in forming a new urban culture. Time was traditionally called *guangyin*, literally, the fleeting light and shadow produced by the movements of the sun and moon.[27] With the introduction of Western clocks, this traditional temporal concept based on the cosmic cycle was replaced with one determined by the mechanical rhythm; a clock that rang by itself signified a time severed from nature. This artificial time enabled the courtesan to have a new "day," which started in the afternoon and ended before sunrise. The gaslights also helped to create this new "nature" by disrupting the rhythm of sunrise and sunset—day was displaced into night. Compared with the old-style bronze mirror that could only display one's face, the modern dressing mirror facilitated a total displacement of the self into an external image that could be gazed upon and remade in line with the latest fashion.

Another element that disrupted traditional ways of life was opium. Opium smoking was perhaps the most common activity in the courtesan house. Like the traditional *ta* (a bed or couch for daytime use), the opium couch (*yanta*) functioned as the center of the living space in the courtesan boudoir. But opium smoking totally changed how the couch was used: the normal upright sitting posture was abandoned as the smoker faced the opium plate: "Wang Liansheng reclined on the right side of the couch to smoke opium, and turned again to the left side to inhale three times; gradually lowering his eyebrows and closing his eyelids, he seemed to be in a state of trance" (24.404). Such narcotic intoxication exemplified the oneiric function of the courtesan house.

Whereas the opium couch offered the client a daytime dreamland, the courtesan's night bed was his ultimate dream space. It was the most traditional item in the courtesan boudoir, which was at once a living room and a bedroom. Framed by elaborate posts, panels, curtains, and a canopy, the bed functioned like a small sleep cubicle, whose ornate outlook conveyed a feel of mystery traditionally associated with female sexuality. It also looked like a sacred and secret alcove at one end of the boudoir: in front of this magical space, the client's desire to penetrate was tamed; he could not demand to stay here at night, but would gladly comply when the courtesan let him share it with her. The bed was usually set in a corner of the room, leaving a narrow gap between its long side and the wall. This hidden space behind the bed was the most secret part in the courtesan house. Here was usually placed a chamber pot, and many important treasures were stored in locked chests.[28]

Next to the bed was a dresser on which were set a gas lamp, a small mirror set, a clock, and some decorative glass items. For the courtesan, as for any woman, grooming was a daily ritual. Sitting next to the ornate dresser and bed, she made herself into an equally ornate item. But here she might also have some quiet time to reflect, as it seemed to be the only sober space between the dream bed and the "public boudoir" of dream life. Here were also found some traditional-style items, including a painting flanked by calligraphy couplets (*yinglian*) hung above the dresser.[29] This arrangement gave the dresser a standing similar to that of the ancestral altar in a house, though it was not at the boudoir's center. The lanterns hung in the boudoir, called *shuhuadeng* (calligraphy-painting lanterns), were also in a traditional style. In addition, the room was decorated with Western-style wallpaper, a practice called *biaofangjian* in the guidebooks (Huayu 1895: 6.5). Hanging traditional calligraphy and paintings on Western wallpaper, or setting modern clocks and glass pieces on a traditional "altar," never was viewed as problematic.

The bed and dresser were at the other end of the boudoir from the opium couch. There was still plenty of space left in this spacious room for important activities such as banquets and tea parties. A small round pedestal table (*bailingtai*) was always set in the room for serving fruit during the tea parties. Depending on the size of a banquet, one, two, or even three square tables were placed together at the center of the room, turning it into a public banqueting room. Food were usually ordered from some nearby fine restaurants. The courtesan house also had a kitchen where servants could make some simple dishes like rice.

In short, the courtesan's body and boudoir were decorated and furnished according to an established convention. The objects on and around her were magical as well as novel, traditional as well as Western-style. But this syncretistic visual profusion was not yet a phantasmagoria of modern consumption. Rather than simply being an object of the modern erotic gaze, the courtesan brought pleasure to her clients mainly through her sweet conversation and singing and decorations around her body represented her respectable status; the expensive jewels solicited from her client were evidence of his persistent devotion rather than an ephemeral display; delicious food and dream-inducing opium played as large a role as the luxurious display inside the house. Nineteenth-century Shanghai had just begun to depart from a tradition in which visual gratification was not as important as the unity of multisensory pleasures. In this process, the courtesan would, as some nostalgic authors lamented, gradually lose her skill in music and the literary arts and be reduced to an object of the gaze, a display of fancy commodities.

It was probably against the backdrop of this transition that the displaced sojourners turned to the courtesan house for a last integrated living experience, for a dream of the lost home. Therefore, the courtesan house was not only a dreamland of marvelous display but also a homelike space for the sojourner's dream life—in contrast to the penury of its visual descriptions, the novel laboriously narrates the living details and "trivial" conversations of the courtesans and their patrons. But more often than not, this combination of the homelike and the marvelous, the new and the old "nature," led to uncanny ends.

Destruction and disillusionment

Even as the courtesan pursued fabulous objects so that they might demonstrate her professional success and her client's devotion to her, the client deemed that by giving her these objects he had made her body and boudoir his own property. Quite commonly, a rich client ordered jewelry, clothes, and many furnishings for a courtesan he kept as his sole mistress. In *Flowers of Shanghai*, Wang Liansheng has such relationships with Shen Xiaohong and Zhang Huizhen: he promises to pay off Xiaohong's debt and helps Huizhen move from an obscure *yao'er* residence to an upscale *changsan* neighborhood, and in return the two courtesans entertain no other clients. As he spends a sizable fortune in fashioning their boudoirs into his homes, he expects that they would be loyal to him. Like the courtesans, he also relies on those objects to secure the relationships.

But as the modern city became increasingly promiscuous, the desire that were unleashed jeopardized any sense of loyalty. When Liansheng finds out by accident that Xiaohong is sleeping with the opera actor Xiaoliu'er, all those "faithful" objects that have made her boudoir his home suddenly turn into uncanny signs—as if they were docile toys becoming animated and rebellious. As he has had these items purchased for her, now he can only destroy them:

> Liansheng was so angry. Turning [away from the back room in which Xiaohong was having the affair], he entered the boudoir and tilted the dresser in front of the bed to the floor; the lamp, clock, mirror set, and glassware on it all fell to the floor and the newly bought bracelets and hairpins inside the dresser might also be broken.... He walked to the opium bed and threw away the opium tray, from which the smoking gears and small decorative items all flew, passing the round table in the center.... [He kicked away two servants who tried to stop him.] With a smoking pipe in hand, he hit every object in the house from left to right, from front to back. Except two gas lamps, the square lanterns, wall lanterns, the glass covers of tables, a wardrobe, and a bed top were all broken into pieces.
>
> (33.456–57; Figure 3.3, bottom left)

As these luxurious items are reduced to shards in the blink of an eye, they become scapegoats for the disloyal person. Just as love can be transferred to these objects, so also can hate and destruction. He has ordered these items to please her, and now he has to destroy them to punish her. Is this not a cycle of fortune from which the modern city dweller can never escape? Actions in the modern city become increasingly senseless, as their meanings are too fast-changing to be coherent. In the end, rather than consolidating human relationships the material items makes them more volatile. This unhappy incident makes Liansheng decide to marry Huizhen instead of Xiaohong. But the outcome of the marriage is worse: he later discovers in his own residence an affair between her and his nephew, who is working for Liansheng there. This time he does not destroy his own house but badly beats Huizhen, whose cries of pain bring no help from the intimidated servants (54.567; Figure 3.3, bottom right). Disillusioned by his romantic failures, he leaves Shanghai for an official position in remote Jiangxi Province.

It was also quite common for some thuggish clients to vandalize a courtesan boudoir. This practice was called *dafangjian*, as a guidebook explains: "Jealousy and rivalry bring instantaneous violence; one man or many called together quickly destroy every item of the courtesan house" (Huayu 1895: 6.5). In the novel, Zhao Erbao stops her courtesan business while expecting to marry her client Shi Tianran who made the promise when he left her for a trip to Nanking, but her long wait ends with the news that Shi has married another woman in Nanking. Her financial debts force her back into the business (62.605–608). One day the thug Lai Touyuan visits her house and becomes displeased at her service; his gang then beat her badly and destroy all her belongings. Being wounded and tired, she falls asleep and has a dream. First she is told that Lai comes back again. When she is about to courageously confront him, several servants come to tell her that Shi, now an official in Yangzhou, invites her to join him there. Overwhelmed with joy, she is about to take that trip, but her friend (and rival) Zhang Xiuying comes and tells her that Shi is already dead. Then the servants suddenly change into demons, trying to snatch her away. At this moment she wakes up, and the novel comes to an abrupt end (64.614–18). Sorrow, hate, joy, and dread swiftly supersede one another in this short dream, which ironically conveys a sober vision of the turn of the fortune in the city. Only in the midst of shards and ruins does Erbao have that vision.

The destruction of the decorative objects might bring sorrow to the courtesan, because they had always conveyed to her a superficial gaiety, which evaporated as soon as they were destroyed. But for a courtesan who had scarcely any business, alone in her room, every image and sound in the house could be a source of sorrow. Li Shufang has contracted tuberculosis and is soon to die, but a heavier blow is that she cannot marry her lover, a devoted client whose family forbids him to take her as his principal wife. One day she tells him about her sleepless night:

> "I was sitting on the couch when it was raining heavily. The raindrops blown by wind hit the glass windows, ping-ping-pong-pong, like some people knocking at them. Even the curtains were blown up to my face. I was so frightened and then went to bed. But I could not sleep, since the house next door was hosting a banquet party, whose drinking noises and songs made my brain hurt. When this party was finally over, the clock kept ticking; I wanted to ignore it, but the ticking sound crawled into my ears. Listening again to the raindrops, [I heard that] they were falling happily. I looked to the sky, which appeared as if it was never going to be bright again."
>
> (18.373)

Approaching death, she hears this world with sharp ears. When the splendid colors escape her sight, she perceives the true meaning of this world: the gay night in the courtesan house is indeed very close to hell. The banqueters, bathing in the light of the superfluous things, do not see the dark side of this dream world. Melancholic Shufang, noticing how fragile and illusory the dream of the courtesan house is, is more sober than the other courtesans. After she dies, her funeral takes place in the house's courtyard and reception hall, while her room is neglected:

> The room has almost been emptied out: all the wardrobes are locked up; two benches are piled on the bed; one of the glass lanterns is broken and dangling,

and appears to fall down soon; some of the painting and calligraphy scrolls on the walls are missing; and chicken and fish bones from an earlier meal are still [on the table] uncleaned.

(43.508)

Shufang's devoted client is shocked to see that her room falls into such a dismal condition so soon after she dies. Only death exposes what lies behind the ephemeral splendor of the courtesan culture.

4   The meeting of courtyard and street

The glamour of the courtesan house was mainly an interior experience, which was to a great extent insulated from the city—a "foreign place" unlike any other cities and towns. As the sojourner's provisional home, the courtesan house certainly sought to re-create the interiority of traditional courtyard house or garden, but under the new urban and architectural conditions the establishment merely retreated to modern interiors featuring the displays of new material culture. Such interior spaces in fact became integrated into the surrounding neighborhood, as they were in a more compact architectural layout and less enclosed by walls.

Most Shanghai courtesans and sojourners lived in housing compounds that were called *li* (and sometimes *fang*). Somewhere between enclosed compounds and open streets or alleys, the *li* were an ambiguous space that combined vernacular and colonial architectural features and accommodated residential and commercial functions as well as residents of diverse backgrounds. Because of this spatial ambiguity, the *li* seemed to be a transitional type between traditional and modern urban space. Indeed, almost all nineteenth-century *li* were torn down and rebuilt in the early twentieth century, and the new compounds were known as the *lilong*—this term was never used in nineteenth-century sources and in this book I use the term "*li*" for that period. The new *lilong* were in even more compact layouts and decorated with Western-style rather than vernacular motifs; yet they retained the hybrid features of nineteenth-century *li* and remained an inclusive spatial type, which is now considered to represent Shanghai cultural identity as well as the city's revolutionary legacy.[1] But it is often forgotten that the first celebrated social space of this building type was the courtesan house of the nineteenth century.

Changing views of the pleasure quarter

Ming-Qing travel notes and vernacular fiction often depicted the courtesan house as an unassuming "small house of blue jade" (*xiaojia biyu*) hiding in a "deep street [or] meandering alley" (*shenjie quxiang*). The only ostentatious display of courtesan culture was seen on some brashly decorated tour boats (*huafang*) that cruised scenic waterways at Jiangnan cities such as Nanking and Suzhou. The *huafang* was for sightseeing as well as a mobile scenery and the courtesan aboard was at once a spectacle and a spectator in the open-style cabin, from which music, songs, and drinking noises spread to neighborhoods by the waterway. The late Qing novel *Fengyue meng* vividly depicted such a scene at Yangzhou:

> [Young loafers from wealthy families] saw a few tour boats coming out of Tianling Water Gate and aboard were courtesans in gaudy dresses and heavy makeup—some groomed as ladies and others dressed as men. They performed a variety of long or short melodies, their music resounding in distant space and their voices lingering around. This scene made the young men restless and they decided to hire a boat to chase those courtesans.
>
> (Hanshang 1991: 1.3)

Such waterways were usually located in commercial or scenic suburbs outside the city walls; they were fluid, open spaces beyond the limit of self-contained spaces organized in line with the Confucian social order. Here the elite enjoyed more interaction with the (sub)urban environment but still retained certain privacy on the slow moving boat. Such tour boats, however, were rarely seen at Shanghai probably because it was merely a frontier town and the area had few scenic waterways (Huang [1883] 1989: 100, 144). The Huangpu River next to the city wall had been frequented by pirates and its waves and tides would have made tour boat trips uncomfortable.

In the early 1850s when the settlements merely consisted of a few houses of foreign merchants along the Huangpu, Wang Tao noted that a few lower-class boatwomen, such as Cantonese *danhu*, offered services to the "black people" of the foreign boats, and along the river and outside the city wall some obscure sex establishments "wove bamboo branches as fences and piled up mud as walls, being extremely damp and narrow" (Wang [1860] 1992a: 5643). Elite courtesan houses were all found inside the walled city at Rainbow Bridge (Hongqiao), Mei Family Street (Meijia jie), Tang Family Street (Tangjia jie), and Mandarin Ducks Pavilion (Yuanyangting). Rainbow Bridge was then a busy street:

> Among the densely built houses to the east of Rainbow Bridge, many rouges and jades in mixed displays were full of splendor. They were divided into distinct houses, the best of which were from Suzhou and Changzhou, the next were from local areas, and the lowest were from the north of the Yangzi. They were all well groomed and dressed, competing with each other for glamour and love. Their dresses rivaled one another to be fashionable. Bright lights shone in their houses night after night and music and songs were heard until dawn.
>
> (Wang [1860] 1992a: 5641)

In the area of Tang Family Street, "though the roads [leading to the courtesan houses] were meandering, many visitors arrived. [The houses had] white walls and bright windows, very simple and elegant; every night when all was quiet, enchanting music spread out from within the walls." By contrast, Mei Family Street "was a remote location, where some courtesans who preferred quiet places to bustling ones rented a house. With beautiful makeup and elegant attires, they highly regarded themselves and considered it a shame to sit together with the music women" (Wang [1860] 1992a: 5642). These discrete locations exemplified the old literary imagery of the small jade house in a deep street, which could only be heard during quiet nights rather than being seen.

Wang fled Shanghai in 1862 because of his alleged association with the Taiping rebels. During his exile in Hong Kong, he was still well informed of Shanghai courtesans by his literati friends and depicted a new scene of the city's pleasure quarter in the late 1870s:

> In the settlements of Shanghai, all street names are innovations, such as Zhaofu (Future Wealth) li, Zhaogui (Future Elite) li, Zhaorong (Future Glory) li, Zhaohua (Future Prosperity) li, East Zhoujin (Day Splendor) li, and West Zhoujin li; in these places are found the best courtesan houses. In addition, there are other *li* with names like Rixin (Daily New), Jiu'an (Enduring Stability), Tongqing (Joint Celebration), Shangren (Promoting Mercy), Baihua (Hundred Flowers), and Guixin (Cinnamon Fragrance); elite courtesans commonly known as *changsan* reside in these neighborhoods. Then, [behind] willowy curtains are music and songs like boiling water, and the doorways and alleys of *pipa* (music instruments) are [full of] rouges and jades that resemble clouds. When the moon is up late every night, parties of songs and dances are held, ten-mile [streets] are filled with intoxicating fragrance, and many flowers blossom in dazzling colors—this can be called "the kingdom of forever spring." Twinkling lights and fire trees indeed create a sky without dark nights. [Visitors] admire the seductive scenes but feel puzzled; all present their utmost postures and appearances in spreading fragrance or competing for charm in the city's every corner. This is indeed a lair for seeking pleasure, a den for dispensing wealth.
>
> (Wang [1878] 1992b: 5686)

This dazzling spectacle contrasted sharply with the earlier scenes of lonely melodies in the city's quiet nights. The courtesans became much more visible in the settlements than their predecessors in the walled city and the auspicious names of the courtesan neighborhoods also made them easily identifiable in the city. The *Shenbao*'s longtime editor Huang Shiquan ([1883] 1989: 144) recorded a similar scene:

> Shanghai has no wonders of painted boats or waterfront pavilions. All elite courtesan houses are located in remote alleys, such as East and West Huifang (Gathering Fragrance) li, East and West Gonghe (Public Harmony) li, Hexing (Joint Prosperity) li, Hexin (Joint Trust) li, Huifanglou (Drawing Fragrance Building), Xiaotaoyuan (Little Peach Origin), and Yuxiu (Nurture Elegance) li, where buildings are deep and alleys are narrow and circuitous. Everyday at sunset, the wind gently blows on silk dresses, music of various instruments is boisterous, and powders and rogues resemble waters and clouds. When visitors

arrive here, they certainly get lost and find it difficult to turn away from the flowers.

While recalling the old imagery of "distant street and meandering alley," Huang presented a dazzling spectacle comparable to the wonder of painted boats and waterfront pavilions. This contradiction between remote location and ostentatious display in the author's nostalgic composition did not fully capture the extent to which the *li* had radically departed from the spatial pattern of traditional *jiefang* (urban neighborhoods). Although being enclosed from the main streets, the interior of a *li* compound had become a bustling place of spectacular views. This spatial innovation had resulted from a joint architectural production by foreign landowners and native construction guilds in Shanghai.

Joint production

The Land Regulations of 1845 allowed foreign merchants in Shanghai to lease land permanently in the designated areas north of the walled city.[2] Once foreign merchants acquired a lot of land, they could build houses for their own use or for sale or rent, but they were not allowed to let them to the Chinese as the settlements were supposed to be reserved for foreign residents only. This official stipulation was soon ignored. From September 1853 to July 1854 when the Small Sword rebels occupied the walled city, foreign landowners built about 800 simple wooden houses along Guangdong Road and Fujian Road in the British Settlement and rented them to Chinese refugees for lucrative profits (Lu and Xu 1999: 91). These hastily built houses formed the first Chinese residential compounds in the settlements. About 8,740 such houses were built in the early 1860s, when the advance of the Taiping rebels drove more refugees to Shanghai from surrounding hinterlands, and the Chinese population in the settlements reached 110,000 (Zou 1980: 3–4, 90–91; Wang 1989: 75).[3] Introducing a speedy way of producing houses in mass quantities, many foreign landowners in Shanghai became the first modern real estate speculators in China.

The houses were of a temporary nature, used by Chinese refugees as makeshift shelters during the civil wars. After the Taiping Rebellion was suppressed in 1864, Shanghai experienced a brief real estate slump as many refugees returned home. However, in the 1870s trade in Shanghai grew steadily, as did the Chinese population in the settlements and the demand for housing.[4] The wooden shelters were replaced by brick and timber houses that were built to form *li* compounds. Most Chinese residents in the *li* now chose to live in the settlements for business reasons while still considering themselves as sojourners in the city. The flourishing real-estate market demanded a new form of dwelling that could be built quickly, on a large scale, and easily transferred between foreign owners and Chinese tenants.

Traditional houses in towns and villages in Jiangnan were built on small scales by individual families who owned the land, followed the traditional house layout, and supervised and financed the construction. The most common indigenous house type in Shanghai and the surrounding rural area was called *sanheyuan* (three-side courtyard). It was usually a one-story brick and timber structure of three or five *jian* (the space between two rows of columns), with main rooms facing south and the central *jian* as the reception hall, or *ketang*.[5] Spacious yards enclosed by low walls were found at its front and back. As the family expanded, more structures would be built along its central axis, forming a set of two or three courtyards in which a family clan lived (Lu and Xu, 1999: 91; see Knapp 2000). Such spontaneous building activities slowly sprawled, sometimes layering upon former ones, and their accumulation often resulted in a picturesque townscape.

Throughout the dynasties of imperial China, this essentially laissez-faire pattern of construction was balanced by certain government controls, whose intensity corresponded to the city's administrative grade in the imperial system. In extreme cases, when new dynasties built new capitals, the centralized planning and construction of palaces, temples, and houses produced cities in a rigid chessboard layout, in which each rectangular block was a walled compound, such as the residential ward—or *fangli*—in the Tang capital Chang'an. The construction of individual houses in the *fangli* was tightly controlled to reflect the official rank of their owners.

The *li* compounds in nineteenth-century Shanghai, however, were built with little government control and in accord with capitalist ways of production. The earliest foreign landowners usually acquired generous lots of land from local owners (with assistance from local authorities when needed), and during the civil wars, they quickly built rows of wooden houses and let them to Chinese refugees. These row houses were rationally organized like military camps with controlled access for better management, and this residential model was inherited by the later *li* compounds (Luo and Sha 2002: 30). With a rigid layout and uniform architectural features, the *li* looked more like a residential ward in the ancient capitals than a vernacular neighborhood. Moreover, the term *li* was apparently borrowed from the ancient term *fangli*. But the *li* never consciously copied the imperial past; it simply reflected a rational, machinelike form common to capitalist and imperial ways of construction, both being translocal in nature. The *li*'s rationalized layout embodied the efficiency of modern capital rather than the austerity of imperial power.[6] Indeed, the mass production of such houses would have been impossible without the settlements' modern banks, which readily financed anyone with a land lease in hand (Lu and Xu 1999: 132; see McElderry 1976; Ji 2003).

The conservative English elite did not deign to build houses for the Chinese. They opposed Chinese residence in the settlement and complained that the cheap houses sheltering Chinese refugees had transformed the settlement into "a native Alsatia, the southern portion being blocked with abominably overcrowded and filthy hovels, fraught with the danger of fire and pestilence, rife with brothels, opium shops, and gambling dens" (De Jesus 1909: 98). The British Consul George Balfour and his successor Rutherford Alcock attempted to keep the settlement exclusively for foreigners because they worried that

> the once Foreign Settlement has become a Chinese town; and, as a natural consequence, has gone through a series of panics during the last few years, lest

it should be given over to sack and plunder on the approach of the [Taiping] insurgents, after the fashion of Chinese cities; – the greatest danger coming from the Chinese population within the boundaries, and in the very midst of which every foreigner now must live. The natives are probably in the proportion of a hundred to one of the foreigners.... It is true, many of the wealthier and better classes of Chinese have taken refuge in the Foreign Settlement; and as they have much to lose, their presence affords a certain security. Yet even this is, after all, worth very little.... And in their train, thousands of Chinese who have nothing to lose, – many of the worst classes indeed, – have also taken up their abode in the Foreign Settlement as an Alsatia, where no law of their own country can reach them; and no power of the stranger exists, to deal with an evil of this nature."

(Alcock 1863: 36–37)

The foreign merchants who came to Shanghai in order to strike a fortune had a different view, which a merchant well explained in a conversation with Alcock:

"You, as H. M.'s. Consul, are bound to look to national and permanent interests – that is your business. But it is my business to make a fortune with the least possible loss of time, by letting my land to Chinese, and building for them at thirty to forty per cent interest, if that is the best thing I can do with my money. In two or three years at farthest, I hope to realize a fortune and get away; what can it matter to me, if all Shanghai disappear afterwards, in fire or flood?"

(Alcock 1863: 37–38)

Alcock was then convinced that he "was losing time in any efforts to stem the tide of land-jobbing and house building for Chinese tenants, who could be found to repay the capital of *land and house* by a two or three years' rent." Thus he ended his "hopeless struggle," and to the landowners' satisfaction, in 1854 the consuls from Britain, America, and France revised the Land Regulations to legalize Chinese residence in the settlements.[7]

Chinese authorities were against the mixed residence of Chinese and foreigners and never officially endorsed the revised Land Regulations. The local gentry held a similar position on the issue, as Mao Xianglin ([1870] 1985: 131) wrote:

Western merchants know only short-term profits but not long-term harms. As prosperity and recession succeed one another in cycles, I think what is considered prosperity is also a decline.... As the [foreign] settlements expand, [local] people's [farming] fields shrink, a little here and a little there, a patch last year and a patch this year. When will this end? Western merchants are profit-driven and want more land as the prosperity of the settlements made it profitable. But this prosperity is in fact brought by the flourishing of Chinese stores and houses and the congregation of [native] merchants and travelers in the settlements. To end this, the Chinese area and the settlements must be separated from one another and the latter are then unable to form a market. Where can they seek profits from then?

Nevertheless, the power of capital broke down the invisible settlement walls that both Chinese and foreign authorities originally wished to retain, and transformed Western and Chinese traditions by juxtaposing one against the other.

The mixed residence of people from different areas of China and elsewhere in the world generated a commercial culture of diversity and economic opportunity. The earliest Chinese residents were wealthy gentry who had fled from the civil wars, and the hovels, brothels, and opium dens so objectionable to the Western elite provided crucial business opportunities for foreign landowners, as wealth shifted from the declining and displaced landed gentry to new urban capitalists. About the latter Alcock (1863: 38) portrayed:

> And as long as there is land still to be bought up, and room to build more houses, and Great Britain supplies means of protection... "all goes on as merry as a marriage bell." Successive merchants, clerks, and storekeepers – generations of them so to speak, come and disappear, stay their time of five or ten years, and carry off a fortune – rejoicing in the Bourbon consolation – *après moi le deluge*! They have snatched wealth out of the fire, and so many others after them, – or if not, *tant pis*! The merchant feels he must be quick in a climate as trying as that of China. He has to snatch a fortune from the jaws of death; – and unless he make haste, it is more than probable he will only dig his own grave, and be snatched away himself.[8]

The earliest real estate developers in the foreign settlements were such firms as D. Sassoon &. Co.; Jardine, Matheson &. Co.; and Gibb, Livingston &. Co., which had accumulated their initial capital mainly through the illegal opium trade. Many early developers, such as the American Edwin M. Smith, started as adventurers or smugglers who improved their situation by striking a fortune, while others built upon their associations with British colonial expansion. For example, Elias David Sassoon came from a Baghdadi Jewish family that, via a close connection with the British Empire, had built a mercantile network from Bombay to Shanghai. This illustrious family history began with Daud Pasha's persecution of Jews in Ottoman Baghdad from 1817 to 1831 that drove Elias's father David Sassoon, the scion of the most eminent Jewish family in Baghdad, to Bombay. Gradually the Sassoons changed their identity from "Oriental" merchant princes to English gentlemen (Betta 2000). This new status belied the fact that their commercial success in China was built upon a long tradition of cross-cultural experience in the East. Their identity as "Westerners" in Shanghai was a social construct for the sake of convenience. Many other adventurers and smugglers from obscure backgrounds now also joined the club of English gentlemen. The real estate market was the ideal field in which they could make such changes.

Foreign real estate owners never dealt directly with Chinese landowners, builders, and tenants. Their land purchases, or permanent leases, were assisted by local land officers (*dibao*), surveyors (*tudong*), and translators (*tongshi*). Mao Xianglin ([1870] 1985: 131) criticized these transactions:

> Though the so-called land lease offers a price, the original landowner can only get thirty or forty percent after deductions by the surveyor, land officer, and translator. Because of this practice, many sustainable families fell into utter poverty. If a leased land were [used as] a farming field, the price paid for it would be reasonable. But Shanghai is a prosperous market town. To the east of the [walled] city, a busy area, housing prices are the highest. Letting a one- or two-*jian* house can bring an income of over a hundred yuan [per year], but a field is worth only a few cents…. North and west of the city there are many farming fields and some graveyards but few houses. The Western merchant makes no distinction between them and sometimes offers a good price, but the land officer who knows the difference colludes with the translator to profit from the transaction. Therefore, these officers try all means to persuade reluctant locals to sell their land and urge Westerners to buy more. There are also some profit-driven [Chinese] folks who buy lands from Western merchants, build houses on them, and then let them for a ten percent profit. In comparison, Westerners gain a hundred times more profits by selling as commercial properties what they have bought as farming fields.

The foreign landowners did not hire Western-trained professionals, such as architects and engineers; instead they relied on Chinese compradors to supervise local contractors and manage the construction and rental of their properties. This joint real estate production of Western merchants and native construction guilds was comparable to the making of hybrid journalism discussed in Chapter 2. Similar to Smith, Earnest Major came to Shanghai as a venture businessman. But unlike the literary "elite" who worked for Major, the Chinese contractors came from the artisan class historically considered to be of extremely low social prestige. However, these contractors soon became nouveaux riches or even real estate tycoons, and their rise in Shanghai contrasted sharply with the fall of the literati into the class of salaried employees.

Smith, who started as a broker for merchants and banks, was among the first to earn a huge profit by building simple wooden houses; he relied on the expertise of Cheng Jinxuan, a Chinese carpenter and the comprador of Smith's real estate company before 1870 (Lu and Xu 1999: 451). Later the Sassoons hired Cheng to manage house maintenance and rent collection. When Cheng saw that many of the Sassoons' houses were in a dilapidated condition and had to be rebuilt, he proposed to rebuild them at his own cost, on the condition that he collect the rent for the next twenty-five years while paying the Sassoons the equivalent of the old rent, and that the houses would be returned to the Sassoons at the end of that period. The Sassoons were happy with this deal. Cheng first rebuilt some *li* compounds near Peking Road where the rent of a house unit was only two to five yuan per month. Employing reusable materials from demolished houses, he built new houses at a cost less than one hundred yuan per unit. He doubled the rents of rebuilt houses and recovered the construction costs within two years. With the same method he rebuilt many other houses owned by the Sassoons (Lu and Xu 1999: 189). By 1890 he had become known as "the king of Chinese real estate."

Few records of contractors such as Cheng have survived. They usually started as apprentices in construction guilds and were at the bottom of the Confucian social hierarchy, but they soon became very rich, as a poet noted at the turn of the century:

> Carpenter Guild (*muzuo*)
> [The head of] every carpenter guild earns a great fortune,
> Building foreign-style houses (*yangfang*) at immense costs,
> Traveling in carriages like rich magnates,
> Sometime returning from work with an umbrella in hand.
>
> Water Guild (*shuizuo*)
> The head alone is able to increase profits,
> And even live in a residence while building high mansions…
> (Yi'an [1906] 1996: 158)[9]

In contrast to the itinerant builders who lived on the job site in other towns, Shanghai contractors appeared as if they were traditional elite. Even Huang Shiquan ([1883] 1989: 111) admired them:

> House construction is contracted by the head of artisans (*jiangtou*). He lives in a grand building, rides in carriages like a member of a prestigious family, and leads hundreds and thousands of artisans. There are distinct guilds among the artisans. Those who build Chinese houses are called *benbang* (native guilds) and those who build foreign houses are called *hongbang* (red guilds). The line between them is clear and cannot be crossed. If a *hongbang* tries to take a Chinese business, all of the *benbang* will rise to attack it; the same will happen if a *benbang* tries at a foreign business. The worst of such conflicts bring gang fights, in which they see each other as enemies, and end up in the local court. This is a bad practice.

Thus, it appeared that the *benbang* built the *li* compounds while the *hongbang* built the Western-style buildings or *yangfang*, which is discussed in the next chapter.

Profiting from the work of lower-class artisans and laborers, the contractors and compradors enjoyed luxurious lives that were impossible elsewhere in China. The rise of these nouveaux riches was epitomized by the careers of Cheng and Silas Aaron Hardoon, the real estate king of early twentieth-century Shanghai who started as a humble Baghdadi refugee employed by the Sassoons. The city was indeed where the obscure became prominent and the traditional social hierarchy was reversed. This reversal should be seen as resulting not simply from the impact of the West on Chinese society, but from the erosion of the established orders of both Chinese and Western communities by new forces generated in the hybrid colonial environment.

Fluid space

The Chinese compradors and contractors had a greater influence on the development of the *li* than their foreign bosses.[10] Their knowledge and experience of local building traditions informed the *li* houses, which looked similar to Jiangnan vernacular dwellings. Built with local materials and technology, the best of these houses retained the traditional courtyard layout and incorporated many local decorative motifs, such as the *matouqiang* (stepped gable), the *shikumen* (stone-framed portal), and the uniform outlook marked by dark tiled roofs and white plastered walls. These vernacular motifs were adopted in a mass production of housing in standardized layouts.

The most common residential unit in the *li* compounds, known as *yijian liangxiang* (one *jian* and two wings), was three *jian* wide, with the middle *jian* as the courtyard and the hall, flanked by two wings or *xiangfang* (Figure 4.1). It was a compact version of *sanheyuan*, consisting of timber structures and brick walls. Passing through the front entrance (*shikumen*) there was a small courtyard, or *tianjing* (literally "skywell," referring to its well-like space), and next to it, the reception hall, or *ketang*. The two wings were used for different purposes, such as studies or bedrooms. Steep stairs at the back of the hall led to second-floor rooms; bright and spacious ones faced south (to the courtyard), and less desirable back rooms, called *tingzijian*, faced north (to the back alley). Behind the main structure was the service area that included a kitchen, a small backyard, storage, and a back entrance. Several units were aligned along an alley, at whose end there was usually a larger unit, sometimes more than three *jian* wide and with a spacious courtyard. Such a unit could be reserved as the residence of the merchant who had built the whole compound.

These houses inherited the traditional layout of courtyard-hall centered dwellings. According to Wang Shaozhou (1989: 45), each of their three *jian* was 3.6–4.2 meters wide and the entire lot was about 16 meters deep (the courtyard was 4 meters, the hall 6, and the kitchen or back room 6), and the houses were spacious. Many tenants of late nineteenth-century *li* were wealthy merchants or gentry, and these houses basically met their need for a large, courtyard-style house. But whereas traditional courtyard houses were built individually and formed an organic sprawl of heterogeneous structures, the *li* houses replicated the same plan and were aligned in rigid rows. The alley (*longtang*) between two such rows was about 2.5 meters wide and led to a perpendicular main alleyway (*long*), 4 meters wide, which cut through the compound linking the streets at its ends (Luo 1991: 19; Figure 4.1).

The orderly layout of the *li* seemed to be consonant with the Confucian spatial order, as exemplified by the rigidly planned imperial capitals. *Li* is an ancient term. In the Han capital Chang'an, a residential area enclosed by walls was called *li*, its four entrances were called *lü*, and *lüli* together indicated this gated residential compound or ward, within which "houses were arranged like combs, and doors and alleys were straight."[11] There seemed to be a rational row alignment of houses in the *lüli*. The Tang Chang'an consisted of more orderly planned residential

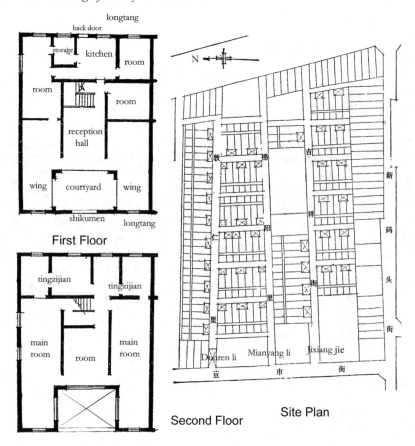

First Floor

Second Floor

Site Plan

Figure 4.1 Left: plans of the *li* house (one bay and two wings); right: site plan of a *li* compound, Shanghai.
Sources: Compilation after Wang and Chen 1987: 9, 39.

wards, or *fangli*, within whose walls residents were tightly controlled and whose four gates closed at night and opened at sunrise (Dong et al. 1982: 29). Suzhou, a provincial capital, also had sixty *fang*, as mentioned in a poem by the Tang poet Bai Juyi (Xu 2002: 23). Though no visual records demonstrate the rational layout of houses inside these ancient wards, they might be similar to, but more strictly planed than, the *hutong* neighborhoods in the last imperial capital Peking, where individual houses were aligned in a roughly rational pattern. In short, the rational alignment of houses in the *li* of Shanghai was not totally unprecedented.

The development of the urban economy from the late Tang onward led to the abolition of the ward system in the major cities of the Song and later dynasties; this was an important component of what scholars consider the "medieval urban revolution" in China (Skinner 1977b: 23–26; Shiba 1970). In the Song capital Bianliang, the doors of houses and shops opened directly onto the streets, while residential neighborhoods, lacking clear walled boundaries, were usually named after these streets. In other words, a location in the city was identified by the name of a street rather than a walled block. In contrast to the Han and Tang capitals, this new, late imperial urban model generated lively urban scenes of commercial and leisure activities, fully liberated from the rigid ward system.

But walls did not disappear from cities in late imperial China; they still enclosed cities and the compounds that housed the imperial and local authorities. Individual residences were also walled complexes. In the meantime, the street was filled with shops and businesses, and often assumed an organic, meandering form in vernacular towns. Important as it was to the booming urban economy, the street was considered indecorous, dangerous, and morally inferior to walled domains. This spatial hierarchy corresponded to the Confucian social ladder, on which merchants were assigned to a very low rung.

While the ancient capitals represented a unitary urban model of walled compounds, the new urban model in the late imperial period consisted of walled Confucian spaces and open commercial streets, which were crucial to everyday life yet marginalized in mainstream discourses. The uniqueness of the *li* in the foreign settlements of Shanghai lay in its synthesis of some features from these two urban models: on the one hand, the mass production of *li* houses was to some extent comparable to the imperial planning of the residential wards; on the other hand, the joint commercial production of the *li* by foreign landowners and local craftsmen, besides adding vernacular motifs to the rational layout, gave a new meaning to the amorphous street—its meandering form already straightened. By integrating the enclosed compound with surrounding streets and shops, the *li* erased the borderline between orderly walled spaces and promiscuous streets, to the extent that the walls' functions of enclosure and protection were weakened.

A *li* compound was bounded by rows of shops facing busy streets. At the back of the shops was a wall enclosing the residential area. As seen in contemporary drawings and photographs, the shops were usually two-story structures with the ground floor open to the street. This uniform, continuous architectural front displayed diverse shop signs and merchandise. Amidst the shop entrances was an opening not so different from the others, except that it featured a distinct stone portal and three characters inscribed above: the first two formed an auspicious word and the last was "*li*" or sometimes "*fang*." It was a *shikumen* leading into the *li* compound (Figure 4.2).

As Wang Tao noted, the street names in the settlements were innovations, departing from the traditional practice of naming a street after a historical figure from the neighborhood or a local business feature, such as Color Clothes Street. Wang's sketch of the walled city mentioned Tang Family Street named after Tang Yu and Mei Family Street after Mei Xuanshi, both of whom were famous figures in local history (Wang [1860] 1992a: 5641–42). The *li* and the settlements, however, were not rooted in any such local tradition, but were built almost overnight on deserted land: "Neglected tombs were leveled and foreign houses were built" (*Shenbao* 1874; Gu 1996: 48). Naming the *li* with auspicious words was probably a measure to improve the feng shui of that inauspicious land, and characters such

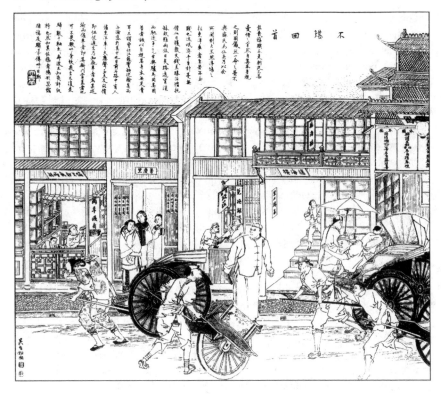

Figure 4.2 Entrance to Puqing li between shops (a boot shop to the left; a bank, a teahouse, and a theater to the right); seven courtesan names posted on the two sides of the entrance. A rickshaw puller who had been an official was running away from a customer who had been his subordinate.
Sources: *Dianshizhai huabao,* May 1884; Wu et al. 2001: 1.29.

as "peace," "everlasting," and "happiness" echoed terms used in the wards of the Han or Tang capital. But unlike the didactic moral terms adopted in the capital, the *li* names were usually about wealth and prosperity, such as Zhaorong li, Zhaohua li, Zhaofu li, and Zhaogui li—*zhao* meaning prospective, and *rong-hua-fu-gui* together as one word meaning glory, prosperity, wealth, and elite. This nomenclature fit well into the settlements' commercial milieu.

Comparable to the gateways (*lü* or *fang*) of the ancient residential wards, two or three *shikumen* were the only unguarded points of entry to the *li*. A nineteenth-century *shikumen* had a decorative architrave and a curving eave in the traditional style.[12] Though called *shikumen* only in Shanghai, this architectural motif also appeared in Jiangnan vernacular dwellings, such as old houses built by Ming-Qing merchants in Hongcun and Xidi in southern Anhui Province (Knapp 2005). The *shikumen* could be seen as a less monumental version of the *paifang*, which probably developed from the *lü* and *fang* in the Han and Tang. As the traditional gateway to a village or urban neighborhood, the *paifang* was often an honorific monument dedicated to a distinguished ancestor of the local clan, bearing a name that defined both the location and that clan. The *shikumen* of the *li*, however, displayed innovative names without any roots in local history and was less conspicuous and monumental than the freestanding *paifang*. Underneath a second-story room, the *shikumen* looked like a shop entrance, especially when it was decorated with business signs, such as those of courtesan houses. This blatant commercial use of a monumental entrance in a residential compound testified to the fact that the traditional borderline between residences and commercial streets was melting away.

Shikumen also appeared inside the *li* compound; they led from the main alleyway (*long*) into the branch alleys (*longtang*) and into individual houses. They all had similar designs but more private doorways became smaller and less ornate. Without these entrances, the *long* leading to the streets would be a throughway and the dead-end *longtang* would also cease to function like a court (*tang*) shared by the residents as a communal space. *Shikumen* not only defined spaces of varying degrees of privacy (street–*long*–*longtang*–house) but also transformed the traffic routes into courtyard-like spaces. This arrangement in fact reflected the traditional layout of a building complex as a series of entrances, courtyards, and halls aligned along the main path. But whereas the traditional layout reflected a strict demarcation of privacy, gender, and social hierarchy, the *li* layout was more fluid and brought together residential and commercial spaces, or courtyards and streets.

In later imperial China the courtyard and the street were antithetical spaces separated by walls: the one represented the elite order and the other the amorphous and vulgar; the one was the center and the other always was marginalized in neo-Confucian ideology. Thus, the house-mansion-palace centered on the courtyard and the shop-along-the-street were two contrasting architectural types assigned to the central and marginal positions in the traditional urban geography.

In the settlements this spatial hierarchy was reversed: the street became an infinitely extending space central to everyday life, while the house had to open itself in order to be a sustainable unit in the city. Though the *shikumen* made the *long*(*tang*) look somewhat like a courtyard, they did not separate it from the street. Commercial activities in streets and domestic lives in houses tended to overflow from these gateways and meet each other in the *long*(*tang*), which then became a key space in the new urban life. The shops around the *li* were usually very small, every inch of their space fully utilized; so too were the houses in the *li*. Though retaining many traditional features, these houses became more compact and their courtyards were too small to be outdoor living spaces, which were so central to traditional domestic life. In comparison, the *longtang* was wider and straighter than a vernacular alleyway.

To make the courtyard appear larger, the house did not have any second-story structure above the *shikumen*, which along with a thin wall separated the courtyard from the *longtang*. This provided an important opening for the well-like space. Through this opening, the second-story windows now looked beyond the wall to the *longtang*. Such an outward-looking feature was more commonly found in roadside shops. Traditional architecture always combined timber frames and solid walls; the openness of the timber structure was more visible in roadside shops than in houses enclosed by solid walls, within which this openness was only found in the rooms facing the courtyard. The *li* house retained this open feature: its reception hall opened to the courtyard via removable door panels, which covered the hall's entire front; wooden walls and large windows filled the rest of the courtyard façades (see Figures 3.3, 4.4). As the second-floor spaces rose above the *shikumen* and the wall, this fluidity between interior and courtyard carried beyond the traditional boundary. This to some extent turned a traditional house inside out. The overflowing of interior space onto the *longtang* also resulted from the fragmentation of walls, as the gables of the two wings flanking the *shikumen* were now pierced by large windows (Figure 4.3). This contradicted the gables' traditional function of containing the fire (*fenghuo shanqiang*). Some elaborate, pavilion-like balconies opened directly to the alleyway or street (Figure 4.4, top left). The integrity and safety of the walled courtyard were sacrificed for the sake of spatial interconnectedness between houses, streets, and the city. Every one could see and be seen by others, as if the city were one busy street.

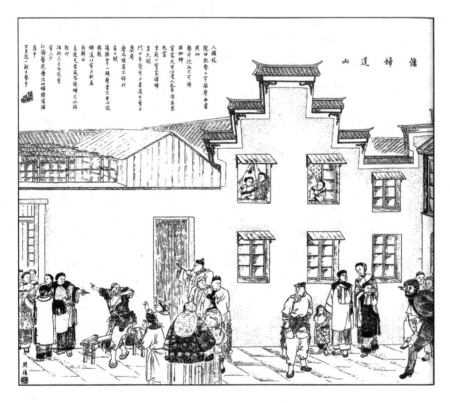

Figure 4.3 A house with modern-style windows in Zhaofu li; in the alley, an itinerant smith was injured in a brawl with a women servant from a courtesan house.
Sources: *Dianshizhai huabao,* February 1886; Wu et al. 2001: 2.260.

Figure 4.4 Illustrations from *Flowers of Shanghai* (1894). Top left: Tu Mingzhu arrives at Gonghe li to attend a banquet in the house of Jiang Yueqin (Ch. 15). Top right: The house of the Zhou Lan puts up the sign of a newly-purchased courtesan (Ch. 3). Bottom left: The house of Tu Mingzhu holds a party that combines Western-style dining with native opera performance (Ch. 19). Bottom right: an opera troupe performs in the courtyard while a banquet party is held in a second-floor courtesan room to celebrate Zhang Huizhen's move into the house (Ch. 5).

Diverse functions

With the spatial innovations discussed above, the *li* houses were used very differently than traditional ones. They became transferable "commodities" rather than permanent homes to which generations of residents had a strong sense of belonging. As temporary lodgings in the foreign settlements, they could easily be purchased and resold, rented and sublet, and their rents were extremely high according to contemporary living standards. The first guidebook to the settlements, *Huyou zaji* (1876), stated:

> Letting houses in Shanghai can bring the greatest profits. In the settlements, six or seven out of ten foreign merchants are doing this business. A house unit, locally called a *zhuang*, has a room upstairs, one downstairs, and an attached kitchen to the back. A street-facing unit costs five or six taels a month; even the cheapest unit in a remote alley costs three yuan. The ancients said that living in Chang'an was extremely costly; now living in Shanghai is more costly.
>
> (Ge [1876] 2003: 86–87)

However costly it was living in Shanghai, more and more immigrants chose it as their new home. The city provided more business opportunities, and high housing values generated income for landowners as well as property agents, wholesale renters, and even individual renters, who resided in one room and sublet the rest of the house to other tenants. Moreover, the *li* house was also a working space where business was conducted and wealth generated, where domestic life and commerce were mixed.

The combination of domestic and business functions was common in traditional houses. The home(land) was always the most important resource of traditional life: a gentry house was where the head of the family managed his businesses; the yard of a peasant house was a working field; and the houses of the *jihu* in Suzhou were small textile factories. But such work involved people within or related to the household and was carried out in a self-contained, family-based network. Only in roadside shop houses were there direct commercial exchanges; they were dormitories at night and had no domestic space in daytime when they merged with the bustling street. The *li* house seemed to be an intermediate between those two kinds of mixed dwelling-work space. The alleyways in the *li* were wide enough for some commercial activities, and the *shikumen* did not separate the residential compound from the street but instead defined different commercial spaces.

The *li* houses were not permanent homes; they were provisional lodgings centering on business activities, and the sojourners' concept of home had to be reinvented. To pay high rents and sustain an expensive urban life, a house was used not only as a home, but as a space that facilitated the constant flow of capital. Merchant residences were used for many different purposes as the sojourners sought every means to maintain their lifestyle or strike a fortune. Thus, extremely diverse functions—residential and commercial, private and public—were found in the *li* compounds.

In the *li* were not only found small neighborhood businesses integrated to the residential space (Figure 4.3), but the city's main businesses in trade and finance also clustered in certain neighborhoods. Among businesses listed in the 1876 guide, twelve silk wholesale stores (out of a total of eighteen) and twelve retail stores were located in *li* compounds; for example, Qingyuan li was home to three wholesale stores and four retail stores. There were also three tea wholesale stores in Zao'an li, two commercial guilds in Nanzhoujin li, twenty-two banks (*huiye* or *qianzhuang*) in Xingren li, and fourteen banks in Tonghe li (Ge [1876] 2003: 343, 357–71, 373–91). By the early twentieth century businesses ranging from press houses to factories to neighborhood stores were all found in the *li(long)* (Lu 1999:138–88). A 1911 guide mentioned 1,125 *li(long)* where hotels and restaurants were found (Luo 1991: 44–46). The *li(long)* also became the haven of the sex trade (Henriot 2001: 220–25).

In the nineteenth century, the most celebrated businesses in the *li* were courtesan houses. The relatively abundant descriptions of these entertainment and sex establishments in the urban literature—including guides, pictorials, and fiction—offer views of the social space of the *li*. The best-known *li* were the locales of elite courtesan houses near Fourth Avenue (Simalu), the city's busiest street, and according to the 1876 guide, one of the city's ten grand scenes was "Visiting Beauties in Guixin [li]" (*Guixin fangmei*) (Ge [1876] 2003: 232).

The *li* houses were not designed and built for any specific businesses, but they could be adapted for all kinds of commercial purposes, just as traditional residences in the walled city could be used as courtesan houses. The Confucian ideology of a social continuum from the state to the family was embodied in a universal architectural layout so that buildings with different social functions had similar physical forms: a palace, temple, or house was always a walled complex composed of a series of entrances, courtyards, and halls. In this context, it was natural that the *li* houses were adapted to many different uses, including courtesan businesses.

As always, the different purposes of buildings were expressed through conspicuous entrance signs. This traditional practice became more popular in Shanghai where a basic building type served multiple purposes. Streets in the settlements were filled with forests of signs, including those bearing names of the *li*. Not associated with any local tradition, these auspicious words absorbed new meanings derived from the social contents located behind the signs. For example, Shangren li was famous for its elite courtesan houses and its signs conveyed that fame to anyone familiar with the city's pleasure quarter. In *Flowers of Shanghai*, when the newcomer Zhao Puzhai wanders on the streets and sees a sign of Shangren li, he recalls some famous courtesans he has heard of and cannot resist entering the compound (2.290). When some courtesans posted their names on the *shikumen* next to the *li* signs, the latter's new connotation was blatant (see Figure 4.2); a bamboo poem said:

Raising [my] head [to look], all the pleasure houses are known;
The names of the beauties are posted on the wall next to the entrance;
Like looking at a list of myriad beauties,
Thousands of famous flowers are labeled in detail.

(Chen [1887] 1996: 89)

Such signs were also posted at the entrances to individual courtesan houses. In the novel, the madam Zhou Lan has just purchased a new courtesan and asks the regular client Hong Shanqing to give the newcomer a name. He suggests "Shuangyu" (Double Jade) and the house immediately posts this name on the entrance (3.294; Figure 4.4, top right). Like a shop sign, the posted name of a courtesan helped to promote her business and spread her fame. While such name plates were daytime business signs for the courtesan houses, the gas lanterns at their entrances and the noises and music of the banquet parties were live advertisements for their nighttime businesses. As quoted above, Wang Tao and Huang Shiquan considered such displays as unprecedented.

Inside the *li*, the new architectural arrangements also facilitated the flexible use of space in the courtesan houses. *Flowers of Shanghai* depicts a famous courtesan's grand residence in Dingfeng li:

> Tu Mingzhu's house is a five-*jian* building. Two *jian* to the west are the main rooms. Among the three *jian* to the east, the middle one is a reception hall, the right one is a Western-style dining room decorated like a crystal palace with white walls, draperies, an iron bed, and mirrors, and the left one is used for holding waiting patrons (*teng keren*) but is called a "study," being decorated with some paintings, calligraphies, and music instruments.
>
> (19.378)

This arrangement modifies the traditional symmetrical layout to accommodate the novel contents. The reception hall is off the center, being flanked by the traditional study and the Western-style dining room, which occupies the central *jian* of the five *jian* house. One day a banquet party is held in the hall to celebrate the birthday of the merchant Li Zhuanhong:

> The wooden panels at the back of the hall have been removed to expose the back room (*tingzijian*), which is set up as a small stage. On its front are hung two rows of lights like pearls; all the screens and curtains are made of finely embroidered silk; and splendid lights and colors are beyond description. At the center of the hall is a Western-style dining table covered with cloth, on which are set knifes, forks, bottles, two glass lamps, and eight glasses, each with a foreign napkin folded in a flower shape.
>
> (19.378; Figure 4.4, bottom left)

This transformation of the traditional reception hall into a combination of a private theater and a Western-style dining room shows the extent to which things Chinese and Western, traditional and modern, elite and popular, are mixed in this house of the chic courtesan. The hall's traditional ritual function is negated as well as reinvented by new "rituals" of entertainment: where the ancestral altar used to stand there is a temporary stage on which some lewd plays are probably performed.

Such a spacious house was rare. A typical courtesan house was shared by three or more courtesans and usually managed by a madam or landlord. An independent courtesan could rent a room from a large establishment to run her own business or have an agreement with the landlord about sharing her business income.[13] Regular business activities such as banquets and tea parties were held in the courtesans' private rooms, but occasionally some important events were observed in the courtyard-hall shared by the courtesans.

When Wang Liansheng's mistress (*xianghao*) Zhang Huizhen moves to a new house in East Hexing li, a party is held to celebrate this event. When Liansheng arrives at the house for the first time, he sees from his sedan the sign "Zhang Huizhen Yu" above the entrance; entering the house, he sees that a band of junior opera actors has set up in the courtyard a small but very colorful stage (5.306). The band is hired for the entire day and night, performing songs and music for the banquet party held in Huizhen's new room upstairs (6.312; Figure 4.4, bottom right). This event honoring Huizhen (and her new relationship with Liansheng) takes place in the communal courtyard as if the unrelated courtesans had formed a family. As the music spreads to the neighborhood, the domain of this communal family is further extended.

The courtesan houses also celebrated important seasonal events in the courtyard-hall. Prior to the three major festivals of New Year, Dragon Boat, and Mid-Autumn when the customers' payments for the courtesans' outcall services in the previous four months were due, the courtesan houses observed *shaolutou*, a ritual to honor the god of fortune, and held banquet parties (hosted by their primary patron). Another religious event popular in the courtesan houses was the *xuanjuan*, during which Taoist priests were called in to sing stories about local deities. One day the house of Wei Xiaxian in Shangren li holds such an event: a scroll of the immortals' images is hung in the middle of the reception hall; four Taoist priests sit facing each other and preach the scripture aloud; incense smokes wind around and drums and bells resound afar (21.392; Figure 4.5, top left).

Serving to hold together the establishment and promote its business, such communal events observed in the courtyard-hall demonstrated that this traditional center still retained its communal function and could be adapted for different uses as it had always been. But in other times, the courtyard-hall was often a neglected space by comparison to the second-floor rooms with better ventilation and views. As discussed in the last chapter, these rooms were even more flexibly arranged to accommodate many functions ranging from private romantic liaisons to banquet parties of up to fifty attendants. The courtesan house had three methods to deal with the situation that two groups of clients visited a courtesan for informal tea parties at the same time: when new visitors arrived and were led by a servant to a room in which the courtesan was still entertaining other clients, she would say: "Lead [them] to a [waiting] room!" (*ling fangjian*); she could also redirect the earlier visitors to a waiting room and let in the new visitors—this method was called "*jie fangjian*" (borrowing a room); or if the two groups of visitors happened to know each other, she could entertain them together in her room—called "*bing fangjian*" (combining rooms) (Huayu 1895: 6.5).

104

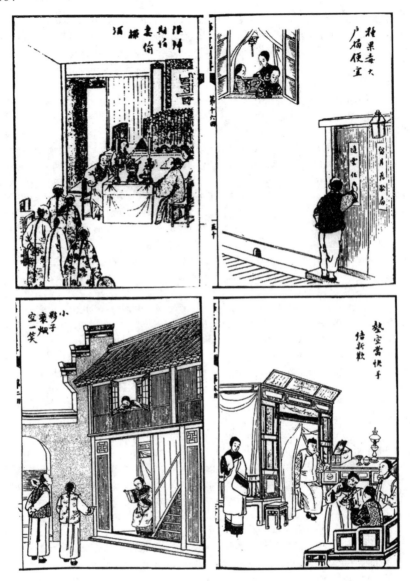

Figure 4.5 Illustrations from *Flowers of Shanghai* (1894). Top left: Taoist priests are preaching scriptures in the house of Wei Xiaxian (Ch. 21). Top right: Li Shifu visits the *yeji* house of Zhu Shiquan while another visitor is entering the house (Ch. 16). Bottom left: Zhang Xiaocun and Zhao Puzhai visit the flower opium house of Wang A'er (Ch. 2). Bottom right: Two servants, Zhang Shou and Lai'an, visit the *yeji* house of Pan San, who is still in bed with a hoodlum (Ch. 5).

That the courtesan's private room above the ground level became the most important business space of a public nature challenged the courtyard-hall's central position. This reconfiguration of traditional space was also apparent in that the formerly invisible, secluded female quarter now proudly looked out to the *long(tang)*, and in some houses directly to the street. The vantage viewpoint from the second floor of this open-style architecture helped the courtesans and their patrons to interact with one another and with the larger urban environment. Visiting Huizhen's new room, Liansheng sees from its balcony the sign of Wu Xuexiang across the *longtang* and then invites her longtime patron (his close friend) to come over for tea (5.306). The novel also depicts many scenes of social interaction between an upstairs room and the alley (Figure 4.5, top right). In the meantime, activities in the courtesan room were also visible from the *longtang*, as a bamboo poem said:

> Zhoujin li has two streets to the east and to the west,
> Where red buildings hide beauties vaguely visible.
> (*Shenbao* 1874; Gu 1996: 56)

As the second-floor space became the center of activities, the courtyard-hall for most of the time functioned as a working space where the servants did various household chores. They usually kept the *shikumen* open for better ventilation and the courtyard was then visible to passersby, forming a continuum with the *longtang*. This courtyard-*longtang* continuum was a fluid and inclusive space where servants from the courtesan houses and merchant residences constantly ran errands and tailors, small vendors, and restaurant or theater messengers regularly visited. It also generated accidental encounters between residents and visitors. In *Flowers of Shanghai*, When Zhao Puzhai sees the sign of Shangren li and strolls into it,

> [he] stood at the entrance [of a courtesan house] and looked into it: a *niangyi* (women servant) with loose hairs was washing clothes in the courtyard and a male servant was cleaning foreign-style glass lamps. A maid about fourteen or fifteen years old, uttering some indistinguishable words, ran out the house and hit Puzhai. Before he became angry, she yelled first: "Don't you hit your Mom! Don't you have an eye!" Hearing her sweet voice and seeing her pretty face, Puzhai forgot his anger and smiled.
>
> (2.290)

Later Puzhai encounters again this maid, called Aqiao, who has quit her unpleasant job in that courtesan house (of Wei Xiaxian) and works in the house of his sister Zhao Erbao. There they have an affair and eventually get married (62.603–606).

The *long(tang)* could also be a place where people engaged in public brawls,[14] and where hoodlums harassed the maids escorting the courtesan sedans. A contemporary report commented on this issue: "To see the violation of etiquette and order, the loss of righteous men, and the filthiest, unheard-of conduct in the world, you must visit [the *li* compounds in] the middle section of Fourth Avenue" (see Figure 3.2).

Elite merchants often avoided such spaces by taking sedans or rickshaws. At banquet times, a *long(tang)* could be crowded with waiting sedans and rickshaws. After a banquet party Lu Zifu and Tang Xiao'an walk out of the house and see that sedans and rickshaws are on both sides of the *longtang*. They turn their bodies to walk through but are blocked by a maidservant who is trying to get through from the other direction (6.314). Such storekeepers as Hong Shanqing often walk in the alley and rich merchants also walk occasionally, but a courtesan always takes a sedan, as her bounded feet prohibits her from walking.

Like the Confucians in earlier times, the merchants considered the street and alley a subaltern space fraught with chaos and danger. While they took advantage of the extension of prosperous streets, their leisurely "stroll" always took place inside the courtesan boudoir, which gave them an illusion of a homelike space, and from which they could see the street while remaining above and apart from it. This visual advantage compensated for the loss of the spacious courtyard, and the elite space was now defined by the high level as the courtyard-hall had lost its central standing. But in the end this final retreat was also full of danger and deception and became part of the street, where personal romances and loves were just like business transactions.

Nonetheless, there seemed to be some secrete spaces in the *li* house that bred genuine but illegitimate loves. Next to the staircase were a couple of small back rooms or *tingzijian* (literally, pavilion rooms) that were sometimes used as the maids' bedrooms but could also be borrowed for secret affairs. It is in such a room that Puzhai and Aqiao have an affair (62.603). On anther occasion when two banquets are held at the same time in the house of Zhou Lan, the *niangyi* Ajin is hiding in a *tingzijian* with her secret lover Zhang Shou, who is the servant of a client in one of the parties (28.428). As detailed in Chapter 3, Shen Xiaohong's secret liaison with the opera actor Xiaoliu'er is in a *tingzijian* when Wang Liansheng finds it out (33.456). Such secret affairs of true passion were considered illegitimate, because they posited a threat to both the traditional Confucian moralities and the business routines of the courtesan house.

In short, the courtesan house epitomized the multifunctional, flexible, and ambiguous social space in the *li* compound. It was a residence as well as a commercial establishment—the resting place of the courtesans and their servants and managers, as well as a "home" purchased by the sojourners. This ambiguous space anticipated a new kind of urban residence, whose free access to public spaces and business opportunities eclipsed the centralized spatial order and rigid boundary of the traditional residence.

Distinct neighborhoods

All nineteenth-century Chinese neighborhoods clustered in the western sections of the then modestly sized settlements of Shanghai. The *li* houses near Peking Road, in the northern part of the International Settlement, were used for merchant residences and commercial establishments such as those listed in the 1876 guide. About four or five blocks south of this business area was the entertainment district, located in the middle section of Fourth Avenue and close to the Racecourse, the French Concession, and the walled city.

Even though different business and residential communities were very close to one another, each *li*, or at least each *longtang*, usually acquired a distinct character by accommodating similar businesses or residences behind its *shikumen*, which, like the entrance of a former grand household, gave a shared identity to a community of sojourners. Residences and courtesan houses rarely shared a *shikumen*. Most sojourners were acutely aware of the social character of every neighborhood. In *Flowers of Shanghai*, when the storekeeper Hong Shanqing knows that his sister, nephew, and niece have moved into Qinghe fang, he is very upset and storms into their house: "This is Qinghe fang. Do you know what kind of place it is?" (31.444–45).[15] Because his niece is soon to open her courtesan business, he feels that his own reputation is being tarnished. As the distinction between domestic women and courtesans was so much tied to the different neighborhoods they resided in, the complicated categories of courtesans and sex workers were translated into a diversified urban geography of fin-de-siècle Shanghai.

Most of the first-class courtesans (*shuyu* and *changsan*) resided in the *li* near the middle section of Fourth Avenue, while many second-class *yao'er* establishments were large Western-style mansions on Chessboard Street (Qipan jie) near the border of the French Concession (see Figure 5.2). Lower-class sex workers also gathered around those areas, although in more obscure neighborhoods consisting of houses different from the typical unit "one *jian* and two wings." The only nineteenth-century *li* to survive in the late twentieth century, such as Xingren li that stood from 1872 until the 1980s, consisted of courtyard houses that were probably used by banks and wholesale stores (Wang 1989: 75). Based on such extant examples, scholars conclude that the *shikumen* house evolved from the nineteenth-century multi-*jian* courtyard house to the smaller single-*jian* house in the twentieth century, implying that the latter did not appear earlier (Luo and Wu 1997; Lu 1999; Zhao 2004). But many contemporary drawings recorded a wide range of building types and neighborhoods in the nineteenth century, and the single-*jian* unit seemed to be more common than other types since it was the only one mentioned in the 1876 guide. Such single-*jian* houses without a courtyard looked like roadside shops and were aligned in rows. Between two such rows was a *long(tang)* leading to a *shikumen* that defined the neighborhood.

The *huayanjian* (flower opium room), a kind of cheap brothel that served opium as well, could be found in neighborhoods of single-*jian* houses (Figure 4.6). In the novel, Zhang Xiaocun tells the newcomer Zhao Puzhai, who is eager to visit a courtesan house, not to visit expensive *changsan* or *yao'er* houses; he then leads Puzhai to a "straightforward place":

They walked to the south, passed Beat-the-Dog Bridge, and arrived in front of a house at the end of Xinjie (New Street) in the French Concession. A dim glass lamp was hung at the entrance. They passed the door and stepped

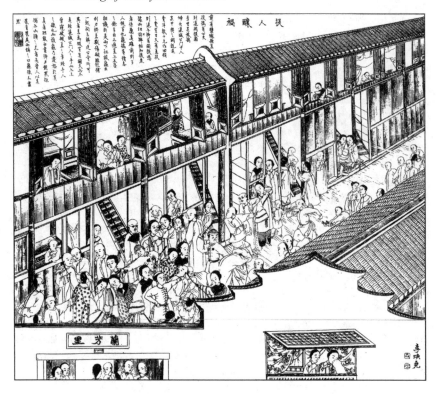

Figure 4.6 Flower opium houses in Langfang li during a police raid.
Sources: *Dianshizhai huabao,* October 1884; Wu et al. 2001: 1.140.

right onto the stairs. Puzhai followed Xiaocun into an upstairs room which was only half *jian* wide. There was a big bed to the left; to the right were a few planks put together as an opium couch facing the stairs. There was also a cedar-wood dresser with chairs by a window.

(2. 287–88)

The illustration of this episode shows a two-story simple house facing a *long-tang* (Figure 4.5, bottom left). Examples of this house type are also found in *Dianshizhai huabao* reports: single-*jian* houses near First Avenue (Damalu), a neighborhood of lower class residents in the Second Long of Xinjie (Wu et al. 2001: 10.288, 7.284). A different kind of lower-class sex worker, *yeji* (streetwalkers), who solicited customers from the street, also gathered in some *li* neighborhoods, such as Ju'an li (see Figure 3.1) and Xinyongqing li; the latter consisted of simple houses equipped with fine *shikumen* but apparently without any courtyards (Wu et al. 2001: 2.151; see Liang 2008a: 497–99).

The sojourners' social status was tied to the kind of social space in which they dwelled. For rich merchants or officials, both their residences and the courtesan houses they visited represented their wealth and elite status. As their friends or acquaintances, the less wealthy merchants and storekeepers also tried to maintain a similar lifestyle. In the novel, Hong Shanqing's relationship with the courtesan Zhou Shuangzhu appears to be a pragmatic liaison necessitated by building a close friendship with the rich merchant Wang Liansheng and others. Just as residing in a distinct neighborhood would improve a resident's social status, patronizing a first-class courtesan helped a customer to join the club of the elite. Thus visiting courtesan houses was part of the sojourners' conscious identity construction.

In late nineteenth-century Shanghai a wide range of extremely diverse sex and entertainment establishments provided services to clients from all walks of life and seemingly formed a hierarchical system. Literati and guidebook authors used the terms *shangdeng, cizhi,* and *pinxia* (upper, second, and lower grade) to rank the courtesans (in the order of *shuyu, changsan,* and *yao'er*) and sex workers; this ranking seemed to have reproduced the social hierarchy of traditional society. But the new urban communities were much more fluid and loosely structured than any traditional community. Whereas the Confucian social hierarchy entailed the top-down praxes of filial piety and subordinate obedience, the system of Shanghai sex trade was full of competitions and rivalries between different kinds of courtesans, and between them and lower-class sex workers. Rather than constituting a set of vertically ranked social groups in a rigid social system, these "business-women" formed segregated as well as fluid communities spreading horizontally in the city's uneven geography.

In structuring this complex world of sex trade, the guidebooks constructed the clearly defined and pseudo-hierarchical categories of courtesans and sex workers. The idea of hierarchy was slightly applicable to the different types of courtesans, as they and their elite customers had formed a loosely structured community through banquet parties and other commercial activities. But it is extremely problematic to apply the idea to all or lower-class sex workers.[16] The relation between courtesans and lower-class sex workers was obviously a matter of class, while within the courtesan class the distinct types reflected the different market values of their businesses rather than forming a social hierarchy. In fact, the terms *changsan* and *yao'er* for the courtesan types indicated how much they charged their customer for dinner and sex.

As the market fluctuated, a courtesan's status changed from time to time. Many courtesan biographies in the guidebooks recorded such changes; for example: "Wang Guixiang, from Suzhou, nineteen years old, residing in Zhaogui li, has an elegant posture, a respectable manner, and a different flavor among the courtesans. She started as a *yao'er* at Chessboard Street; in [1889] she became very famous and moved her residence and became a *shuyu*."

In *Flowers of Shanghai*, the borderlines between the different kinds of courtesans are porous as well as quite noticeable. When Wang Liansheng helps Zhang Huizhen move to a better neighborhood, he asks Hong Shanqing to come over to her old residence in Xiangchun li, where it was dark without any lights. Shanqing sees that Huizhen looks courteous and approachable and reckons that she is a *yao'er* residence courtesan. He then asks her where she is moving to.

She says: "Dajiaoyao's house in East Hexing li, across the street from the house of Wu Xuexiang." Shanqing asks: "Are you renting a room or working for a landlord?" She answers: "Renting a room, thirty yuan a month" (4.299). Xuexiang is a *changsan*; apparently Huizhen is moving to an elite neighborhood. Later Xuexiang and Huizhen and their patrons become friendly neighbors (5.308-309).

The borderlines between the different kinds of lower-class sex establishment were even less clear. In the novel, the merchants' servants visit some *huayanjian* or *yeji* houses while running errands for their maters (Figure 4.5, bottom right). One day a few servants visit an obscure brothel in Xinjie:

> Zhang Shou asked: "What kind of place is this? You folks really know how to have fun!" Changfu said: "What would you say?" Zhang Shou said: "I think it looks like nothing: not a *yeji* house, a *taiji*, or a *huayanjian*." Changfu said: "We are supposed to be in a *huayanjian*. But as they have other visitors in the house, they led us to this place. Do you understand?"
>
> (5.305)

The different forms of sex trade could have indeed confused the lower-class sojourners. The three kinds of brothels Zhang Shou mentions were detailed in the nineteenth-century guidebooks, which considered the *taiji* as the most despicable where pimps made sexual liaisons for customers and domestic women. Like the *huayanjian* and *yeji* houses, the *taiji* were usually found in obscure neighborhoods, which sometimes even attracted gentry-class customers (Wu et al. 2001: 7.185).

The class distinction between courtesan houses and cheap brothels, like that between merchants and their servants, was much more strictly observed. But even this borderline between the elite and the lower class was sometimes overstepped. The novel gives a vivid example of such transgression. In the teahouse Huayulou (Flower Rain Building), the merchant Li Shifu is attracted to the *yeji* Zhu Shiquan, who is there looking for customers, and then visits her house regularly but secretly. Later his servant Kuang'er discovers this secret:

> [In running an errand for their masters, Kuang'er and Changfu] walked to the end of Stone Road (Shilu), and saw Shifu walking alone toward the west. Kuang'er was surprised: "Why is he going there?" Changfu said: "Maybe to see a friend." Kuang'er said: "It doesn't look like so." Changfu said: "Let's go there and have a look." They followed him at a distance and saw he entered Daxing li. They stopped at the entrance and looked into the alley where Shifu stopped and knocked at a *shikumen* door. A smiling old woman brought him in and then shut the door. Kuang'er and Changfu then walked into the alley but had no idea of what kind of house that was.... When they were wondering, a *yeji* in red face and green hair opened the upstairs window and appeared to be speaking to someone below. Shifu was right behind her. While the servants were running away from Shifu, the old woman came out. Changfu boldly asked her: "What is the name of the 'girl' (*xiaojie*) in your house?" She looked at them and changed her face: "What girl? No nonsense!"

She then left them. Kuang'er said: "Perhaps it is a family." Changfu said: "Must be a *yeji* house; if it were a family, she would have yelled at us more angrily."

(26.418–19)

Later that night, Kuang'er visits the *yeji* Pan San but his romance is ruined by the hoodlum Xu Maorong; this makes him very jealous of his master's "cheap deal." The next day, he breaks into that *yeji* house in Daxing li, with the excuse of delivering a message to Shifu, and embarrasses him. But after his secret is discovered, Shifu visits the *yeji* more frequently (27.423–24). His purpose of seeing the *yeji* is different from that of other merchants in having courtesans as their social partners. Living with his servant in a hostel, he is old and lonely and craves a more homelike place; he says: "If you want a woman, why to visit the *changsan*, *shuyu* or even *yao'er*? There are some down-to-earth (*shizhai*) stuffs." He always tries to avoid attending expensive banquet parties hosted by his friends, and prefers to visit the *yeji* house in private. In the house, when the *yeji* and her madam treat him with home-style meals and tell him that he is their only patron, he probably feels really at home. But the house apparently has other customers and Shifu eventually contracts syphilis from the *yeji*—a huge price paid for crossing the borderline.

There are more examples of border crossing. Zhao Puzhai and Zhang Xiaocun visit both *yao'er* houses and *huayanjian*. Visiting a *huayanjian*, Puzhai is once badly beaten by some thuggish servants who are the house's regular visitors (17.371). These fictional episodes realistically reveal the sojourners' uncertain social status as well as their acute class awareness. The borderline between the elite and the lower class was indeed vigilantly patrolled, but it hardly prohibited transgressive behavior in the fluid space of the *li* neighborhoods. Whereas in a gentry household border-crossing affairs—e.g., between a master and a maid— were hidden behind the walls, in the *li* neighborhood such affairs became more common and visible. The ways in which Kuang'er finds out his master's secret and humiliates him testify to this visibility and the lack of rigid social hierarchy in the new urban community.

The novel figuratively compares the different courtesans and sex workers to myriad colorful flowers drifting on the sea. Enjoying the splendid view of these flowers, the sojourner walks on them but does not realize that underneath them is water rather than land and he eventually falls into the sea (1.279–80). This allegorical scene represents the sojourner's downfall in the modern city where the firm ground and solid walls melt away. The novel indeed depicts a fallen world, in which the traditional hero is dead and, taking his place, dozens of characters come by and go away just like passersby on a busy street.

As traditional bonds and boundaries had to a great extent dissolved among the displaced sojourners, the *li* and the city at large became an encompassing street, a fluid world with a floating population and enchanting views. The literati poet Yuan Zuzhi marveled:

Wonderful Shanghai!

Wide avenues tell of the foreign settlements:
Thousands of houses and doors are all open paths;
Leading to every direction are broad and smooth streets.
This instructs me to sing of an all-around tour.

(Quoted in Huang [1883] 1989: 142)

Enjoying this freedom from the self-contained household and rigid social hierarchy, the sojourners were increasingly submerged in the city's sprawling commercial fabric and uneven geography. In contrast to traditional homeowners residing in a set of courtyard spaces, they were merely passersby with uncertain identities and fortunes on the city's promiscuous streets, where the neo-Confucian ideal of social order and hierarchy had always been compromised. This is the true picture of the social space in the *li*, where the courtyard adjoined the street as the latter expands infinitely in the city.

5   Ultimate ingenuity, amorphous crowds

While the new spatial arrangements in the *li* compounds entailed a changed notion of residence—as an integrated part of the city's commercial fabric rather than a self-contained realm—the sojourners' everyday life and leisure activities took place beyond the *li* and involved a range of public spaces, such as broad avenues, teahouses, and exotic shops. Like the *li* compounds, these new spaces were hybrid-style and represented the native adaptation of Western spatial types. The sojourners also adopted a new lifestyle that was marked by pleasurable pursuits after visual attractions in the new urban environment. As this chapter shows, the sojourners still framed this environment in mythic and natural imageries rather than in line with a new public order, but their dense gathering in it nonetheless made them behave collectively like a new urban public or modern masses, thanks to the new economy of visual communication and commodity exchanges.

Influenced by Jürgen Habermas's (1989) seminal idea of the public sphere in modern democratic society, historians of urban China have examined the new developments of Western-style print media and native commercial guilds (*huiguan* or *gongsuo*) in the late Qing treaty ports (Rowe 1984, 1989; Wagner 1995, 2007a). The guilds as the social organizations of commercial sojourners were considered China's indigenous civil societies and therefore key to the formation of Chinese modernity. But scholars have paid little attention to the new public spaces and the material and technological urban conditions that developed in the treaty ports. Whereas the native guilds in Shanghai fragmented the sojourner community along the traditional lines of native-place heritage (Goodman 1995), the city's public spaces brought together the sojourners from diverse backgrounds and classes, potentially forging them into a new urban public. The ideal of the public, this chapter suggests, was embodied in the new urban environment no less than new social organizations.

The challenge of human ingenuity

In the last quarter of the nineteenth century, Shanghai surpassed Suzhou as the most attractive tourist destination in Jiangnan. More and more visitors and sojourners toured the city and their passion for its new industrial marvels marked a departure from the established ideal of travel, which was still cited in nineteenth-century guidebooks as a foil to the hedonistic tour (*yeyou*) of the city:

> Like an arrow on a stretched arch, a man should direct his ambition toward all places. Traveling amidst famous mountains, great rivers, towering buildings, and flying pavilions, he beholds upward to appreciate the magnificence of the universe and looks down to survey the prosperity of myriad creatures. Thus, his eyes are riding and his heart flying: this is enough to bring the ultimate visual and acoustic pleasure.
>
> (Meihua 1894: 1.1)

The ideal of travel was to appreciate natural wonders in this vast country. Though buildings and pavilions were also appreciated, they were considered to be of a lesser aesthetic value than mountains and waters. The preface of the illustrated guide *Shenjiang shengjing tu* (1884) explained the relationship between natural wonders and manmade structures:

> The renowned wonders of the world are those created by the heaven and those made by man. Mountains hide elegance; water and mist are nebulous— these are created by heaven. If they are supplemented with pavilions and terraces and enclosed with balustrades, the latter are made by man. When the heavenly-created and the manmade are combined all wonders can be found; by contrast, manmade scenes without heavenly craft are attractive to vulgar folks and repulsive to viewers of good taste.
>
> (Wu 1884: 1.3)

This positioned heaven/nature (*tian*) and man (*ren*) in a hierarchical relation: it was only in the order of *tian* that the unity of nature and man could be maintained. The mythic concept of *tian* gathers together the different notions of sky, nature, heaven, and divinity in the Western languages; this linguistic ambiguity to a great extent erased the distinction between the divine and the mundane, the supranatural and the natural. Unlike the God in the Judeo-Christian tradition, *tian* was a natural rather than supranatural concept. While the God had since the Renaissance become a humanist construct to legitimate man's domination of nature, *tian* always demanded man's subservience to nature in order to maintain the nature-man unity (*tianren heyi*). The concept of *tianren heyi* was central to feng shui practices that sought to site and shape manmade structures in harmony with natural creations (Feuchtwang 1974; Knapp 1999: 29–39). Thus, the "pavilions and terraces" were not so much monumental structures on their own as insubstantial additions to the natural beauty of their sites. They followed the form of nature rather than remade it into artificial forms.

Such scenic structures were often located in remote country sites, quite different from "manmade scenes without heavenly craft," which were usually found in some urban sites. The natural wonders were indeed far from cities which would be "attractive to vulgar folks." Yet the *tianren heyi* ideal was also embodied in the relationship between country and city. All human settlements—villages (*cun*), market towns (*zhen*), and walled cities (*cheng*)—were to be in harmony with the country and natural landscape. While the organic growth of vernacular towns and villages formed picturesque townscapes, the planning of the imperial capital embodied a constructed cosmological order. The continuous network of settlements of various sizes and locations formed a rural–urban continuum (Skinner 1977c, 1977d), in which there was relatively little contrast between hinterland and city, except the imperial seat which represented a different *tian*, namely the imperial power. The urban development of Shanghai, however, challenged this organic configuration of nature-man and country-city and generated a cityscape that contrasted sharply with the country's vernacular and imperial landscapes. The preface of the 1884 guide celebrated this new development:

> Displaying the extraordinary and extolling the marvelous is completely different from common ideals and designs and has not existed in the Middle Land (Zhongtu) since the ancient times. What are considered as ultimate human ingenuity challenging the heavenly craft (*renqiaoji er tiangong duo*) attract even the well-learned elite to view first for pleasure. They should not be evaluated according to heavenly interests. The wonders of Shanghai are like them. Shanghai used to be a remote corner of Songjiang County. Since [the 1840s], it has been opened to Chinese and foreign merchants and many from the Great West (Taixi) have gathered here. Our dynasty set aside a foot of offshore land to contain them and designated it a trading port. Soon it became a great metropolis in China. Its magnificent and orderly monuments, grand waterfront mansions, and strong and firm growth are without comparisons in other towns: the high masts and fast ships densely aligned along the Huangpu are from many foreign countries; the towering buildings and splendid pavilions exuding colors of gold and jade are the Westerners' abodes; in a fine day after a light rain, those agilely turning to the left and to the right are playful carriages; the curvy eyebrows, blossoming cheeks…. are from the romantic pleasure quarters. Lightening gas turning into lanterns, underground tunnels transporting fire, the high and the low are all illuminated and nights become days, decorated with sprawling marvels, illusory scenes, and theatrical outfits. All these dresses, vehicles, instruments, and utilities constitute a different heaven and earth.
>
> (Wu 1884: 1.3–4)

These spectacles of "ultimate human ingenuity" challenged the heavenly craft and thereby disrupted the unity of nature and man. But visitors and sojourners in Shanghai were not told to embrace them and abandon the established values in nature and the country. In the preface, the admiration of towering mansions and high masts contrasted with the characterization of the city as merely "a foot of offshore land." This small site set aside from the vast country to keep the foreigners at bay also brought into it a larger and different world, namely the "Great West." The contradictory senses of the little city and the large world

Figure 5.1 The Bund in the International Settlement.
Source: Wu 1884: 1.56.

reflected the author's bewilderment, which echoed Wang Tao's earlier characterization of Shanghai as a city "of a bucket size, yet with airs from four seas."
By emphasizing the littleness of the settlements, the preface retained a pride
about the Middle Land's huge expanse. But this little city nonetheless breached
the continuous landscape of the self-contained territory and the established values were in crisis—the country and the city were opposed rather than unified;
so too were nature and man.

A new imaginative geography then took form; central to it was no longer the
vast country as a seamless landscape but a tiny site filled with dense and towering
buildings—a urban locale which became distinct from the surrounding hinterland while being connected to what is beyond the country, beyond the visible and
tangible. This connection was via an invisible, ultradistant dimension that could
be emblematically represented by the height of urban structures (or the masts of
ocean boats). Whereas a vernacular settlement extended horizontally, merging
into the country or natural landscape, the new urban wonders clustering in the city
confronted its natural surrounding with their phenomenal height. With more articulated vertical dimensions, the new houses and mansions stood detached from
one another and from their natural surroundings rather than formed a continuous sprawl hugging the ground. The vertical dimension had been associated with
heavenly or imperial structures, such as sacred pagodas and the golden roofs in

the Forbidden City, but now Shanghai blatantly stole this heavenly dimension as if it were an imperial seat. Indeed the city was developing into a (colonial) capital of Western imperial powers and thereby challenged *tian* or the old imperialism of the Middle Kingdom.

Aside from introducing the new dimension of space, the development of settlements also demonstrated a new sense of time and history. The preface traced this development back to the transformation of a deserted grave land:

> The earlier situation of this small land was like this: white bones held up the sky, yellow bushes covered the ground, wild animals and birds cried, and ghost fires flied. It was called a deserted land similar to the remains of the dead. But within a few decades, grand streets and markets have taken form and are crowded with people; outreaching avenues have been built and marvelous goods are stored—this glamour and prosperity is the best in the world. Is this a heavenly creation to which man merely adds decorations or the ultimate achievement of the power of man?
>
> (Wu 1884: 1.5)

In retrospect, a prosperous site was usually considered to have developed from a mythic, vital origin imbued with auspicious essence or good feng shui. By contrast, the preface depicted a sterile land with scenes of death, quite different from the flourishing cornfields and idyllic villages observed by the first foreign settlers.[1] One wonders why the author imaginatively reconstructed this ghastly and desolate scene of the past against the current prosperity. While dramatizing the rapid urban development, the passage also implied an illegitimate origin of the new urban wonders. Both the deserted grave land and the new urban wonders negated heavenly creations or natural forms of life: the one was nature appearing as death and the other consisted of spectacles of flourishing artifice. If the new wonders indeed grew out of the sterile land so objectionable according to the normative standard, then they became something beyond that standard.

The author of the preface did not mention that Shanghai had already developed into a bustling market town before the arrival of the British. He could have made a connection between the settlements' new wonders and the walled city with a flourishing commercial suburb, and seen the former as an expansion of the latter.[2] Instead, he considered the settlements as a rootless development on a sterile land unrelated to the old city and suburb, basically a novelty imported from the outside. This rootlessness would have (il)legitimated an innovative urban culture that challenged the old ideal of nature-man or country–city unity. The natives indeed called Shanghai an "alien place" (*yichang*), which appeared to be superimposed onto the established rural–urban geography. Instead of forming a continuum with the hinterland, the *yichang* was connected to a new (imperial) world beyond China and hence became distinct from the rest of the Qing Empire.

Yet there were no indications of historical progress in the imaginative transformation from the deserted grave land to the new wonders. While contrasting the city's "bucket size" with the vastness of the Middle Land, the author compared the transformation with natural ones:

> But oceans and fields, mountains and valleys, are in constant motions without unchanging rules. Where to find the colors and forms of the clouds and mists that pass before our eyes? Could they be predicted by those who are used to seeing ordinary things?
>
> (Wu 1884: 1.5)

This comparison with the mythic *canghai sangtian*—the natural, cyclical, yet unpredictable transformations of seas and farming fields—contradicts the previous statement that the "ultimate human ingenuity" should not be evaluated according to heavenly interests. This incongruence betrays the author's complex mentality, which was filled with admirations as well as doubts about the shocking development. Instead of envisioning a progressive history, he conceptualized the new urban wonders in mythic imageries and thereby reduced them to part of natural formation, similar to the formless clouds and mists that passed before his eyes.

Marvels on the Bund

The wonders of the settlements were epitomized by Western-style mansions erected along the waterfront of the Huangpu. In 1846 when the British Consul Rutherford Alcock first arrived in Shanghai, "there were but three or four houses on the 'Bund,' or river front" (Alcock 1863: 35). Two years later, Wang Tao, at the age of nineteen, visited Shanghai from a small town near Suzhou and was amazed by his first glimpse of the Bund:

> As soon as we got up the [Huangpu], I found myself all at once in a different world. As I looked out from the boat I was in I could see an expanse of mist and water, and bristling through it a forest of masts. All along the bank of the river were the houses of foreigners, which seemed to me then to tower into the sky with their upper storeys.
>
> (Wang 1985: 9809–10; quoted in McAleavy 1953: 4)

As the humble predecessors of the "towering buildings and gorgeous pavilions" shown in Figure 5.1, these houses usually had three or four stories, tall enough to inspire awe from hinterland visitors who had seen few structures more than two stories high. A turn-of-the-century historian described their hybrid architectural style:

> The newly finished establishment.... well built though sportively described as of the "compradoric" style of architecture, from the designs of some being, it is said, left to the discretion of the compradors; and yet some were not altogether devoid of elegance, being in the Italian villa style orientalised by

the addition of verandahs, and generally with gardens, where amidst thriving home flowers, pheasants were to be seen sometimes.

(De Jesus 1909: 46–47)

The term compradoric was a pun on comprador and Doric; the natives simply called these buildings (and their style) *yangfang* or foreign buildings.

Introduced to Chinese treaty ports from European colonies in South Asia in the early nineteenth century, the *yangfang* was a building in a square plan, surrounded by verandas, and topped by a pyramidal or hipped roof. It had almost equal measures in height, width, and depth. This rather bulky, cubic, and free-standing structure looked sharply different than the linear extension of Chinese shops and the horizontal sprawl of traditional dwellings, whose vertical dimension was embodied negatively in the courtyard that let in heavenly elements rather than in any structure soaring toward sky, and whose profound depth was hidden in the alternating layers of structures (entrances and halls) and spaces (courtyards) extending along a set of axes or paths. The (invisible) depth and (lack of) height in traditional houses conveyed these social meanings: the mysteriousness of private space (or the inner quarter) and the unity of nature and man. In contrast, the *yangfang* displayed an overwhelming volume, whose width, depth, and height were merely abstract geometric dimensions devoid of any social meanings.

The display of this abstract volume as detached architecture was perceived as extremely novel. Literati visitors composed bamboo poems to marvel at the *yangfang* on the Bund:

> One hundred feet tall buildings detached on the four sides,
> Have in the middle windows filled with glass;
> Foreign buildings are better than mirage buildings;
> Who reads poems about mountain immortals and sea paradises?
> (*Shenbao* 1874; Gu 1996: 48)

For Chinese sojourners, these free-standing buildings seemed to be also "detached" from reality. The "real" townscape was always a labyrinthine sprawl of adjoining house complexes and "deep streets and meandering alleys," in which no architectural facades except bleak walls were displayed. By contrast, the settlements' open waterfront and wide avenues aligned with distinctly articulated *yangfang* looked like the mirages or immortals' abodes. Many new architectural features also seemed surreal:

> Foreign buildings glow like gold and jade,
> Iron as their balconies, stone as walls;
> It is fortunate to have glass windows on the four sides,
> Night comes as usual with moonlight like frost.
> (*Shenbao* 1874; Gu 1996: 48)

Iron, stone, and glass were very different from traditional building materials such as timber and brick. The glass windows appeared to be most fascinating, as Huang

Shiquan ([1883] 1989: 132) admired: "Glass came from foreign countries, produced from sands, mud, and black lead being fired. Set into windows and screens, it makes you feel light and spacious, without any dusts and stains. Compared to silk and paper screen, it is much better." He also mentioned there was a glass factory in Shanghai.

While the Chinese poet imagined moonlight coming in through the windows—a literary trope of homesickness—the foreigners mainly used them as lookouts. In fact the windows did not let in any gaze from outside, thanks to their Venetian blinds, which was mentioned as a novelty in another poem (Gu 1996: 349). Thus the transparency of these windows was only in one direction, that of looking out but not of looking in. In contemporary drawings, the *yangfang* windows appeared as abstract and opaque architectural motifs (Figure 5.1; see Figure 1.2), while the windows of Chinese houses were often depicted to reveal interior scenes (see Figures 4.3, 4.4).[3] The *yangfang* facade displayed stone walls, balconies, and windows but concealed the interior, which was comparable to the inner quarter of a Chinese house hidden behind layers of walls. This inner quarter was open to a walled garden, while the *yangfang* interior look out through the window onto a garden, which, however, was not enclosed by high walls and was totally exposed to passersby:

> Low walls surround a high building;
> Fragrant grass like a carpet gently hugs the ground,
> Added with a few exotic flowers;
> The passersby turn around to look again.
> (*Shenbao* 1874; Gu 1996: 49)

This open display of a private garden also appeared surreal and attracted curious gazes of Chinese passersby, who would have considered that such visual treasures signified wealth and should then be concealed and protected. Another poem addressed this concern:

> Low carved walls surrounding on the four sides,
> Spring colors in the garden not to be concealed,
> This building exudes a flow of gold and silver;
> Who dare to take this fortune mountain from the Persians?
> (Huang 1857; Gu 1996: 350)

The last line implied that only the Westerners could afford to show off their wealth. For the natives, any displays of wealth to outsiders would make the house vulnerable.

The *yangfang*'s open façade and garden and concealed interior were comparable, and in contrast, to the dual character of the Chinese house: porous rooms open to the courtyard but enclosed by solid walls from the street.[4] The permeability or openness of the Chinese house, as Ronald Knapp (2000, 2005) argues, was one aspect of a remarkable continuity of form throughout history. Such building types as *xuan* (pavilion) and *xie* (pavilion by water) were skeletal structures filled with windows or panels on the four sides. Except that of a roadside commercial establishment, the open and porous structure was meant to be in harmony with nature, either in a scenic location or a walled garden, rather than displaying wealth to the public or inviting exchanges with the urban streets, which were always considered to be promiscuous and unworthwhile. The unity of nature and man could only be maintained in self-contained spaces; by contrast, there were no shared ideals and interests among people in fluid urban spaces.

The marvels on the Bund, however, presented a different picture: while private interiors were sealed off from nature, the display of grand facades and gardens and legible urban layout created a spectacular order, which turned formless and fluid streets into monumental avenues. As noted above, this new order of "human ingenuity" was considered to be a challenge to the "heavenly craft." In fact it also represented a new kind of imperial power that challenged the heavenly power of the Chinese empire. But for nineteenth-century sojourners, the spectacle of the Bund was marvelous rather than imperialist; they then conceived it in mythic rather than political imageries and imagined the *yangfang* as the abodes of immortals or exotic Persians. However surreal they looked, these colonial edifices were real buildings built by Chinese compradors and contractors, who would then reinvent the *yangfang* type in the making of the Chinese quarters located behind the Bund.[5]

Flowers of Chessboard Street

In the early 1860s when the advance of the Taiping troops drove many refugees to Shanghai, Chessboard Street (Qipan jie) and Fifth Avenue (Baoshan jie or Wumalu) were the busiest Chinese streets in the British Settlement. This area was of quite a distance from the Bund and close to Yangjing Creek (as the border between the Settlement and the French Concession) and to the walled city. Later urban literature traced the origin of the city's prosperity back to these streets where entertainment businesses first flourished, as did this poem about Chessboard Street:

> Perpendicular streets delineated like a chessboard,
> Perplexing mundane roads are seen together.
> Qin buildings in the east corner and Chu mansions in the west,
> Who can look at them from outside the game?
> (Ge [1876] 2003: 238)

These streets in a chessboard layout seemed to be molded after the legible urban fabric of the Bund, but they were densely aligned with buildings and became rather "perplexing" (*fenyun*). "Qin buildings" and "Chu mansions" (*qinlou chuguan*) alluded to the pleasure houses or *tang(zi)* in the area. A *tang* was a sex and entertainment establishment employing up to fifty *yao'er* (second-class) courtesans. Such businesses were established to meet the demand of wealthy refugees who crowded into this "bucket-size" city; the *tang*'s large scale was comparable to that of foreign businesses in the settlements and would not be allowed in other Chinese cities. In contrast to "small houses of blue jades" in Jiangnan pleasure quarters, the grand *tang* houses were large *yangfang*, which Wang Tao ([1878] 1992b: 5688) described as "multistory buildings exuding colors, reflecting each other like gold and jade." A bamboo poem depicted them as "clusters of three-story buildings of songs and dances" (*Shenbao* 1872; Gu 1996: 10).

A later drawing in *Dianshizhai huabao* (1890) showed such a building: Hongshun tang at Chessboard Street. It appeared as a monolithic volume, quite different from traditional architecture as the composite of brick walls and timber components (e.g., pillars, beams, and panels); its windows looked like holes on the walls rather than spaces between skeletal frames; its entrance was an unadorned *shikumen* (stone portal), above which was a simple wooden balcony in a hybrid style (Figure 5.2). This building was much less monumental than the colonial mansions on the Bund, and was surrounded by alleys rather than an open garden and wide avenues. The alley in front of it was too narrow for a complete view of its façade—its roof and maybe a third floor were not shown in the drawing based

Figure 5.2 Customers attempted suicides in Hongshun tang at Chessboard Street.
Sources: *Dianshizhai huabao*, June 1890; Wu et al. 2001: 7. 104.

on an alley view. Apparently, buildings at Chessboard Street reproduced the *yang-fang*'s stocky, monolithic volume but not its surrounding open space. The next building shown in the drawing was only a few feet from Hongshun tang. Such architectural production resulted in extremely dense neighborhoods.

Surrounded on three sides by the pleasure houses at Chessboard Street and on one side by Yangjing Creek was the famous teahouse Beauty Water Terrace (Lishuitai), which according to later authors was the first of its kind in the settlements. Teahouses were popular leisure spaces in late Qing cities; they could be roadside buildings in busy urban areas or open-style pavilions in scenic locations, and visitors could enjoy tea and surrounding natural or urban sceneries. In the settlements, many innovations were added to this type of leisure space. The grand interior and tall and open structure of Beauty Water Terrace offered the sojourners views which they had never seen before. Many bamboo poems celebrated this unique structure; one said:

> A three-story building high by the riverside,
> Its four sides filled with glass windows open to all directions,
> To see flowers or quench thirst all visit here;
> The ultimate scene and love are in Beauty Water Terrace.
>
> (*Shenbao* 1874; Gu 1996: 54)

Obviously the teahouse was a voluminous and freestanding structure in the *yang-fang* style, but it also inherited many features of the *xuan*, such as the continuous windows. It in fact combined the *xuan*'s openness with the *yangfang*'s huge volume.

While on the Bund they admired the *yangfang* from a distance, in the Chinese quarter the sojourners could climb up onto the top floor of the teahouse and look out. But there was no open waterfront or wide streets around the teahouse; nor was it open to a view of real flowers in a traditional garden. If its open-style architecture was meant to be in unity with nature, where could natural sceneries be found in this dense urban quarter? Across the narrow streets were many *tang* with windows and balconies facing the teahouse, and visual exchanges between these buildings became the dominant attraction, as another widely circulated poem portrayed:

> Surrounding the building's four sides are flowers like a sea;
> Aligning along the balustrades they were for you to appreciate.
>
> (*Shenbao* 1872; Gu 1996: 9)

The appreciation of this sea of "flowers" indicated a reinvention (and parody) of the ideal of nature-man unity in this city of "ultimate human ingenuity." As discussed above, the sojourners' comparison of the Westerners' mansions to the immortals' abodes or mirages entailed a wish to "naturalize" those new symbols of trade, industry, and imperial power. Similarly, their depiction of women on display as "flowers" also sought to reframe the prosperous Chinese quarter in a natural imagery. This vegetal form of beauty in the male eye best captured female sexuality as the natural and testified to the sojourner's wish to objectify the courtesan. His gaze at her reduced her into a dead object, which could not return his relentless gaze. The city's new spectacles indeed invited such gazes, which did not make much distinction between dead objects or living beings.

At that time, "elegant ladies arrived from all directions, like rolling clouds and mists; this is a grand spectacle of the settlements" (Wang [1878] 1992b: 5686); this spectacle of seductive women (mainly courtesans and various sex workers) indeed rivaled that of the marvelous Bund. Compared to the sea, clouds, and mists, these women became a new embodiment of nature; a pleasurable communion with them would recover the loss of heavenly craft in the city and ease the traumatic feeling inflicted by the civil war. Imagined as an antithesis of domestic women, the women on sale resembled a new kind of "wild nature" for the sojourners. While a journey to pristine mountains and forests was to appreciate the sublime and apprehend the transcendental, a hedonistic tour (*yeyou*) in the settlements revolved around the immanent views of the "flowers."

Both the "flowers" and the "immortals' abodes" were a kind of dream or mythic images that mesmerized the sojourners. But whereas the grand mansions and wide avenues were perceived as surreal, the teahouse in the crowded urban quarter made private dreams real and concrete. The mansions and avenues represented a new but alien public order, while the teahouse reinvented the native experience of nature-man communion. The poems recorded this experience with a feel of intimacy as if it were in a private garden, but it was in fact about seeing those "public" women in a quite public setting.

As in other towns, the Chinese streets in the settlements were promiscuous and chaotic spaces. They became "invaded" by the courtesans' private boudoirs, which appropriated the new kind of architectural space as a stage for their seductive display. This display of private pleasure would have been a threat to the rigid social order maintained in the walled household or official complex. As such spaces of traditional power could hardly be found in the settlements, there seemed to be a lack of public or communal order in the sojourners' Shanghai. Nor was the legible layout and spectacular order of the Bund found in the Chinese quarter, in which the *yangfang* was reinvented as an even more hybrid spatial type. Its grand volume was combined with fluid space and porous structure, and its potential of creating a larger rational urban layout got buried by the dense cluster of buildings and the rampant display of the "flowers."

As urban spaces and characters were experienced as if they were mythic or natural beings, such as flowers, clouds, mists, immortals, and mirages, they did not embody any shared codes of public conduct. In teahouses and streets, the sojourners were concerned only with their private interests. In this safe haven from the devastating civil war, they were also free from the traditional controls of family patriarchs and local rulers, and then enjoyed the new urban pleasure to its fullest extent.

When many sojourners returned home after the Taiping rebels were defeated in 1864, the settlements experienced an economic slump. But Shanghai soon recovered from this temporary recession and developed rapidly from 1870 onward. Then

Figure 5.3 Visitors fell from a broken balcony of a building that used to be the teahouse
Beauty Water Terrace.
Sources: *Dianshizhai huabao,* May 1886; Wu et al. 2001:3.44.

the busiest Chinese street was Fourth Avenue, a few blocks north of Chessboard
Street, which had become a second-class area. The first guidebook to the settlements recorded that Beauty Water Terrace had been converted into an ordinary
building (Ge [1876] 2003: 149). A later report in *Dianshizhai huabao* commented
that ever since the Taiping turmoil was over, the teahouse's business had declined
and its ownership had changed through many hands. As the busy market relocated
to Fourth Avenue and the elite courtesan houses also moved away, the "sister flowers" of this area could hardly attract any "elegant customers." One day, a courtesan
and her maid climbed up onto a balcony of the poorly-maintained teahouse to
enjoy the view and fell from the balcony as its handrail gave away (Figure 5.3).

Streetscapes of Fourth Avenue

Now the best views of the "flowers" were found in the middle section of Fourth
Avenue. As shown in Figure 5.4 from the 1884 guide, the avenue was a wide
thoroughfare teeming with carriages, rickshaws, sedans, and pedestrians, more

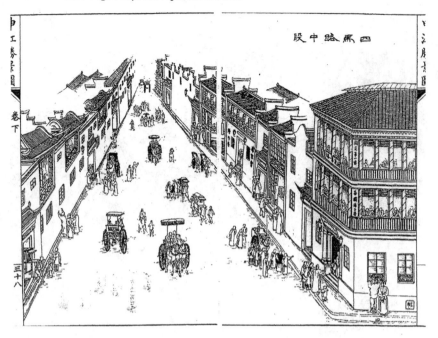

Figure 5.4 The middle section of Fourth Avenue.
Source: Wu 1884: 2.38.

spectacular than Chessboard Street. On both sides of the avenue were aligned two-story buildings in the Jiangnan vernacular style and a few taller *yang-fang*-style buildings. They appeared to be the street sections of *li* compounds, whose main entrances, *shikumen*, are shown in the illustration. As discussed in Chapter 4, elite courtesans known as *changsan* resided in these compounds, and their sedan chairs are shown in the illustration: two in the middle of the avenue and another coming out of a *shikumen* in the far left. Most of their establishments were inside the compounds and could not be seen from the street, but some houses had balcony-like rooms open directly to the street. Three such rooms, fashioned like ornate pavilions, were shown in the left of the illustration; women in them were interacting with men on the street (see Figure 5.7 below for a better view of such a room). Such street-facing establishments were sometimes called "painted buildings" or *hualou* (Gu 1996: 54), and their ornate windows or balconies had made the street famous for its exhibition of the "flowers," as a poem said:

> Rouges and jades stream out of the walls and fill the streets,
> At twilight, rolling up curtains and leaning against windows.

The poet noted: "Many pleasure houses, especially those on Fourth Avenue, have street-facing windows. After four o'clock they all open the windows and let [passersby] to look in" (Chen [1887] 1996: 89).

While such windows opened to a Western-style avenue, they were quite different from Western-style windows, which as noted above were for looking out but not for looking in, being part of the façade that concealed the interior. Georg Simmel (1997: 68) analyzes this style of window in comparison with the door:

> Yet the teleological emotion with respect to the window is directed almost exclusively from inside to outside: it is there for looking out, not for looking in. It creates the connection between the inner and the outer chronically and continually, as it were, by virtue of its transparency; but the one-sided direction in which this connection runs, just like the limitation upon it to be a path merely for the eye, gives to the window only a part of the deeper and more fundamental significance of the door.

This insightful analysis of the window of a masonry building sealed off from its environment does not apply well to a porous Chinese building of brick and timber. On the one hand, the inward-looking Chinese house strictly controlled any openings on its outer walls: any out-looking window were eliminated and direct views through the main entrance were blocked by a screen wall; such measures aimed to protect the house from any outer forces that might disturb its inner harmony or feng shui. On the other hand, any windows that did open to the street or the courtyard connected the interior and the outdoor in both directions, and thereby functioned similarly to the door in Simmel's analysis. In fact, the window and the door were often the same thing in a roadside shop or a room facing the courtyard.

Windows facing Fourth Avenue allowed views in both directions. In contrast to Western-style windows on opaque façades that presented a uniform and abstract spatial order, these Chinese windows breached the walls that maintained the traditional spatial order by displaying secret boudoirs to the street crowds. Indeed, the view of a beautiful woman through a window, in an open pavilion, or on a tour boat had previously been found only in secluded gardens or marginalized spaces of floating communities. Now such seductive views were seen everywhere on the street, and the balconies and second-floor windows became no different from ground-floor shop openings which displayed goods and commercial signs.

On Fourth Avenue were also found the spectacular façades of grand teahouses, such as Building Number One (Diyilou), Splendid People Club (Huazhonghui), and Five-Story Building (Wucenglou), which all surpassed the earlier Beauty Water Terrace in scale and glamour, while inheriting its open and hybrid architecture style. Splendid People Club and Building Number One were shown in the illustration as a two-story vernacular style building and a three-story *yang-fang*, respectively (middle right and far right in Figure 5.4); Five-Story Building was depicted in a drawing in *Dianshizhai huabao* (left in Figure 5.5). Similar to Beauty Water Terrace two decades earlier, these teahouses attracted visitors to view "flowers" from their windows, as a poem said:

> A multistory house highly built emits secret emotions;
> With the pure fragrance of fine tea,
> By bright windows on the four sides, it was delightful to have a sit;
> Across the wall you can also call a dear girl.

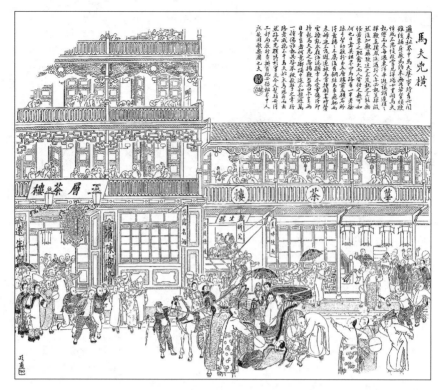

Figure 5.5 A carriage accident in front of the teahouse Five-Story Building.
Sources: *Dianshizhai huabao,* July 1892; Wu et al. 2001: 9.152.

The poet noted: "Such teahouses as Splendid People Club and Four Seas Rising Peace (Sihaishengping) have windows open to every direction and are surrounded by pleasure houses. Visitors who have acquainted girls in these houses often chat with them and make explicit gestures. These all happen under public views and no one is surprised" (Chen [1887] 1996: 83). While these visitors were no longer war-time refugees, they still enjoyed the freedom to pursuit private pleasures that was not possible elsewhere in China, and their indiscreet conduct in public spaces again testified to the lack of public order therein.

The viewers of the "flowers" too had become part of the avenue's seductive spectacle, which was as "perplexing" as that of the earlier Chessboard Street. An enigmatic poem that accompanied the illustration of Fourth Avenue highlighted this display of urban characters:

> Five-color horses and seven-scent carriages,
> In the midst of colorful silk dresses were prosperous gateways.
> Men in embroidered gowns, women in gaudy rouge,

Standing shoulder to shoulder in intimate conversations.
Where to find the magnates and kings?
In front of those doorways where myriad couples are.
Pearl flowers and jade trees fill the city;
No one knows any sorrow about being a visitor in this world.

(Wu 1884: 2.39)

In contrast to the "deep streets" of Jiangnan cities, this wide avenue and its open-style buildings exposed the pursuits of private pleasure by the "magnates and kings," who were as much on display as the "flowers." If the latter were rediscovered as the natural in the bustling street, would the city's new magnates potentially restore the heavenly order to that space? But they were in fact nouveaux riches or spendthrifts rather than real magnates or kings; and their indiscreet conduct and changing fortune made the street more confusing and disorderly. Though without the old heavenly order, the new urban space was still naturally configured; it in fact resembled a forest teeming with creatures.

A spectacular view of this forest could be enjoyed from the tallest building on Fourth Avenue. Visiting Shanghai in the early 1890s, Chi Zhicheng ([1893] 1989: 159) experienced such a view:

My friends and I climbed up onto the top floor of Five-Story Building and looked down: sedans moved like wind, men and rickshaws ran like horses, carriages flied like dragons, [and all these looked as if they were] rolling waves and thousands of troops passing by with waving banners; the crowds were like gatherings of ants, their voices were like humming of bees, and they also looked like flocks of fish, ducks, and geese that were winding toward us. Suddenly I heard music, songs, joyful chats, and clinking of jewels, but these noises came to me from the mid-air and it was not clear if they were from nearby or far away, from above or below. It was so cold out there that my body could not stand. I looked back to my friends and joked: "I have heard of ancient immortals who stood on the top of the clouds to survey the world below. This is just like that."

In this bird's-eye view, the street appeared as a mythic natural landscape: the crowds appeared as ants and bees while the vehicles looked like mighty dragons and ocean waves. The abstraction of sound enhanced the mythic vision: the visible was not heard and the audible not seen; all were obscure and unclear as if they were in a dark forest. The viewer then dreamed that he himself had become a mythic figure who stood above this forest to inspect the prosperity of its various creatures. But as soon as he was back in the street, he would just be one of the ants he had seen from above.

Indeed, as the modern street was experienced as a natural phenomenon, both superhuman and subhuman forms of life (and things) were found in it. The sojourners were not the first who rediscovered this promiscuous "nature" in the street of the modern metropolis. Victor Hugo wrote of the street of nineteenth-century Paris:

> What had happened on this street would not have astonished a forest. The tree trunks and the underbrush, the weeds, the inextricably entwined branches, and the tall grasses lead an obscure kind of existence. Invisible things flit through the teeming immensity. What is below human beings perceives, through a fog, that which is above them.
>
> (Hugo 1881; quoted in Benjamin 2003: 36)

Benjamin explains this passage: "In the crowd, that which is below a person comes in contact with what holds sway above him. This promiscuity encompasses all others. In Hugo, the crowd appears as a bastard form which shapeless, super-human powers create from those creatures that are below human beings." The crowds on the modern street appear superhuman and take on mythic forms precisely because they consist of people from all walks of life.

The crowds on Fourth Avenue included not only the "flowers" and "magnates" but also rickshaw pullers and sedan carriers. As discussed in Chapters 3 and 4, servants, peddlers, hoodlums, and thuggish gangs engaged in a wide range of productive and destructive works in the *li* compounds. Their unruly activities also spilled over onto the main streets, and sometimes their brawls and other violations of the settlements' regulations led to their arrest by the police. Unable to pay the fines, they were then forced to work in the municipal construction projects. A bamboo poem recorded a street scene of such convicts:

> Iron chains tie together many convicts,
> Being punished, they break stones and grind sands for days.
>
> (Chen [1887] 1996: 81)

A report in *Dianshizhai huabao* (1887) depicted a team of forced laborers in a road construction work. The reporter's criticism of this practice exposed the darkest spot of the "urban jungle":

> Visitors admire the settlements' broad and smooth avenues. They are indeed spectacular, but according to my view, they are also thorns and traps—what to admire? Do you see those whose bodies sweat, whose feet are painted, and who were shackled in long chains to pull the stone roller? Any Westerners among them? Drive them, beat them, shout at them, and humiliate them. Thus, the city's thoroughfares are built with Chinese flesh, blood, and tears. The Chinese should not and cannot have the heart to admired this!

Thus, the avenue in a superhuman form was in fact "thorns and traps" that turned the basest urban characters into a kind of superhuman force. The team of convicts depicted then appeared disciplined and orderly (Figure 5.6).

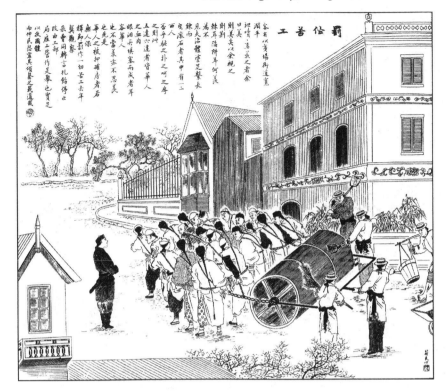

Figure 5.6 Chinese convicts in a road construction work.
Sources: *Dianshizhai huabao,* April 1887; Wu et al. 2001: 4.8.

The city indeed buried Chinese bloods and sweats underneath its Western-style buildings and streets. Anticipated by this illustrated report, an awakening sense of Chinese nationalism would eventually drive native intellectuals to protest against Western imperialism. Like the nineteenth-century reporter, they focused their attention on the iron chains as the symbol of colonial oppression while neglecting the fact that the Chinese (or dwellers in any modern city) had created for themselves a new urban condition which was equally imprisoning. In fact, the iron chains was an ancient coercive disciplinary apparatus that was only occasionally put into effect in the modern city; the dominant capitalist disciplinary practice was in fact through everyday "training" in the new urban space.

Spectatorship of street events

The mythic view of Fourth Avenue the sojourners evoked implied that the new urban space was populated by natural creatures with survival instincts. Similar to transitory spaces in Jiangnan market towns, the modern street enhanced the old apathy between strangers rather than giving them a shared sense of common destiny or universal brotherhood.[6] The only common character of the sojourners seemed to be that they were all curious spectators on the street. Thus, the lack of public order persisted in Shanghai's native quarters except when some extraordinary spectacles imposed an unusual order on the naturally configured street.

Wide and straight avenues were also built in imperial China. The ceremonial pathway, usually as the central axis of the imperial capital or a provincial administrative seat, regularly displayed the ruling authority through ritual performances. But only the selected elite were allowed to participate and view these ritual displays in the walled-in, tunnel-like avenue (Wu 1999: 85–89). While no imperial rituals were performed in such county seats as Shanghai, the local magistrate and his entourage regularly paraded through the main streets—however narrow and crooked they were—to create a moment of public order.

Fourth Avenue was straight and wide and could stage grand ritual displays, but the native authorities were not allowed to parade on this street in the International Settlement. The only spectacles that approximated that parade seemed to be the carriage rides of elite courtesans and their patrons, which astonished first-time visitors such as Chi Zhicheng ([1893] 1989: 161):

> Dusts suddenly rise, frightening noises thunder, and the gorgeously dressed and groomed have already passed through flowers and willows. The pedestrian welcome their arrivals and look back to their departures, his eyes dazzled and his heart lost.

Whereas the "flowers" seen through the street-facing windows represented a lure of the forbidden pleasure and a threat to the public order, fabulously-dressed courtesans in open-style carriages temporarily brought order to the street as this glamour parade turned the formless crowds into a uniform mass of spectators. The more extraordinary such a spectacle was, the more orderly the spectatorship was. When the public performances of the elite courtesans went wrong, the street crowds become more apprehended by their fall from grace. A report in *Dianshizhai huabao* (1888) detailed a brawl between two elite courtesans on Fourth Avenue (Figure 5.7):

> On the nineteenth of the last month, my friends [and I] climbed up into Splendid People Club. Suddenly an uproar of loud cries and applauses came from the street; [we] opened a window and saw two courtesans in two carriages in a rapid chase. The courtesan in the front carriage stood up, turned back, and pointed her fingers at the courtesan in the back and cursed her; the latter also stood up and fought back. Their ferocious gestures were evenly matched. At that time, [we heard] the noises of running carriages and the onlookers' laughs, cries, and applauses but [could] not [make out] the courtesans' quarrels. Nonetheless, [we] saw their cherry lips open, white arms upheld, rouges mixed with sweat, and willow eyebrows frowned—a different kind of amazing gesture.

For the male gawkers shown in the drawing, this "different gesture" was more gratifying than the everyday scenes of the "flowers" and carriages.

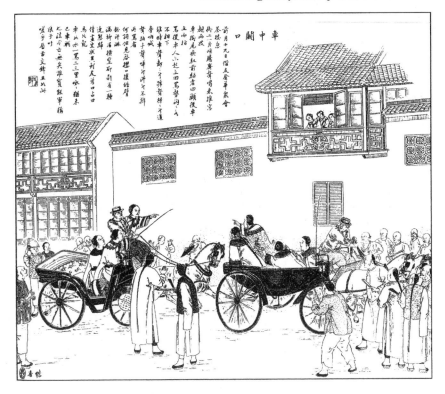

Figure 5.7 Two courtesans in a quarrel in two running carriages on Fourth Avenue.
Sources: *Dianshizhai huabao,* July 1888; Wu et al. 2001: 5.91.

The courtesans now consciously displayed their iconic images on the street, but this newly-gained privilege occasionally exposed their private life to public views, especially when competitions and rivalries between them led to their indiscreet public behaviors. When such an established public character revealed her secret persona, it immediately became a subject of public interest—in fact, a subject of private interest shared by the masses. Like other spectators, the reporter of the courtesans' brawl exploited it for his private pleasure. After returning home, he asked an artist to make this drawing and a friend to compose a poem and published them in the pictorial. Thus his private exploitation of the incident became a public one. This exploitation was not just one of women by men. In addition to a crowd of male gawkers, two women also enjoyed the melodramatic performance of their elite sisters from the window of their boudoir on the opposite side of the street. They seemed to have forgotten their own performative role on the street and turned into a part of the mass spectatorship under the spell of the unusual event.

Other kinds of sensational incidents in or around the major teahouses were regularly reported in the pictorial (e.g., Figures 5.5, 5.8, 5.9, 6.1). They ranged from brawls to robberies to traffic accidents, and always attracted a crowd of onlookers, who appeared quite passive and were apathetic to people involved in the incidents. While having come to the street for different reasons, these onlookers temporarily forgot their own businesses and took part in the collective spectatorship of the incident that evoked a catastrophic scene of tragedy or death. Thus the naturally-configured street metamorphosed into a space of public crisis, in which the quotidian life of lure and ennui came to a halt and the crowds succumbed to an extraordinary order.

The effect of a shocking incident on individuals in the crowds was magnified by the new type of urban and architectural space, which attracted greater and denser crowds than old-style streets and functioned as an open theater of street dramas. Here sounds and images got separated; individuals could see the incident but had to guess its meanings from whatever hearsays they could make out of the drowning urban noises. Such contingent and often distorted individual perceptions added up to the equally contingent and distorted collective perception of the incident. As long as it was seen as a marvelous spectacle of comfortable distance, the spectators remained a passive and apathetic crowd. But when the incident was perceived as an imminent threat that involved the onlookers, this perception would then drive them into a mass reaction that was often more catastrophic than the incident itself.

As reported in *Dianshizhai huabao*, in the night of the ninth of the first lunar month in 1886, a fire broke out in Building Number One and alarmed residents in the neighborhood of courtesan houses behind the teahouse; many ran out onto the streets in panic (Figure 5.8, top). Fortunately the firemen put out the fire in time and only the teahouse was destroyed. Five years later, the pictorial reported another fire alarm in the same location, where the teahouse was rebuilt and renamed Up One More Story Building (Gengshangyicenglou). A paper lantern caught fire in the wind at the entrance of a storytelling house next to the teahouse. One cried "fire!" and dozens of other passersby also shouted out the alarm, which immediately triggered a panic reaction among the teahouse customers. They rushed through the stairs and hallways in order to get out and many were injured in this stampede (Figure 5.8, bottom). Thanks to the hearsays of a few passersby, the petty lantern accident caused a catastrophic mass reaction, which contrasted sharply with the passive spectatorship of the street dramas.

The dense gathering of individuals in the public space caused everyone's behavior to be influenced by the others'. This interconnectedness between individuals resulted in a great degree of conformity in their reaction to unusual happenings, from which a new urban public emerged. This public, however, was an unpredictable "creature," which selfishly exploited scenes of fallen characters as well as overreacted to some petty crises. Benjamin (2003: 36–37) reflects on the origin of this monstrous creature in the modern city:

> A street, a conflagration, or a traffic accident assembles people who are not defined along class lines. They present themselves as concrete gatherings, but socially they remain abstract—namely, in their isolated private concerns. Their models are the customers who, each acting in his private interest, gather at the market around their "common cause." In many cases, such gatherings have only a statistical existence. This existence conceals the really monstrous

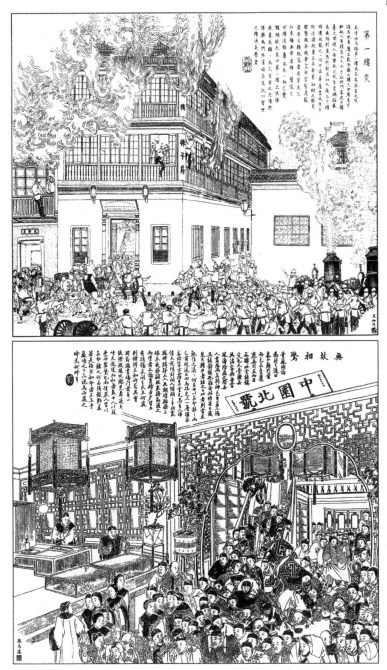

Figure 5.8 Top: A fire broke out in Building Number One and alarmed nearby residents.
Bottom: A false fire alarm caused a stampede in Up One More Story Building.
Sources: *Dianshizhai huabao,* March 1886, May 1891; Wu et al. 2001: 2.288, 8.41.

thing about them: that the concentration of private persons as such is an accident resulting from their private concerns.

He also points out that totalitarian states can politically manipulate this existence by rationalizing it and giving "free rein to both the herd instinct and to reflective action."[7]

In late nineteenth-century Shanghai, the colonial authorities had no political agendas for or against the Chinese sojourners, while the sojourners who paid taxes to the governments in which they were not represented had little or no consciousness of local or national politics. But the new urban environment nonetheless "trained" them to become a new kind of masses, whose "herd instinct" and "reflective action" as activated by the fire alarm incident could potentially be exploited for political ends. A couple of decades later when the city became a center of the Chinese nationalist movement, the perceptions of national crises effectively forged the urban crowds into a new Chinese mass of solidarity.

When the passersby overreacted to the lantern accident, they did not think of the consequence of their action. By contrast, modern politicians and activists do calculate, or miscalculate, the result of their conscious and systematic exploitation of the herd instinct of the masses. The precondition of such exploitation was that the individuals had lost the faith in their personal fate. The report of the fire alarm criticized the loss of composure of teahouse customers rather than blaming the passersby for their exaggerated cries. The reporter cited an ancient parable of a general remaining calm in front of a crumbling mountain, and reckoned that if these customers had calmly accepted their fate (*anmingtingzhi*), the disaster would not have occurred.

As an ancient myth, a person's predetermined fate or destiny invokes the death instinct to balance the survival instinct.[8] In a panic crowd, this balance is lost as the individuals' survival instincts enhance one other and turn into a herd instinct. In modern mass politics, the myth of the personal fate (death instinct) was replaced with the construct of a collective destiny (rationalized herd instinct), and the poesy of individual life with the statistical existence of the masses. The modern state then seeks to control and manage this statistical being by making it an object of scientific knowledge.

The decline of the old myth began in the sojourners' street in which the crowds were trained by a new visual economy to behave collectively and uniformly, regardless of the diverse backgrounds and destinies of the individuals. Yet these individuals were not just passive spectators of the "flowers," carriages, and street dramas; they were all consumers (or customers) gathering at the everyday marketplace around their "common cause."

Markets in the teahouses

As China's greatest trading port, Shanghai was indeed a grand marketplace that attracted more and more sojourners from the hinterland. This marketplace was epitomized by the major teahouses on Fourth Avenue, in which visitors not only enjoyed tea but also purchased goods, narcotics, and even human bodies. These teahouses were all multi-functional commercial space, and Building Number One was considered the greatest among them. Huang Shiquan ([1883] 1989: 109) described this teahouse:

> A three-story *yangfang* surrounded on the four sides by glass windows, it looks like a crystal palace on a fine day. Its upper and middle floors can accommodate over a thousand visitors, and also have additional private rooms for smoking opium. Its ground floor is a billiard room (*danzifang*). In its opening days it was so famous that all new visitors in Shanghai flocked here, but recently it is often frequented by policemen, detectives, maidservants, secret lovers, and other obscure characters. The young men and women of elegant styles then prefer to visit Splendid People Club.

The building's entrance showed a long flight of stairs directly to the street (Figure 5.8, top). The stairs led to the second floor and continued upward in a top-lit atrium, which united the rigidly divided floor spaces. This continuous flow of interior space in a skeletal timber structure was quite comparable to the fluid space in the modern architecture of steel and reinforced concrete. A *Dianshizhai huabo* report depicted this grand interior: "Tables and seats are clean, halls and rooms are deep and spacious, tea is refreshing, and 'flowers' are dazzling. Customer can also play billiard games or smoke opium. Everyday from noon to midnight it is a bustling place" (Figure 5.9). The formless street crowds were also found inside the grand teahouse, as it attracted a wide range of customers from elite merchants to rickshaw pullers and was frequented by peddlers and *yeji* (streetwalkers) who operated their small businesses in the crowds.

Late Qing and early Republican teahouses had always been the hub of diverse activities for people from all walks of life (Qin 1998: 1004). But whereas old-style teahouses provided intimate social spaces for local customers who often knew each other well, the new architectural space of Shanghai teahouses accommodated large crowds, who were strangers to one anther and not attached to any particular teahouse. The new teahouses differed from those in other towns as much as Fourth Avenue differed from a vernacular street.

Sensational events were staged inside the teahouses as often as on their surrounding streets. As illustrated in Figure 5.9, a courtesan visited Building Number One with her maid and a waiter flirted with the maid. She mocked him as being poor and lustful and he insulted her back. This verbal exchange led to a physical brawl between the waiter and the courtesan's madam who had just arrived. The customers got up from their tables and couches and gathered around the brawl to view. Like the street crowds, these gawkers enjoyed the spectacle in the open and well-lit interior space around the central staircase.

The novel *Flowers of Shanghai* vividly portrays a busy scene in Huayulou (Flower Rain Building) where the merchant Li Shifu regularly visits for tea and

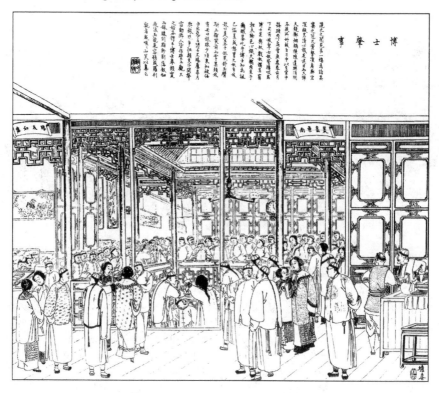

Figure 5.9 A brawl between a waiter and a madam in Building Number One.
Sources: *Dianshizhai huabao,* December 1884; Wu et al. 2001: 1.191.

opium. One day after lunch, he climbs up onto the third floor of the teahouse, in which the business is just getting busy:

> Shortly after, many tea and opium customers arrived with great noises as if they were rushing tides, and no empty seats were left. Many peddlers constantly walked in circles in the midst of the crowds of customers, soliciting them to buy food, toys, and other goods, which the peddlers held in their hands, on their shoulders, or in front of their chests. Shifu was not interested in them. He was looking for a *yeji*, as this teahouse is a well-known place to "hunt for *yeji*." Countless *yeji* arrived here in groups, chatting, joking, and making explicit gestures.
>
> (15.361)

A filthy-looking *yeji* waving a gaudy handkerchief approaches Shifu but cannot get his attention. She then walks away and chats with a waiter. In the chat, she laughs, curses, and throws the handkerchief to the waiter. The waiter dodges, hits a peddler, and causes his goods to fall scattered all over the floor. Seeing this accident, the *yeji* quickly runs away, while two maidservants walk by and

Figure 5.10 Customers joined the *yeji* for tea in a teahouse. The report noted that since
waitresses were banned in the opium houses, the teahouses' business had
improved.
Sources: *Dianshizhai huabao,* September 1891; Wu et al. 2001: 8.141.

trample over a mirror and a thermometer. The peddler then quarrels with them for
compensation. In the end, the waiter gives the peddler a little money to settle the
dispute. In the teahouse, Shifu eventually finds a *yeji* he likes, while other customers also enjoy tea, opium, and food.

In such a teahouse, customers, vendors, and goods were mixed and sometimes
indistinguishable from one another. The peddlers were small mobile "stores" of
commodities and the *yeji* were a unique form of "commodities" that was always
on the move. The customers enjoyed a changing display of these commodities
without leaving the seats. The *yeji* and peddlers were also visitors in the teahouse,
and their busy solicitation was combined with idle wandering or chatting. Some
yeji ordered tea while making gestures to well-dressed male customers, and many
a young man could not resist the seduction and joined their table (Figure 5.10).
In these *yeji* the commodity, seller, and consumer were one. They were the
true lovers of the crowd, and considered everyone in it their potential patron.
In the city, the apathy and indifference between individuals in the crowds
seemed to be balanced by the unbounded love of the commodities.

If these commodities had a soul, it "would be bound to see every individual as a buyer in whose hand and house it wants to nestle" (Benjamin 2003: 31). Marx and Benjamin invoke the concept of commodity-soul to illustrate the phenomenon that commodities displayed in modern shops have acquired a personality in interacting with the consumer. In the nineteenth-century teahouses, the commodities were not yet separated from the bodies of the *yeji* and peddlers, whose personalities indeed interacted with the customers. They would have personified the later commodity-soul, but their servile solicitation seemed to wield far less power over the customer than the silent display of commodities in modern shops. The term *yeji* was also used to refer to some unemployed male laborers who solicited manual services from travelers at some major streets and docks (Ge [1876] 2003: 123–24). The way in which the *yeji* and peddlers marketed their bodies, manual labor, or goods made the customer feel as if he were a master being served by his slaves. As long as the commodities were identified with such wretched bodies, they lacked the power (or visual allure) to captivate the customer. By contrast, when commodities confront the consumer directly in the modern shop, they have acquired a new personality that would captivate the consumer.

Though the teahouses' architectural space was anachronistically similar to that of modern department stores, the chaotic mix of people, noises, and narcotic and visual pleasures in the teahouses contrasted sharply with sanitized visual allures in the department stores. The teahouses still resembled the old-style marketplace or bazaar. Unlike the teahouses frequented by the *yeji*, the elite courtesan houses at Fourth Avenue were exclusive spaces. As I have shown in Chapter 3, the courtesan boudoir was decorated with luxurious objects, which enhanced the courtesan's attraction and even helped her to maintain control over her long-time customer. These objects, including furniture, mirrors, lanterns, paintings, and clocks, were all industrial products purchased from the market. The fashionable display in the courtesan boudoir then reflected a new visual culture of commodities that was emerging in the city's novel shops and boutiques.

Shops on First Avenue

Fourth Avenue was the city's native entertainment center where the dominant attractions were spectacles of human bodies and performances, as a poet described:

> People are myriad, courtesan houses and *yeji* nests are aligned;
> Theaters, teahouses, and restaurants make travelers forget their homes.

In comparison, First Avenue (Damalu or Nanking Road), the main east–west thoroughfare in the International Settlement, was a busy shopping street, about which the same poet noted:

> The whole street is full of shops of decorations and jewelry;
> Next to them are silk and cloth stores.

Supplemented with many Western-style goods,
There are marvelous products glittering in precious colors.
(Yi'an [1906] 1996: 107)

Most native shops were in the ground floors of two-story vernacular-style build-ings, usually as the street sections of the *li* compound; these shops were fully open to the street (see Figures 4.2, 6.12). On First Avenue there were also some large shops enclosed by high windowless walls, on which were displayed an ornate entrance portal (*shikumen*), a shop sign, and advertisements in bold Chinese char-acters. Without these commercial signs, the shops would have looked similar to traditional-style mansions (see Figure 6.11, far right).

Shops that specialized in industrial or Western-style products (*yangguang huo*, literally foreign and Cantonese goods) were usually in *yangfang*-style buildings. About this type of shops, the 1876 guide noted:

> Among the shops of foreign goods run by Westerners, Hengdali [Vrard &. Company] is the most distinguished, specializing in clocks, thermom-eters, music instruments and boxes, magnifiers, and medical equipments—each kind has many varieties. Among those run by the Chinese, Yuesheng Quanheng is outstanding, storing all kinds of foreign and Cantonese goods. There are about a hundred other stores of this kind in the settlements and the walled city.
>
> (Ge [1876] 2003: 139–40)

As depicted in a *Dianshizhai huabao* report, Quanheng appeared to be a spa-cious *yangfang*; the entrance was kept open to attract passersby but it also pre-vented curious onlookers from entering (Figure 5.11). Inside the shop, customers were dazzled by the display of novelties, including elaborate chandeliers, clocks, and vases, as the report commented:

> [If a customer] steps into it for a quick look, [he] would not be able to distin-guish the grand from the delicate, the refined from the crude, [his] eyes would be dazzled, and [his] soul lost. This situation is just like when [a man is alone] on an obscure mountain path and cannot handle things around him.

The report recorded an accident in the shop. A rich customer was buying a Western-style water pump in the shop and other customers gathered around him to look at the pump. He broke a glass lamp by accident and a falling shard hurt a child among the onlookers. The shop then asked the customer to give the child's family some money for taking care of the wound. Accidents and crowds that were more frequently found in the teahouses occasionally took place in such a Western-style shop too.

In *Flowers of Shanghai*, one day the courtesan Wu Xuexiang and her patron Ge Zhongying visit Hengdali, which appears in the illustration to this episode as an exquisite Western-style building on First Avenue. The windows on its ornate façade look opaque rather than transparent and the entrance door was

Figure 5.11 A child hurt in an accident in the shop Quanheng.
Sources: *Dianshizhai huabao,* May 1886; Wu et al. 2001: 3.31.

shut rather than kept open (Figure 5.12, left). When Xuexiang and Zhongying get inside:

> Seeing various colors and strange things, they felt dizzy and shocked; look-ing at this and then at that, they did not know the names of most products; having no time to ask for these names, they only had a quick look. The sales-men displayed many items, which were switched on to amaze visitors: many artificial birds flapped wings and singed; various fake animals danced; and a group of four or five bronze foreigners played trumpets and strings, beat various instruments, and created a set of grand melodies. Countless other gadgets were also shown. Zhongying only picked out some useful items, while Xuexiang liked a watch set into a bracelet and wanted to buy it.
>
> (6.311)

The sojourners would not consider this "boutique" as their dream world; rather, they were confused and bewildered by the products on display while also admir-ing them (see Huang [1883] 1989: 137–38).

Figure 5.12 Illustrations from *Flowers of Shanghai* (1894). Left: Zhongying and Xuexiang enters Hengdali (Ch. 6). Right: Yao's wife dines with Ma Guisheng in a Western-style restaurant (Ch. 57).

Such a shopping scene is rare in the novel. When a rich merchant, such as Wang Liansheng, wants to buy expensive gifts for his courtesan mistress, he often commissions a friend who is familiar with purchasing such items. Hong Shanqing is an expert "broker" in such commissions (see Des Forges 2007: 114–21). For nineteenth-century consumers, words from their friends were more reliable than the visual display of goods. At different social levels, the goods spoke to the buyer via trustworthy friends, cordial vendors, or solicitous peddlers. These traditional ways of shopping were soon to recede to the background (but not to disappear totally) as a new style of shopping took over the main street in which the silent, impersonal images of commodities confronted the buyer directly. And First Avenue, or better known as Nanking Road, soon superseded Fourth Avenue as the ultimate dream world of a new generation of Shanghai consumers.

6   The mingling of magnates and masses

The "boutiques" of industrial novelties and the courtesan houses were more exclusive spaces of consumption than old-style stores and the teahouses. In such exclusive spaces the new visual culture of commodity economy would eventually captivate the consumers by offering them a dream that they could all enjoy a world of fantastic displays like the "magnates and kings." The city's irresistible seduction derived precisely from the illusion that this dream of exclusivity was within the reach of every individual. This illusion then brought together the city's "magnates" and masses, not only on the streets and in open-style teahouses but also in a range of interior spaces sealed off from the surroundings.

Just as the openness and articulateness of Western-style architecture on the Bund was in fact perceived through viewing a display of opaque façades that concealed interiors, the cosmopolitan glamour of the modern city was also a superficial display that hid its exclusivity. Like the exotic boutiques and courtesan houses, other kinds of entertainment spaces were also quite exclusive, featuring splendid interiors or offering escapes from the street crowds. This chapter examines the restaurant (*jiulou*), opium house (*yanguan*), storytelling house (*shuchang*), theater (*xiyuan*), carriage ride (*mache*), and garden (*huayuan*). While these leisure spaces were constructed with different degrees of exclusivity and catering to customers of different classes, they all separated or distanced the customers from the street crowds by walls or movement. This spatial strategy of exclusion was not always effective as the spaces were nonetheless connected to the streets where the magnates and masses always mingled and their fortunes and social status changed.

Restaurants

Unlike the inclusive teahouses, the restaurants of the settlements provided exclusive social spaces for elite merchants to hold banquet parties. Gathering Harvest Court (Jufengyuan) was mentioned in the guidebooks and *Flowers of Shanghai* as one of the fine restaurants. It was illustrated in a *Dianshizhai huabao* report as part of the background of an unrelated story. In contrast to the adjacent *yangfang*-style teahouse, the restaurant looked like a traditional mansion with an elaborate stone portal (*shikumen*) and stepped gables (*matouqiang*); it selectively invited customers into a discreet dining space away from the bustle of Fourth Avenue

Figure 6.1 Up One More Story Building (left) and Gathering Harvest Court (right) on Fourth Avenue.
Sources: *Dianshizhai huabao,* February 1889; Wu et al. 2001: 5.236.

(Figure 6.1). As in an elite courtesan house, here the customers enjoyed wine, food, music, and the company of first-class courtesans and would not like to be distracted by views of the "flowers" through open windows. While the teahouses were the hotbeds of the lower-class sex trade, the businesses of the fine restaurants were closely associated with the courtesan houses, to which the restaurants regularly delivered food and sent outcall tickets for the courtesans.

There were different kinds of restaurants that offered a variety of cuisines: the Cantonese and Western-style ones were especially noted in the guidebooks. The renowned Cantonese restaurant Old Flag Prosperity (Laoqichang), as depicted in *Flowers of Shanghai*, was decorated in an elaborate style: all screens, balustrades, windows, and doors were made of delicately carved hardwood; all curtains and draperies were of painted or embroidered fine fabrics; and its traditional architectural components and furniture items were glowing and glittering, not to mention those exotic flowers and plants, famous calligraphies and paintings, and precious antiques and collectibles on display (50.548). Obviously, the elite customers visited the restaurant not just for fine food and Cantonese courtesans (Wang [1878]

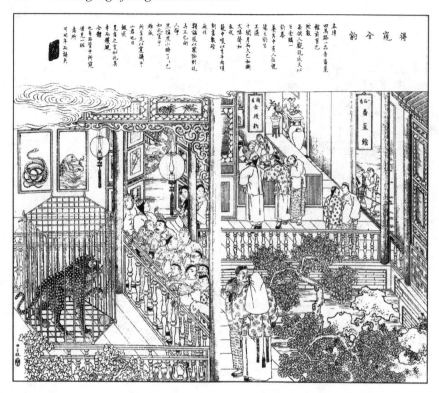

Figure 6.2 A leopard displayed in the entrance hall of First-Class Flavor.
Sources: *Dianshizhai huabao,* February 1885; Wu et al. 2001: 1.254.

1992b: 5703); they also wished to experience the dream lifestyle in the palatial interior. This short-lived experience was quite typical of the urban life led by the nouveaux riches.

The city's Western restaurants that served foreign customers were called *waiguo caiguan* (Ge [1876] 2003: 144–45), while the Western-style restaurants for Chinese customers were called *fancaiguan* or *dacaiguan*. The first of the latter type was Yipinxiang or First-Class Flavor (Meihua 1894: 1.2, 2.8); its entrance hall, shown in Figure 6.2, was fashioned in a traditional style and staged a display of snakes and a leopard to attract customers. This exotic display probably implied something new and unconventional about this "barbaric" (*fan*) restaurant. The hall adjoined a small courtyard garden of rockeries and plants, which recreated a mineral and vegetal form of nature to complement the display of the wild animals. The entrance hall was not fully open to the street; but through the doorway, passersby, such as the rickshaw puller in the illustration, could have a glimpse at the marvelous displays in the hall. Similar to the front courtyard of a traditional-style mansion, this entrance hall was an elegant transitional space. The dining rooms upstairs were usually quieter and smaller than the banquet rooms of Chinese-style restaurants.

Chinese secret lovers (*pingtou*) often chose Western-style restaurants as the locales of their secret liaison. While romantic liaisons with the courtesans were normally found in native-style restaurants and theaters, an illegitimate affair with a domestic woman could only be sanctioned in an exotic and discreet space such as First-Class Flavor. In this exclusive space the elite domestic women "benefitted" from the decline of traditional moral standards as other women did in the teahouses. In 1897, *Dianshizhai huabao* reported that two married couples who were having affairs with each other's spouse unwittingly celebrated the Mid-Autumn Night in two adjoining rooms of First-Class Flavor. An acquaintance of the two husbands was surprised to discover their secret meetings and curiously looked into one of the rooms. The man inside got angry: "Who is this crazy man who dare to spy on another man's wife! He must be arrested and sent to the police." The acquaintance retorted: "Stand up and have a look! Each of you drinks with the other's wife. Knowing no shame, you still want to report to the police for justice. Do you want everyone to know your secret affairs?" The two couples then felt very embarrassed (Figure 6.3). The illustration showed two intimate dining rooms partitioned by screens in the traditional (or Japanese) style; each room was

Figure 6.3 Two couples with their spouses swapped dined in First-Class Flavor.
Sources: *Dianshizhai huabao*, November 1897; Wu et al. 2001: 14.269.

eclectically furnished with a private table for two, Western-style chairs, electric light bulbs, a dressing mirror, and a bonsai.

While old-style dining spaces were off-limit to domestic women, the novel and exclusive Western-style restaurants sanctioned exceptions. In *Flowers of Shanghai*, when the merchant Yao Jichun does not return home one night, his wife is worried; next day she calls out his regular courtesan host Ma Guisheng to the Western-style restaurant Huzhongtian on Fourth Avenue. When the outcall ticket arrives in Guisheng's house, Jichun just wakes up from the drinking of the previous night.[2] He tells Guisheng not to go, fearing that she and his wife would end up in a brawl. Guisheng says: "If she wants a fight, why has she chosen a Western-style restaurant for it?" When she arrives in restaurant, Yao's wife greets her nicely, takes her hand, and sits with her in a foreign-style sofa. Yao's wife orders five Western-style dishes and asks Guisheng to dine with her. Guisheng only has a taste of each dish and probably feels uncomfortable to dine in a restaurant, because a courtesan on an outcall duty is supposed to sit, sing, and sometimes drink but never to eat. When Guisheng proposes to sing a song for Yao's wife, she declines. Her main purpose in meeting Guisheng is to discuss Jichun's recent activities. The meeting goes very well, and in the end she tells Guisheng: "Since my husband is your regular patron, I now hand him over to you. He is now in the foreign settlements (*yichang*); don't let him make any calls on other courtesans. If he does, let me know" (57.578–80; see Figure 5.12, right).

In this highly unusual meeting, the domestic woman and the courtesan, who have been each other's rivals, form an "alliance" against their man. They have jointly devised tactics to deal with him and eventually gained a certain independence from him. Such intimate relationship between women was previously found only between wives and maidservants in the domestic inner quarter hidden behind walls. In Shanghai, the Western-style restaurants provided discreet spaces in which domestic and other kinds of women could liaise with their secret lovers or with other women. The flourishing of such public but exclusive spaces entailed a "liberation" of the elite women from the domestic quarter and an expansion of their social circle. This novel development was sanctioned by Western- or hybrid-style material culture adopted in the new type of native spaces. As the male-dominated space became accessible to women, its fraternal image was then tinged with a lesbian color.[3]

Opium houses

While the fine restaurants' private banquet rooms entertained merchants, courtesans, and occasionally their wives or secret lovers, popular restaurants—not to mention those cheap food stores on every street corner—could be found in such teahouses as Five-Story Building, which in fact combined opium rooms (*yanjian*) with a restaurant (Meihua 1894: 1.2). Opium rooms were found in other teahouses too. In these rooms, the customers not only smoked opium but also enjoyed the waitresses' (*nütangguan*) cheap sexual services. A kind of lower-class brothel known as *huayanjian* (flower opium rooms), as noted in Chapter 4, also combined opium and cheap sex. The elites blamed these lower-class establishments for causing the decline of moral standards:

> Since flower opium rooms appeared, the pockets of small peddlers and poor laborers have been emptied. Smoking a box [of opium] costs only a hundred copper cashes [about seven cents of a yuan], which also buy the pleasure of touching and stroking a waitress. One yuan can buy the ultimate pleasure. Therefore, it is often seen that rickshaw pullers, with their sleeves rolled up, run like flying to earn two or three hundred cashes, of which dozens are spent on food and boarding and the rest all squandered in the opium houses.
>
> (Huang [1883] 1989: 102)

Some opium rooms "where dirt and scum were hidden and the elegant folks avoided were even better [decorated] than the teahouses" (Chi [1893] 1989: 159). There was also a kind of large opium houses called *yanguan*, such as Southern Honesty (Nanchengxin) in the French Concession with a lavishly decorated interior:

> All beams and columns are painted and carved; all pillows, couches, tables, lights, plates, cups, and bowls are glamorous and elegant. The hall is decorated with Chinese and foreign flowers and the rooms with famous paintings and calligraphies. In summer, many manually-powered fans (*fengman*) make [customers] forget the scorching sun outside; in winter, myriad furnaces make [them] unaware of the ices and frosts that cover the ground. A huge mirror is set in the middle of each couch: when gaslights are on in the night, lights and mirrors reflect one anther. This makes [visitors] feel as if they were in a world of glass, a universe of jewels; their eyes are dazzled and their minds are puzzled.
>
> (Chi [1893] 1989: 160)

This spectacular interior was also an "exclusive" space for lower-class consumers—a dream world away from the bustle of the street, from everyday toils. Indeed, those who were excluded from the glittering world of the nouveaux riches could at least purchase a dose of narcotic and then feel as if they lived like immortals.

The first guide to the settlements also elaborated the interior glamour of the major opium houses and noted: "With one or two hundred cashes, a customer can visit a house with his friends to get high. In the afternoon and evening, visitors arrive like tides and their breathes and opium smokes mingled, forming a thick fog. Non-smokers can hardly stay there for a moment" (Ge [1876] 2003: 150). A bamboo poem said:

> Opium couches are set perpendicularly to the east and to the west,
> Each has a bright light for smoking bamboo pipes.

> Across from the aisle people meet but do not see,
> As if they were in clouds.
>
> (Chen [1877] 1996: 83)

An opium house was called Mianyunge or Sleep Clouds Building. In the "cloud" the visitor not only got high but also enjoyed the company of the waitresses:

> The world of smoke and flowers is a paradise of love,
> Leaning to jades and cuddling rouges in front of the couch.
>
> (*Shenbao*, June 15, 1889; Gu 1996: 419)

A series of poems published in 1872 depicted the waitresses as

> A team of big feet (*dajiao*) all dressed up,
> Driving every visitor frantic.

or as married female servants (*niangyi*):

> When it is asked whether *niangyi* are useful,
> All say they can help elegant ladies to groom;
> Now they become the partners of the opium lights,
> Half boldly flirting and half being coy.
>
> (*Shenbao*, July 4, 1872; Gu 1996: 24)

The *yeji* (streetwalkers) also visited opium houses to look for customers and were sometimes arrested by the police for their misdemeanors. A *Dianshizhai huabao* report (August 1888) showed three convicted *yeji* in a huge cangue exhibited at the entrance of Southern Honesty. The official who ordered the punishment said: "Southern Honesty is a big business and these convicts I send to it will be its great advertisement. That opium house should reward them." The spectacle drew a huge crowd and the police had to use water canons to keep order (Wu et al. 2001: 5.139).

The business of the opium houses had become so licentious that the International Settlement prohibited them from hiring waitresses, but the French Concession did not have such regulation. Consequently the opium houses in the Concession flourished while the teahouses in the Settlement became extremely busy and were frequented by the *yeji* (see Figure 5.10).

In the teahouses and opium rooms commodified bodies, material goods, and narcotics freely mingled with one another, obscuring the distinction between the high and the low in the "urban jungle." As the city developed, however, this formless and dangerous mix gradually receded to the background while the main streets became dominated by sanitized spectacles, such as the equally seductive display of commodities on First Avenue. This development reflected the transference of sexual libido from the body to material objects and the visual display or abstraction of female sexuality in the public spaces.

Storytelling houses

Different kinds of commercial and entertainment spaces seemed to be randomly combined in fin-de-siècle Shanghai; even an opium room and a storytelling house (*shuchang*) were put together in the teahouse complex Splendid People Club (Chi [1893] 1989: 160). For the customers, this combination seemed to have remedied the loss of the waitresses' bodies in the opium room with the images and voices of the *shuyu* (first-class courtesans), who were then the stars in every storytelling house and made the elite's exclusive pleasure accessible, if only halfway, to the masses.

Once female sexuality was freed from the confined domestic quarter, it was freely combined with things in the market, from opium couches to banquet tables. But the more it mingled with these things, the more it was reduced to a few fragmentary sensations, eventually to purely visual ones. In the *yeji* and opium women sex had been separated from its reproductive function and become solely a source of carnal pleasure; in the exquisitely dressed *shuyu* female sexuality was reduced to acoustic and visual sensations, as her body was beyond the reach of her audience. The more her sexuality was reduced, the more it was capable of entering the masses. The abstract images of her sexuality then captivated the masses like the aura of a distant and elusive goddess—a sex goddess of seduction and incomplete gratification. As the modern masses wanted to bring into their life everything distant, they had to be satisfied with such halfway gratifications, taking seduction as gratification, fragmentation of sexuality as sexuality. The ultimate gratification was then permanently deferred in the modern city.

Unlike official and private courtesans owned by the court and aristocratic families, the late Ming *mingji* (famous courtesans) ran their own business in the floating world of Jiangnan; they mainly served the elite class. When Shanghai became a city of "mixed residences" in the 1850s, the *shuyu* emerged as a kind of independent entrepreneurs (Henriot 2001: 23). Compared with the late Ming courtesans, they were more visible in public and served a broader clientele. Rather than being the (female) "slaves" of a (male) master, they claimed to be professional storytellers who "sold their art rather than body" to the urban public, who would appreciate their voices and images as refined art. This new profession showed how the ancient art of seduction survived in the age of mass consumption. As the "magnates and kings" had disappeared, the *shuyu* had to cater to an expanded clientele, which as a statistical existence was more reliable than a few elite customers. She then became a dream image for the masses rather than a complete person for the privileged few.

While inheriting the role of historical courtesans, the *shuyu*'s profession was also modeled after the male storyteller who entertained people from all walks of life in teahouses and streets. Her hybrid role was then known as the "female story-singer" (*nüchangshu*): she "sang" rather than told stories. Chi Zhicheng ([1893] 1989: 157) sketched the evolution of storytelling art in Shanghai:

The storytelling house is the so-called [house of] "telling long stories" (*shuo-dashu*). Recently, some people inherited Liu Jingting's wit, Yudiao's clarity, and Madiao's gravity,[4] and took the stage to perform storytelling; their voice, gestures, and facial expressions were so vividly presented. But since the storytellers lost the skills and made their listeners fall asleep, they have relied on the beauties of [Shanghai] to attract more audience, inviting famous courtesans to join the performance. Before they tell a story, a courtesan sings a prelude song (*kaipian*), and during the performance she also acts out dialogues [with the male storyteller].[5]

It seemed unlikely that Shanghai's prosperity had not attracted skilled storytellers from nearby urban centers. The decline of storytelling art was due to the change in the audience rather than the shortage of skilled storytellers. Benjamin (1968: 91) points out that boredom is the nest in which the storyteller spins his tales:

> Boredom is the dream bird that hatches the egg of experience. A rustling in the leaves drives him away. His nesting places—the activities that are intimately associated with boredom—are already extinct in the cities and are declining in the country as well. With this the gift for listening is lost and the community of listeners disappears. For storytelling is always the art of repeating stories, and this art is lost when the stories are no longer retained.

The sojourners were no longer the good audience of old-style stories because their life lacked boredom. In the city, they were always excited by a rapid succession of diverse but primarily visual sensations. The more such fleeting sensations the sojourner encountered, the bigger his appetite for them was, and the less he was able to remember them as long-lasting experience, which was precisely the condition of good storytelling art.

Like a sage, the storyteller passed on his experience to the listeners and offered them valuable counsel. His art originates from the fabulous tales which a mother tells to her curious child so that the child is carried away by them and falls into dreams. This gender ambiguity of the storyteller—a maternal male—probably had made it easier for the *shuyu* to take on his role in Shanghai. But the *shuyu*'s listeners or, rather, beholders were looking for short-lived images of beauty rather than a maternal character. Displaced into this "foreign place," they had suppressed their longing for maternal love, or their homesickness, with repetitive searches for transitory visual and acoustic pleasures. For them, the *shuyu* was an objectified (or masculinized) female character whose performance just provided such pleasures and also reenacted in an oneiric fashion their frustration in remembering the rapidly succeeding sensations in their life.

The long marvelous legends (*chuanqi*) were no longer heard in Shanghai storytelling houses. The *shuyu* only "performed" short stories about love and romance, such as *Baishe zhuan* (The white snake legend) and *Yu qingting* (The jade dragonfly). Yet few of the city's courtesans had adequate storytelling skills at all, while every storytelling house listed more and more courtesans as its performers to attract visitors:

> Since [the *shuyu*] Yuan Yunxian became famous in storytelling (*shuobai*), two, three, or more courtesans have been invited onto the stage; those who cannot sing a *kaipian* choose to sing Peking Opera songs (*erhuang xiaodiao*) instead. Because listeners like songs rather than stories, singing has replaced storytelling and the

storyteller retreats to the back stage playing instruments for the singers. This is how Shanghai's storytelling houses are different from those in other towns.

(Chi [1893] 1989: 157)

As the male storyteller fell into obscurity, the *shuyu*'s art was also in decline. Originally only those who could tell (or sing) long legends were called *shuyu* or *xiansheng* and they would refuse to sit together with any courtesans (*ji*). There was once a *shuyu* association (*gongsuo*) that issued licenses to qualified performers at the cost of thirty *yuan*. Later, all courtesans who could sing short songs claimed to be *shuyu* or *xiansheng* and no qualifications were needed at all (Wang [1887] 1987: 373; Meihua 1894: 2.5).

While the new courtesans' beautiful faces and glamorous attires, as Wang Tao observed, were all unique, their style was rather banal compared with the earlier *shuyu*. Since it was difficult for the courtesans to acquire the skills of telling long legends or short stories, many chose to sing Peking Opera songs instead, which had become extremely popular in the city. But the soaring Peking Opera tune was not suitable for the "southern courtesans," whose faces and necks turned red in stretching their voice (Wang [1887] 1987: 372–73). This inelegant performance in the connoisseur's eyes was a sensational scene for other viewers who were always eager to see novel performances. A poem said:

A tune of Peking Opera surprises all the seated.
A woman's mouth can even utter male voices.

(Chen [1877] 1996: 89)

Displayed to the urban public, the onstage courtesans were just one of the city's exotic spectacles. In April 1887, *Dianshizhai huabao* reported that the owner of Yeshilou invited a "Western courtesan" (*xiji*) to singing the obscene song *Shiba mo* (Eighteen touches) every few days and the performance was tasteless. The report also noted that the storytelling houses on Fourth Avenue had made the street quite noisy (Wu et al. 2001: 3. 317).

According to the guides, the twelve storytelling houses of fin-de-siècle Shanghai were all located at Fourth Avenue. A house would hire twenty courtesans for the day act (in the afternoon) and another twenty for the night act. The names of these courtesans were posted at the entrance and a man was hired to announce the names to passersby on the street (Chi [1893] 1989: 157). It cost a customer little to enter a storytelling house, drink tea, and listen to songs. For those who could not afford to visit the courtesan houses, visiting a storytelling house was the easiest way to view the elite courtesans and enjoy and comment on their looks and performances (Meihua 1894: 2.5). In order to attract more visitors, a house always has about ten courtesans sitting on the stage and taking turns to play tunes and sing short songs, as a bamboo poem said:

Various instruments played, many [courtesans] seated,
They rival one another like lady troops.

> Once [a courtesan] is ordered to sing a song, [her] price doubled,
> Complacent like a crane standing above a flock of chicks.
>
> (Chen [1887] 1996: 89)

This spectacle was the male visitor's ultimate dream: the elite courtesans competed with each other to please him as if he were a king loved by his palace ladies. Thus the old polygamist dream survived in the public display of the courtesans, which made the audience believe that they were as privileged as the rich. This illusion then satisfied the masses' desire to bring into their private life all that were distant and auratic.

The elite courtesans did not display themselves or perform to gratify the poor who only paid for entering the house, but they could hardly tell between the rich and the poor in the audience. Sitting idly on the stage, a courtesan waited for a rich customer who would request her to sing a song and thereby make her a star in the house. If she saw acquaintances in the audience, she would beseech them to order songs. Like her audience, she also believed that the city's glamour and wealth would eventually make her a "queen."

It cost a customer one yuan to order a courtesan to sing a song. On one occasion, a well-dressed young man ordered fifteen different courtesans in Ranking Jade House (Pinyulou) to sing sixteen songs and the house thought that he was a fortune god, but in the end he did not have enough cash to pay for any of those songs. The house detained him and sent for his family to ransom him. But the family had no money either and begged the release of their son (Figure 6.4).

The most famous *shuyu*, however, rarely performed in the houses that listed their names; they performed in a house only when they were called to it by some customers who ordered a set of songs.[6] When such an event took place, the house would be crowded with listeners (Wang [1887] 1987: 373). A bamboo poem depicted:

> The noise of the storytelling house soars toward the sunset sky,
> The manager and waiters shoulder to shoulder;
> Suddenly hearing that the glamorous storyteller arrives,
> Everyone opens eyes to see Yunxian.
>
> (*Shenbao*, July 5, 1872; Gu 1996: 25)

This poem dedicated to Yuan Yunxian, of whom Huang Shiquan ([1883] 1989: 116) wrote a short biography, was from the series "Nütanci xinyong" (New poems on female lyric singers), published in the *Shenbao* to celebrate the twelve most renowned "storytellers" in Shanghai. In the same month, the newspaper published another series of poems featuring thirty woman storytellers (Gu 1996: 362–63). The authors of these poems and the print media certainly helped the elite courtesans to reach a broad audience and become cultural icons, while at the same time reducing them to merely names or literary images.

The literati-journalists could hardly afford to order songs from the famous courtesans, but through visiting the storytelling houses and banqueting in restaurants

Figure 6.4 Ranking Jade House detained a customer who ordered sixteen songs but had
no money to pay.
Sources: *Dianshizhai huabao*, March 1894; Wu et al. 2001: 11.53.

and courtesan houses, they enjoyed the courtesans' performance and considered
themselves to be its connoisseurs. From the 1870s onward, they regularly elected
the best-known courtesans in the city and compiled a series of "flower lists"
(*huabang*), which were originally inspired by the Twelve Beauties of Nanking
(Jinling shi'erchai) in the novel *Dream of the Red Chamber* (Wang [1878] 1992b:
5753–63; Yeh 2006: 227–30). As in Shanghai there were no such grand houses
and gardens as those in the novel, the literati constructed a new "flower country"
(*huaguo*) by composing and publishing lists of courtesan names.

In 1877, Gong Zhifang, whose talent Wang Tao compared to that of famous Tang-
Song poets, compiled a flower list of twenty-eight "storytelling goddesses" (*shuxian*), each represented by a precious flower and highlighted in an eight-character
short verse. His friends were so impressed with the list that they urged him to release
it to the public, but he thought that publishing his wanton words would "blemish
the jades" and his personal preferences would not please the different tastes of other
people. Nonetheless, he was persuaded to let others make copies of the list, which
became highly sought for in the city (Wang [1878] 1992b: 5754–55).

At the turn of the century, the making of the flower lists by the new tabloid presses parodied Western democratic elections and in the early Republican period the most famous courtesans were titled "the President and Prime Minister of the Flower Country" (Henriot 2001: 65–68; Yeh 2006: 231–36). As this development continued, the old (polygamist) dream of beautiful and talent women evolved into a constellation of the stars in the dream world of mass consumption.

Theaters

The great teahouses also hosted storytelling performances by the *shuyu* during the busiest hours of a day, and they were much larger establishments than the twelve storytelling houses. The city's commercial theaters (*xiyuan* or *chayuan*) were also large establishments and staged non-stop performances every day from afternoon to dawn, as a poem said:

> Large and small theaters are all over the street,
> Music and songs make every night a Lantern Festival.
> (*Shenbao* 1872; Gu 1996: 357)

If every night indeed became a festival, then this festival had lost its uniqueness. In contrast to this everyday commercial festivity, the traditional religious festivals that honored local deities with opera performances functioned as cathartic events for the local community. For the socially underprivileged, such a festival was an exciting break from daily boredom and the normative social order and its opera performance took on a secular form of entertainment. The local gentry, however, would consider such performances to be vulgar and cause moral decline because they lured domestic women who were otherwise strictly confined to the inner quarter. Rich households hired opera troupes to perform in their houses rather than letting their ladies go to the communal festivals.

In 1887, a *Dianshizhai huabao* report commented: "Many women get into temples to burn incenses and watch theatrical performances, but demure and chaste ladies never want to go. When such a boisterous event is held, those who like to dress up and show off call forth their sisters to attend it together." The report illustrated an opera performance at the inauguration of a renovated village temple near Shanghai, showing two actors in huge masks and Taoist gowns, a band of musicians, and a courtyard full of spectators. Better seats on a second-floor gallery were reserved for some ladies with children, while women in the courtyard had to buy a seat on a temporary platform in order to avoid jostling with male viewers. A few mischievous boys went underneath the loosely-planked platform and poked the women from below with sharp bamboo sticks. Adding to the women's misery, the shaky platform eventually collapsed and they all fell and lost their shoes and hairpins. The report concluded: "They arrived [in the theater] with high spirits but went home depressed, and their private parts had been violated...." (Figure 6.5)

In late nineteenth-century Shanghai, the commercial guilds (*huiguan*) were powerful institutions; they sponsored a range of religious events and opera

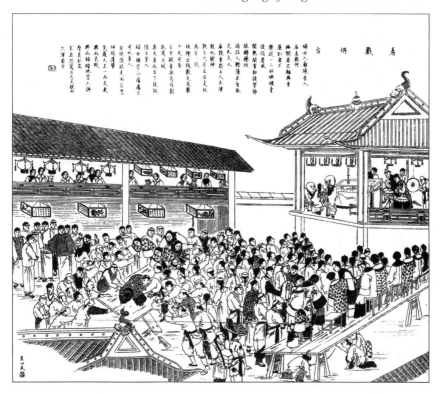

Figure 6.5 An accident in a village temple theater near Shanghai.
Sources: *Dianshizhai huabao,* April 1887; Wu et al. 2001: 3. 318.

performances that reflected the native cultures of the business sojourners (Goodman 1995: 103–106). Like the temple theater, the *huiguan* theater comprised an elevated and roofed stage and a courtyard auditorium surrounded by two-story galleries on the three sides. Such a theater also attracted unruly crowds. In June 1884, *Dianshizhai huabao* reported an event in the theater of a Cantonese *huiguan* in Jingkou, a port city by the Yangzi River west of Shanghai. Honoring Guandi, the god of righteousness and trade, the event featured extremely loud noises of gongs and drums, which drew a passerby into a crowd that was making its way into the already overcrowded theater. In the crowd, he was pushed by people from behind and could not escape; he cried for help but no one heard him in the noisy theater. Not until blood gushed out from his mouth did people stop the performance and send him to the hospital; but it was too late to save his life. The theater, the reporter commented, was a dangerous place that every filial son who cherished his life should avoid (Wu et al. 2001: 1.50).

The courtyard-stage layout of the traditional festival theater, as seen in the above examples, seemed to be a variation of the courtyard-hall layout that was widely adopted in Chinese architectural complexes. But folk rituals in a festival

theater were quite different from the neo-Confucian household rituals that sancti-
fied the normative social order. While the courtyard layout represented the timeless and unchanging, the festival events ruptured the continuum of everyday life
by reenacting legends and myths as crises. Through such crisis-like events in the
theater the local community would accomplish a collective catharsis. By contrast,
the commercial theaters in the settlements were everyday entertainment spaces in
which opera performances seemed to have lost their original function of inducing
a community catharsis.

Commercial theaters first appeared in late eighteenth-century Peking and inherited the rupturing or subversive potentials of the festival theater. The court patronage of the Peking Opera had contributed to the success of these theaters, but the
imperial authority also considered them as the hangouts of ruffians, slackers, and
insurgents and issued dozens of edicts regulating their construction, location, and
clientele (Goldstein 2003: 755). Shanghai theaters followed the Peking model but
their commercial operations were not constrained by any court regulations. For
example, their daily advertisements of plays and actors in the *Shenbao* were quite
unique in China at that time.

Located at the heart of the Chinese quarter in the settlements, the grand theaters
such as Red Laurel Court (Dan'guiyuan) and Gold Laurel Court (Jin'guiyuan)
were the city's most spectacular entertainment spaces, which even attracted a couple of curious foreign spectators on occasions. One evening in the early 1880s,
three or four Europeans accompanied by their Chinese interpreter visited Gold
Laurel Court and one of them published an account of the visit in the English-
language journal *Shanghai Mercury*.[7] As an outside observer, the author depicted
a detailed picture of the theatrical space of late nineteenth-century Shanghai. He
first described the theater's surroundings:

> The theater is a large square building, standing off from the side of the street,
> and the approach to it is by a broad alley, the two-storeyed shops and tea-
> houses on either hand being lighted up, and the frontage of the theater itself
> illuminated; [Fourth Avenue] is crowded so densely with [the Chinese], that
> it is difficult to walk along amongst them, and the entrance to the theater is
> also crowded—[rickshaws] and sedan chairs and their coolies being chief
> obstructions. The loud beating of gongs, the singing or rather screaming of
> actors, and the laughter of the [Chinese] inside, are heard as soon as we come
> to the entrance, and our friends are fully convinced that the fun is already
> going "fast and furious."
>
> (MacFarlane 1881: 39)

As the theaters attracted visitors of different classes, the crowded streets leading to their entrances were quite chaotic and occasionally staged street "dramas."
In 1890, *Dianshizhai huabao* reported a fight between the Sikh guard of Heavenly
Blessing Court (Tianfuyuan) and a hoodlum who attempted to enter the theater
without a ticket. The drawing showed the theater's entrance in the *shikumen* style
right next to a shop house. A sedan chair carrier, a food peddler, and the running

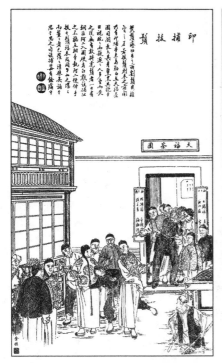

Figure 6.6 Public brawls at the entrances of Heavenly Blessing Court (left) and Heaven Immortal Court (right).
Sources: *Dianshizhai huabao,* October 1890, January 1889; Wu et al. 2001: 7.271, 5.203.

hoodlum mingled with a crowd of well-dressed visitors in front of the entrance. An earlier report in the same pictorial showed the entrance of Heaven Immortal Court (Tianxianyuan) in the *paifang* style next to a snack stand and a tobacco shop. A visitor who was looking at the latest program announcements posted on the entrance was hit by his nemesis with filths (Figure 6.6; another theater entrance shown in the far right of Figure 4.2).

Entering the lobby of Gold Laurel Court, the European visitors were greeted by a number of Chinese attendants and saw that "the box office and cloakroom are amalgamated, and are in form more like a small shop, with a large counter, than anything else." An attendant led them walking through a shaky staircase and the front and right galleries to a private box "fitted up in tolerably decent style." From the box, the visitors enjoyed a view of the stage and auditorium below:

> The area or pit of the theater is marked off in a square surrounded by wooden railings; the space is filled by five rows of small tables, and five or six in each row; each of these tables is sufficient for accommodation of four persons, who sit on small wooden chairs. The whole of this part was packed with Chinese;

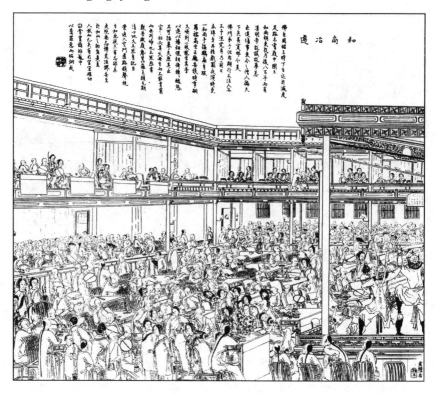

Figure 6.7 An interior view of Red Laurel Court.
Sources: *Dianshizhai huabao,* September 1884; Wu et al. 2001: 1.129.

judging by their appearance the majority were merchants, or shopkeepers, or at least in tolerably good circumstances; they were all well dressed, the dark purple cloak or jacket being the general array. Outside the rails, there is a space [a]round three sides of the building for a cheaper class of seats, and the occupants were one mass of blue cottons. In the galleries, which are only of small breadth, part of the left hand side was occupied by one or two private boxes and the rest was laid out with small tables and chairs; the front gallery, of considerable length, and greater breath than the others, had no private boxes at all, but had one row of the tables as the "front seats," and behind them a passage through which we had passed, while further back, and more elevated, there were several rows of table. The right hand gallery was chiefly composed of private boxes, and the one reserved for our accommodation was close to the stage, and about ten feet directly above the side of it.

(MacFarlane 1881: 40; see Figure 6.7)

This hierarchical seating arrangement, as reflected in the ticket prices, sought to construct a new social order.[8] The new audience then would have been more orderly than the crowds in a local festival theater. But as men and women from all walks of life were closely seated or mingled in the auditorium, it still looked like a chaotic street. A wide range of theatergoers with different looks and characters was vividly portrayed in contemporary bamboo poems (Gu 1996: 22–24, 357–58). In a theater were often seen a "dandy" with

> Peking-style smoking pipe and Peking-style boots,
> And a pair of sunglasses always in his hand;

and an elite courtesan who

> In summer dressed in light fabrics and in winter in precious fur,
> Fresh, fashionable flowers worn in her hair, with a very amused face.
> (*Shenbao* 1874; Gu 1996: 22)

The courtesans and their patrons were the distinguished visitors in a theater, which provided them special "flower tables" filled with fruits and flowers in fine glasswares (Huang [1883] 1989: 117). Wang Tao ([1878] 1992b: 5690) described theatergoers who called out the courtesans: "At night, they get into the theater and have call-tickets sent out, and slowly the [courtesans] arrive, whose shadows and scents are mixed with melodies and songs. They look to the left and then to the right, and really feel delighted." As reported in *Dianshizhai huabao*, even a Buddhist monk was once seen sitting at a flower table in Red Laurel Court (Figure 6.7).

In a busy theater were also seen many *niangyi*, who "put away their smoking pipes and talked with their heads low," and some domestic women of different ages, who wore "fashionable dresses and hairdos and looked straight to the stage without talking" (*Shenbao* 1874; Gu 1996: 23). Except the domestic women who concentrated on the opera performance, others were more or less talking, looking around, and showing off. These offstage "acts" by the audience became an integrated part of the theatrical spectacle, while at the same time making the auditorium look chaotic and bustling like a teahouse. The theaters indeed served tea and were called *chayuan* (literally, tea court), which sounds similar to *chalou* (teahouse). The unruly crowds in the teahouses were also found in the theaters. This theatergoing style continued in the early twentieth century until modern-style playhouses were introduced and audience etiquettes were promoted (Goldstein 2003).

The theatergoers were more engaging in and distracted by offstage activities when less known actors performed on the stage. When the star actor performed in the main evening act, the attention of all audience would be drawn to the stage. Thanks to the latest illumination technology, the stage itself was a great spectacle. The European visitor depicted the stage of Gold Laurel Court:

> The stage is a wooden platform, standing four feet above the level of the floor of the house, and two huge pillars stand at each of corner in front of the stage, for supporting the roof; but they are also made use of for very primitive gas fixtures in the way of foot lights, and two or three brackets

project from the pillars giving the light of a few burners to the stage, others to the gallery, and others to the pit; the rest of the house being tolerably well lighted by gas. The pillars are also utilized in another way than for gas fixtures, for about fifteen feet above the stage, a horizontal bar is fixed in them, on which acrobatic performances are given. As seen from the front, there is a large ornamental board stretching across the pillars, and on it there are [sic] in huge gilt letters the name of the theater. There is no scenery about the stage; the back of it is only a partition, composed chiefly of panels, in carved wood.

(MacFarlane 1881: 40)

This stage still looked like an elevated traditional-style pavilion but was much more elaborate and technologically advanced than that of a festival theater which operated under natural daylights. The opera plays performed on the stage were also different from local opera genres.

One of the city's earliest theaters, Triple Elegance Court (Sanyayuan) specialized in the classical court opera Kunqu. This elegantly-versed opera genre did not appeal to a broad audience and the Kunqu troupes (*wenban*) soon went out of fashion. The Anhui troupes (*huiban*) dominated Shanghai theaters since the theater Full Court Fragrance (Mantingfang) was established in the 1860s, but they were soon rivaled and outperformed by the Peking troupes (*jingban*), especially when new theaters such as Gold Laurel Court and Red Laurel Court hired star actors (*mingjue*) from Peking. The influences of the Peking troupes were noticeable in the courtesan houses and storytelling houses, where the courtesans performed Peking Opera songs, and in the everyday streets: "Since the Peking troupes arrived in Shanghai, most officials, merchants, scholars, and common folks had dressed in the Peking style" (Ge [1876] 2003: 108–109).

In addition to these professional troupes that dominated the great theaters, itinerant troupes that specialized in the local genre Flower Drum Opera (Huaguxi) were also active in late nineteenth-century Shanghai. They performed in teahouses and streets for lower-class audiences, as Huang Shiquan ([1883] 1989: 104) noted: "Vagabonds and unemployed actors gather some local courtesans, wearing light makeup and costumes to perform; their licentious gestures and obscene voices should not be heard and seen." Compared with professional troupes that were all male (or rarely all female), such a mixed troupe performing romantic dramas was considered to be obscene by the elite. Flower Drum performances first appeared outside the New North Gate of the walled city and near Auspicious Street (Jixiang jie) in the French Concession. After the local Chinese authority banned such performances, they took place only in covert venues. A poem said:

The music of the Flower Drum has ceased for six years,
But it is said that new tunes are to be played soon;
Enchanting songs fly from a teahouse corner,
To earn some cashes from local peasants.

(*Shenbao*, February 27, 1888; Gu 1996: 416)

While professional male troupes dominated the commercial theaters, female troupes performed Mao'erxi in the courtesan houses and other private venues (see Figure 4.4, bottom left).[9] A Mao'erxi troupe comprised amateur actresses (i.e. courtesans), who played both male and female roles:

> Suddenly their tender voice raised and their tune changed,
> Slanting mandarin hats on their quivering hairdos,
> They changed outfits of men and women in a blink of the eye:
> The puzzling male and female forms all indistinguishable.
>
> (Ge [1876] 2003: 259)

No stars emerged from the amateurish performances of Mao'erxi and Flower Drum Opera, while a professional troupe's rise and fall was closely related to the quality of its star actors (Chi [1893] 1989: 156). The operation of the commercial theaters began to center on the star actors rather than the troupes at the turn of the century (Yeh 2005). These star actors contrasted sharply with the actors of the itinerant troupes hired to perform in temples, guild houses, or private residences for festival events. The latter were considered to be of the lowest social class and the troupe owner's private property.[10] Their performance merely boosted a festival celebration rather than being appreciated for its own aesthetic appeal; being viewed as the puppets (*kuilei*) of the gods, they could not emerge from the theatrical roles with distinct personalities that the audience might adore. By contrast, the stars of the commercial theaters had become the city's cultural icons with distinct personalities, which penetrated the everyday life of mass consumers rather than honoring the gods as symbols of local communities. This development showed that after its separation from the rupturing festivals, the theatrical spectacle functioned to maintain the normative order of capitalist production by redirecting the masses' destructive potential to individual consumptions of visual sensations rather than giving it a collective catharsis.

The male actors playing female roles (*dan*) were appreciated for their beauty (*se*), being aesthetic rather than sexual. Huang Shiquan described the *dan* actor Zhou Fenglin who had specialized in Kunqu but changed to Peking Opera: "About twenty years old, he has a rounded figure like the moon and a smooth face that outshines flowers; his composure is full of grace, being fluent, sharp, fragrant, and leisurely" (Huang 1992: 4853). Huang collected the biographies of Zhou and other well-known actors in Shanghai and numerous dedicatory poems to them into a work titled *Fenmo congtan* (On powder and ink), which seemed to have been inspired by Wang Tao's earlier work on Shanghai courtesans. Like the courtesan, the *dan* actor of aesthetic appeal was also a metaphor of ephemeral fortune in literati writings. Huang ([1883] 1989: 101, 111) nostalgically recalled that some earlier actors had vanished without a trace after six or seven years of performance, while some other actors "in old age and of fading beauty" discarded by Peking theaters came to Shanghai and became extremely popular because the city's theatergoers always craved new things.

Probably to emulate the *dan* actors, many courtesans chose to sing Peking Opera songs rather than old-style prelude songs. But the *dan*'s elaborate theatrical costumes were not seen outside the theaters. The courtesans probably wanted to be visually distinct from the *dan* actors, whose unique beauty could not be reproduced in the courtesans. As Wang Tao ([1878] 1992b: 5694) noted, women's fashion followed what was on vogue in the courtesan houses, while men's clothes imitated the outfits of male characters (*sheng*) on the theatrical stage. The city's "dandies" were fashioned like the *sheng* actors, probably because the courtesans adored them and often sought romantic relationships with them. Actors of warrior roles (*wusheng*) were most attractive to the courtesan; she was drawn to their dazzling acrobatic actions, whose virility was as illusory as the *dan*'s feminine beauty. Around the turn of the century, the affairs of famous actors and courtesans were widely circulated through the city's tabloids. Thus, after theatrical spectacles became affairs of everyday consumption, the theatrical roles and plots expanded into the "off-stage" lives of the actors and courtesans, whose abstract images then appealed to an even broader audience.

Street parades

Folk festivals had not disappeared from nineteenth-century Shanghai; their celebrations were more often seen on the streets than in local temple theaters. In late imperial China, a wide range of religious and secular events took the form of street parade, which would transform the everyday street into a space of sacred rituals or mundane revelries. Imperial and local authorities regularly exhibited official rituals as well as convicted criminals via parades on the ceremonial pathways or busy streets of capitals and towns. In contrast to these official processions, local folk parades featured unruly crowds and usually addressed to the world of the dead. But the borderline between official and folk rituals was quite vague. For example, the city god (*chenghuang* or wall and moat) was worshiped by both local officials and populace. The god ruled ghosts, as the magistrate did local residents. The god's "kingdom" influenced the mundane world, as the spirits of the deceased were believed to protect or ensure the good fortune of their living descendants. While the gods and ancestral spirits were worshiped in temples or households, those who had died without any male descendants became homeless or orphaned ghosts (*guhun*). The street rituals sought to pacify these wandering ghosts.

The city god of Shanghai (i.e. the walled city) was a deified local historical figure, Qin Yubo, who initially declined to serve the first emperor of the Ming but later became a court official (Mao [1870] 1985: 48–49). The god (i.e. his statue) periodically inspected his realm in a procession (*jingyou*) that would drive away the homeless ghosts on its path while relieving their hunger with burned paper ingots:

> Every year, on the Qingming, Hungary Ghost Festival, and first day of the tenth month, the residents [of the walled city] carried the city god in a procession to the Northern Altar, where they offered sacrifices. The celebrants, with their paraphernalia, sedan chairs, and the like, blocked streets and alleys. There were at least seven hundred horses in the procession. Local courtesans,

their hair pinned in a bun, dressed like convicts from ancient times, chained and shackled, were carried in sedan chairs, following the horses. This was their "fulfillment of vows." Frivolous young men mingled with the procession in order to view and comment on those women, taking it as a great amusement. Respects for the god had degenerated into bawdiness.[11]

(Wang [1875] 1989: 1.12–13)

This procession, called *saihui* (or *saihui yingshen*), was a cathartic communal event comparable to rowdy actions in a local festival theater. Playing ghosts or convicts seemed to be a protest against the ruling authority and a disruption of the normative order of the living world.

The celebration of the Buddhist-inspired Hungry Ghost Festival (on the fifteenth of the seventh month) by local communities throughout China usually took the form of extravagant *saihui* that symbolically traveled from the world of the living (*yang*) to the realm of the dead (*yin*). This imaginary journey transformed the quotidian streets into a dreadful route of wandering ghosts—a liminal space that resembled a pristine way (Figure 6.8). Benjamin (1999: 519) reflects on the difference between the street and the way:

"Street," to be understood, must be profiled against the old word "way." With respect to their mythological natures, the two words are entirely distinct. The way brings with it the terrors of wandering, some reverberation of which must have struck the leaders of nomadic tribes. In the incalculable turnings and resolutions of the way, there is even today, for the solitary wanderer, a detectable trace of the power of ancient detectives over wandering hordes. But the person who travels a street, it would seem, has no need of any way-wise guiding hand. It is not in wandering that man takes to the street, but rather in submitting to the monotonous, fascinating, constantly unrolling band of asphalt. The synthesis of these twin terrors, however—monotonous wandering—is represented in the labyrinth.

The contrast between nomadic route and modern street reflects the different wanderings of the old tribe and the individuals of the modern city. We have seen the pleasure "wanderings" of individual sojourners in the streets of the settlements; the local community of the walled city or a community of sojourners also occasionally took a symbolic excursion through these streets.

The long agrarian tradition of Chinese society preserved little memory of its remote nomadic past, but wars and natural calamities periodically drove Chinese peoples into waywise excursions searching for new settlements. The dread of these painful relocations seemed to be relived in the collective rituals of the territorial cults of gods and ghosts. In a local community, the terrors of wandering and incalculable turnings survived in periodic crises and the threshold experience of ghostly parades.

Streets in vernacular settlements were narrow and crooked and looked more similar to a pristine way with unpredictable turnings than a modern street. When Western-style streets first appeared in the settlements of Shanghai, the natives

Figure 6.8 A Hungry Ghost Festival parade at Suzhou.
Sources: *Dianshizhai huabao,* September 1886; Wu et al. 2001: 3.155.

marveled at the spectacular views, such as that of the Bund (see Figure 5.1), and they as individual wanderers would submit themselves to the monotonous order of the straight and broad streets. But when the rituals of the local territorial cult were performed on these streets, they transformed into a ghostly way with unpredictable turnings.

On the birthday of Tianhou (Heavenly Queen, the patron goddess of seafaring) in 1884, a procession escorting the goddess's statue started from the old temple at the East Gate of the walled city, traveled northward along the Bund and through the settlements, and ended in a new temple dedicated to the goddess in Hongkou north of the Suzhou Creek. *Dianshizhai huabao* used two full pages to cover this event: the procession was led by a loud band of cymbals and gongs, the carriage of the statue of the goddess, procession directors on horses, and a splendid parasol that displayed the names of the donors; participants in various theatrical costumes, ladies in gorgeous attires, and boys and girls dressed like immortals followed; Cantonese merchants and "dandies" in fashionable dresses mingled in the procession, which also include incense burners, a music band, and junior actors

Figure 6.9 A procession escorting the statue of Tianhou traveled through the foreign settlements.
Sources: *Dianshizhai huabao,* June 1884; Wu et al. 2001: 1.55.

performing on three mobile stages. As Tianhou was also worshiped in their home-towns, Cantonese and Fukienese sojourners joined this local event with offerings of roasted pigs and goats (Ye 2003: 199–200; Figure 6.9).

The contrast of Figure 6.9 with Figure 5.1 showed the extent to which this indigenous event had transformed the Western-style avenue on the Bund. The artist's pictorial distortion of the straight street into a zigzagging path implied that the boisterous parade had subverted the street's monotonous order. But the illustration merely followed the convention of *saihui* representations, which always featured a meandering path staging the parade's waywise course, and belied a real spatial development: in the conflict between the local parade of the old city and the new urban space of the colonial settlements, the modern space and policing in fact disciplined the unruly parade. As the procession attracted crowds of spectators along the street, the settlements' police forces, the pictorial reported, took care of every detail and had every aspect under control. Consequently, all participants decorously behaved.

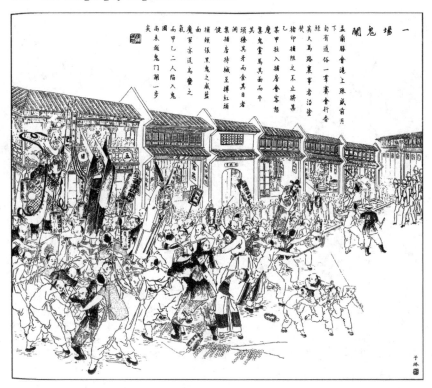

Figure 6.10 A clash between the police and a *saihui* parade on First Avenue.
Sources: *Dianshizhai huabao,* September 1887; Wu et al. 2001: 4.137.

The city's new spatial order was also in conflict with the "local" parades of the sojourners' communities. The sojourners worshiped the gods of their native places in their hometown associations or guild houses, which regularly sponsored opera performances or parades associated with the cults, especially during the Hungry Ghost Festival (Goodman 1995: 91–103). Displaced from their native soil, the participants of these *saihui* probably considered their sojourns in the city similar to the wanderings of the orphaned ghosts or convicts they played, and their rowdy actions often invited police interventions.

In 1887, *Dianshizhai huabao* depicted a clash between the police and a *saihui* parade on First Avenue. Rather than bending the straight street, the artist showed that the parade was out of its place on the street aligned with uniform shop houses. Because the parade burned paper ingots in the street, the police intervened and arrested two participants. The parade then gathered more people to fight the police in the station. The drawing dramatized this event as a street fight between policemen and the *saihui* participants: "The red-turbaned police emanated black ghost power. The blue-faced devil troops exhibited barbarian rabble spirit" (quoted in Goodman 1995: 95; Figure 6.10). Both the parade and the police were instrumental in producing a collective order, but whereas the parade sought to surmount the dread of death by invoking the territorial spirits and inducing communal catharses, the police symbolized and enforced the abstract quotidian urban order that was alienated from any local territories and communities. In the drawing, the gods' majestic effigies were falling quickly in the face of the advance of a foreign police squad.

The new spatial order was translocal and was best embodied in the orderly processions organized by the colonial authorities. When the former president of the United States Ulysses Grant visited Shanghai in 1879, the International Settlement held a parade of firemen (Huang [1883] 1989: 113–14). In 1887, the celebration of the Golden Jubilee of Queen Victoria featured the marching of troops, elephants, and firemen (Wu et al. 2001: 4.95). The Chinese spectators admired this colonial event no less than the exotic circus plays and horse races held in the city.[12]

In November 1893, the Municipal Council (Gongbuju) organized the Jubilee of the International Settlement and invited Chinese trade guilds to participate in the parade. The guilds responded with great enthusiasm and contributed more money to the celebration than the Western community.[13] The city's Western- and Chinese-language media covered this event in details. A special issue of *Dianshizhai huabao* included eight illustrations that depicted the jubilee parades of the firemen and seven Chinese guilds—one of them shown in Figure 6.11—which formed a continuous procession on First Avenue. In contrast to the usual representations of *saihui* in a diagonal and zigzagging movement, the illustrations show the parades in a straight movement and strict profile, flattening all their contents onto a horizontal strip that extends from left to right. This "monotonous and fascinating" extension would manifest the general themes of progress and discipline in the celebration of this "Model Settlement."

In the procession, ghost fires and unruly crowds were replaced with glittering lanterns and orderly spectators. The city's colonial media reported that the "dense congregation" of Chinese spectators was well behaved and kept to its designated place, demonstrating "the amenability of the Chinese native when he comes under firm and friendly control" (*North China Herald*, November 24, 1893; quoted in Goodman 2000: 901). But the colonial control of the native parades was not as successful. These parades had their own agendas and were still comparable to the old-style *saihui* in many ways, such as adopting traditional paraphernalia. For example, the banners, lanterns, and mobile stages in the Ningbo parade were imported from the City Temple Association of Ningbo (Goodman 2000: 907). The expense of the parades came from the contributions of individual stores, which requested the parades to pass their street. When the Cantonese parade was about to enter a street that was not in the officially designated course, it was blocked by the police. Frustrated, the parade dispersed rather than proceeding to the Bund (Goodman 2000: 912–13). The foreign spectators were quite disappointed:

> It is unfortunate that owing to some misunderstanding the Chinese procession got separated from the Firemen, and… turned around, so that the people along the Bund north of the great triumphal arch never saw it at all…. on

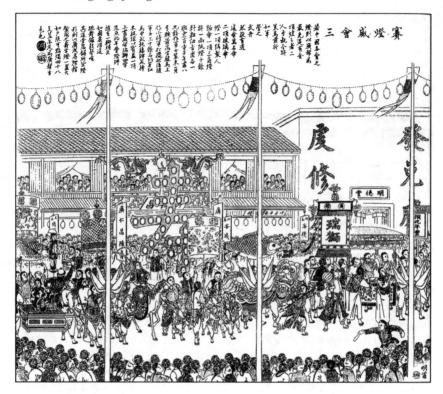

Figure 6.11 The Cantonese parade on First Avenue in the Jubilee of the International Settlement.
Sources: *Dianshizhai huabao,* December 1893; Wu et al. 2001: 10.282.

> Saturday… again there was some misunderstanding, and though fragments of the procession were seen from time to time…the expected general Parade of the Guilds was a failure.
>
> (*North China Herald*, November 24, 1893; quoted in Goodman 2000: 901)

This failure resulted from the different expectations of the natives and the colonial authorities of the parades. The colonial authorities wanted them to be part of a grand spectacle of the Model Settlement shown to the world, while the native merchants merely wished the parades to bring them good fortunes by passing their streets. This conflict of interests between the "local" and the colonial would soon evolve into that between Chinese nationalism and the Western imperialism. Preoccupied with the latter conflict, the liminal experience of public parades or protests in early twentieth-century Shanghai addressed relations between imagined de-territorialized worlds rather than between the living and the dead in a local society.

Carriages and rickshaws

The settlements' broad streets not only staged the orderly modern-style festivals but also facilitated everyday communications and sightseeing in the city. The 1884 guide celebrated a view of the Bund:

A broad and straight street, as smooth as a grindstone;
Dusts stick to the ground do not rise.
Rickshaws and carriages arrive here in teams,
Riding into the British Settlement of the Great West.
(Wu 1884: 1.57)

The immense resources spent in constructing such streets would be comparable to the resources which local Chinese authorities deployed in building city walls, gates, and bell towers. Except the grand avenues for imperial rituals, urban streets were usually narrow, dusty, and rugged and accommodated the slow traffics of pedestrians, sedan chairs, and small vehicles.[14] By contrast, the settlements' thoroughfares (*malu*) were designed for Western-style carriages, which the foreigners first introduced as a fast and majestic means of communication.

The native merchants and courtesans soon emulated the foreigners and regularly took carriages rides to "boost their pleasant gatherings and broaden their hearts and souls." In fact, the carriage ride became one of the urban wonders celebrated in the guidebooks. A Chinese carriage rental business was running and for two yuan one could rent a carriage for half a day to cruise the Bund and the main streets or take an excursion to the suburbs. By the early 1890s, there were more than 2,000 carriages in Shanghai, but they were not as safe as the foreigners' vehicles (Ge [1876] 2003: 95; Chi [1893] 1989: 160).

For the Chinese elite, the carriage ride was less a means of everyday commuting than an occasion of pleasurable tour, supplementing everyday trips in sedan-chairs or rickshaws. When a courtesan was on an outcall duty, she took a sedan chair, whose curtains hid her from crowds in the streets and alleys. Riding in an open-style carriage, however, was for her a break from daily routines and the crowded *li* neighborhoods and a leisurely trip sometimes enjoyed with her long-term patron or devoted lover (often in a separate carriage). They would cruise the thoroughfares to enjoy fresh air, open spaces, and exotic cityscape; on a hot summer day, they could also catch cool breezes from the Huangpu River. Some new courtesans regularly took carriage rides to attract potential customers (Han [1894] 1998: 35.464–65).

Thus the sojourners had "domesticated" this imported means of communication as a new indigenous form of travel that seemed to have reinvented the old-style pleasure tour on an ornate boat (*huafang*) that cruised scenic waterways in the Jiangnan region. As old Shanghai had neither scenic waterways nor "the wonders of ornate boats and waterfront pavilions," the local courtesans had to join the city god parade "to please the god as well as to show off to their clients" (Huang [1883] 1989: 144, 111). In the settlements Western-style streets and carriages

Figure 6.12   The courtesan Lu Lanfen saw her patron riding a carriage with the courtesan
Lin Daiyu and hired a rickshaw to chase them; the chase ended in a crash that
threw Lu out of the rickshaw and exposed her tiny feet.
Sources: *Dianshizhai huabao,* September 1897; Wu et al. 2001: 14.209.

fulfilled some functions of the waterways and tour boats. The carriage ride had
become a new form of pleasure tour for both sightseeing and showing off; the
outrageous costumes and reckless conduct of the carriage riders were highlighted
in the late Qing media and fiction (Yeh 2006: 62–68; Des Forges 2007: 96–98).

Staging the self-display of elite passengers, the carriage ride nonetheless maintained a comfortable distance between them and the street masses, thanks to the
carriage's speed and high seats. There was in riding a carriage a sense of superiority which was absent in walking on streets or alleyways; in a fast moving carriage the nouveau riche enjoyed "streetwalking" from a vantage point of viewing
while the courtesan seduced the public on the street but remained distinct from
the streetwalker (*yeji*). The courtesan then attained an iconic image that had never
been seen before, though this image was often tarnished by her own indiscreet
conduct. Like the *yeji*, the courtesans displayed on the streets were a threat to the
public order: brawls and reckless chases between rivaling courtesans in carriages
were sensational stories reported in the contemporary media (Figure 6.12; see

Figure 5.7); lewd behavior between some courtesans and their patron was also spotted in running carriages (Wu et al .2001: 14.205, 14.233).

A few star courtesans were even reported to have romantic affairs with carriage divers (*mafu*), who were imagined as virile characters in the late Qing fiction (Des Forges 2007: 97). In contrast to the coolie class of sedan carriers and rickshaw pullers, the drivers seemed to have acquired an elite status in taking charge of the majestic carriages. They behaved as if they were a new kind of masters on the street, as a *Dianshizhai huabo* report depicted:

> On the streets of the settlements, a carriage driver holding the leash comes along. He would hit with his whip rickshaws that are slow in making the way for his carriage and beat pedestrians he encounters. He then races away and nobody can catch and arrest him for justice. Such drivers become more and more reckless and nothing can be done about it.

The report illustrated an accident on Fourth Avenue: a middle-aged woman was hit by a carriage to the ground; luckily, she was not seriously injured and managed to get up. The driver then yelled to her: "Are you blind? Stand in the middle of the street and don't know to make the way for carriages! Whose fault is it if you are hurt? " He attempted to beat the victim but was stopped by indignant onlookers. The report urged the Municipal Council to punish such vicious drivers (see Figure 5.5).

The Council issued a few traffic rules, which were noted in the guidebooks: "Carriages must not speed while passing a bridge; carriages and rickshaws must have their lights on when riding at night"; and "a carriage can take no more than five passengers" (Ge [1876] 2003: 1.4; Huang [1883] 1989: 146). In spite of these regulations, many carriage accidents were reported in the media.[15] These accidents showed that the sojourners' appropriation of the modern means of transportation also sanctioned their reckless and wanton conduct that had never been seen before.

Showing little sympathy to the victims in these accidents, the media explained their misfortunes in terms of supernatural causes or karmic retribution. Indeed, the fall of these people symbolized the changing fortunes in the city, which had made the borderline between the elite and the masses quite permeable. Unlike the ostentatious carriage drivers, rickshaw pullers were humble and servile, but many of them had fallen from an illustrious past (see Figure 4.2). A bamboo poem said:

> Half of rickshaw pullers used to be rickshaw passengers;
> Do they remember the embroidered silk-gowns they used to wear?
> All their fortunes spent on the [courtesan] beds and running like a horse,
> They toil in dust and wind all year long.
>
> (Chen [1877] 1996: 81)

In *Flowers of Shanghai*, when Zhao Puzhai has squandered all his family's saving in the city's pleasure quarters, he becomes a rickshaw puller rather than returning home. When his family come to Shanghai in order to bring him home, his sister Erbao asks him why he did not return home. He cannot answer and she then says: "You must have been too attracted to Shanghai. Pull a rickshaw, seeing here and watching there. How wonderful that is!" Puzhai is embarrassed by this comment and remains silent (29.433).[16] If such rickshaw pullers could enjoy the city's marvels as much as the rich did, then the pleasure in the modern city was marked by the downfall rather than the illusion of grace.

The fall from grace which marked the everyday life of the elite as well as the masses arrived in tandem with a newly-gained freedom. In the courtesan houses and teahouses female sexuality was freed from its maternal destiny, while in the theaters and the streets the sojourners enjoyed the spectacles without paying homage to the gods and spirits, being freed from the dread of Death. This freedom paradoxically entailed a downfall from submission to godlike grace to repetition of hellish pleasures. With this change, the mourning over the inevitable destiny was superseded by the compulsory fondling of the city's dead body—namely the new industrial cityscape of seductive spectacles.

Gardens

The sojourners' carriage rides usually followed the enclosed route of Fourth Avenue, Stone Road (Shilu), First Avenue, and the Bund in the International Settlement (Yeh 2006: 71; Des Forges 2007: 97). This circular tour without a destination seemed to be mainly designed for the endless self-display of the courtesans and their patrons within the native quarter bounded by these busy streets, except the Bund where they enjoyed waterfront views and exotic facades of Western mansions—a different world from the native quarter. There was also a public park on the Bund, which would have been an ideal destination for the sojourners' tour. But it was reserved for foreign residents only and was not even mentioned in the nineteenth-century guides for Chinese pleasure tours (except in Wu 1884: 2.18). The sojourners' oblivion to the racist management of the park by the colonial authorities contrasted sharply with the later anti-imperialist discourse of the park as an infamous site of national humiliation.[17]

Parks or gardens were ideal destinations for the elite who wanted an excursion away from the crowded and promiscuous urban quarter. Traditional-style gardens in the walled city, such as the East and West Gardens of the City Temple, were also tourist attractions. The West Garden (Yuyuan) was sold by the Pan family to the transport merchants in 1760 and later became part of the prosperous marketplace surrounding the temple; the picturesque pavilion in the garden's artificial lake was in fact a busy teahouse (see Figure 1.3). The famous City Temple market of antiques and artworks often made visitors unaware that they were already within the "sacred" temple complex:

> Shanghai City Temple has natural sceneries,
> Taking many pavilions and terraces as a marketplace.
> (Chen [1877] 1996: 85)

No carriages could pass the narrow streets surrounding the temple and gardens in the walled city. The sojourners in the settlements then took a different road trip for a new idyllic destination.

In the early 1860s, foreign settlers built a road to Tranquility Temple (Jing'ansi), about two miles west of Fourth Avenue. The courtesans and their patrons then visited the temple by carriages, took a rest in the woods, and then returned to the city. Soon a garden, called Shanghai Garden (Shenyuan), was built next to the temple and opened to the public as a commercial establishment. As illustrated in the 1884 guide, the garden had a Western-style entrance and main building, which was used as a teahouse; there were some traditional-style corridors and pavilions at the left side of the main building (Figure 6.13). According to a *Shenbao* report, the building could accommodate two hundred visitors. Although there was no traditional landscape of hills, rockeries, ponds, precious flowers, or ancient trees in the garden, it still attracted many visitors:

> Every night in late summer and early autumn, many visitors arrive in the garden with their courtesans by carriages. At most they would order some tea and a few dishes; tea costs about one cent and a dish costs ten cents; foreign drinks and tobaccos are also available but few order them.... Some get here by rickshaws, which other visitors despise for their vulgar looks, and do not order any tea at all.
>
> (*Shenbao*, August 1886; quoted in Xu and Xu 1988: 314)

The garden's business declined when Fool Garden (Yúyuán) was built next to it in 1890. According to Chi Zhicheng ([1893] 1989: 161–62), the grand buildings and fine furnishings of Fool Garden was the best of all Shanghai gardens and attracted many visitors. These new-style gardens brought together men and women who had not previously been seen together in public. They probably emulated the Western couples seen together in the public park.[18]

In *Flowers of Shanghai*, courtesans and their patrons sometimes take carriage rides to Bright Garden (Mingyuan), located next to Tranquility Temple and probably modeled after Shanghai Garden or Fool Garden. One day, Wang Liansheng and his courtesan mistress Zhang Huizhen, along with another couple, visit the garden:

> In the garden, the lawn looks like embroidered fabric, green peach trees have just bloomed, and bird singings herald the spring of Jiangnan. It is Sunday; fine sky, fresh air, and warm breezes; many visitors who have gotten here by about forty carriages observe the early spring ritual; no empty seats in the pavilions and on the terraces are left. Ladies' hairpins and men's hats shine together and their different shoes mingle; wine mists have just evaporated and tea vapors rise again. This is more exiting than a *wuzhehui* [pancaparisad, a Buddhist congregation that makes no distinction between social classes].
>
> (9.325–26)

Figure 6.13 Shanghai Garden (Shenyuan) next to Tranquility Temple.
Source: Wu 1884: 2.28.

This native crowd of men and women on the Western-style lawn would contrast with any private gatherings in the gentry gardens or on suburban scenic sites of other towns. The visitors seem to have enjoyed the combined new urban excitement and unchanging idyllic pleasure. But the garden soon turns out to be as dangerous and chaotic as a city street. In the crowd, the opera actor Xiaoliu'er, whom Liansheng recognizes, rudely stares at Huizhen. A little later Liansheng's another courtesan mistress Shen Xiaohong arrives with her *niangyi*. She accuses Huizhen of stealing Liansheng from her and starts to beat Huizhen. Liansheng tries to stop Xiaohong in the fight which also involves the *niangyi*. Eventually a foreign policeman called to the scene ends the messy brawl between the four people (9.327).

Whereas Bright Garden turns into an extension of the dangerous street, the novel constructs a dream garden away from the city: Bamboo Hat Garden (Yiliyuan) owned by the rich merchant Qi Yunsou. After the literati characters Gao Yabai and Yin Chiyuan are introduced in the thirty-first chapter, the novel juxtaposes idealized portrayals of parties in this garden with realistic narratives of affairs in the courtesan houses in the *li* compounds. The nostalgic parties feature poetry compositions and literary games based on the classical learning and the merchants and courtesans admire the talent and humors of Yabai and Chiyuan. The traditional-style garden consists of ponds, rockeries, pavilions, and a main building called

Grandview Building (Daguanlou), and appears to be influenced by Grandview Garden (Daguanyuan) in *Dream of the Red Chamber*. In this earthly paradise (*shiwai taoyuan*) away from the streets and alleys, the generous merchants, witty literati, and gifted courtesans forget their mundane concerns and cultivate their aesthetic sentiments, especially during the celebration of Qixi (Chinese Valentine) (38.482–40.496).

But the fictional construct of this garden is full of irony and the garden eventually does not protect the characters from dangers in the city (Des Forges 2007: 167–68). Rather than advocating conservative ideals against new developments in the city, the novel portrays literati and courtesans who stick to old ideals, such as Fang Penghu and Wen Junyu, as laughable and out-of-fashion characters (47.530–31, 59.591–93). Affairs in Bamboo Hat Garden constitute not so much a nostalgic reconstruct of the literati tradition as a parody and critique of it: words taken from the classics are used in profane drinking games (39.485–86, 41.500–501); pornographies are appreciated as fine works of art (40.496); and an obscene essay is admired as the ultimate marvel (51.549–50). These decadent activities are led by Qi Yunsou, dubbed "the Master of Grand Romance" (Fengliu guangda jiaozhu), whose hedonistic followers used the garden merely as a hideout from dangers in the city's pleasure quarter.

The location of Bamboo Hat Garden, as described in the novel (38.482), matches with that of Zhang Garden (Zhangshi weichunyuan), a private property of the official-merchant Zhang Shuhe. This modern-style garden was developing into the city's most influential public space when Han Bangqing published the novel from 1892 to 1894. As a member of the literati circle around the *Shenbao*, Han probably visited the garden, where were held the birthday parties of the poet Yuan Zuzhi and the *Shenbao* editor He Guisheng in 1886 and 1890, respectively (*Shenbao*, October 8, 1886; May 4, 1890; Xiong 1996: 35). We might assume that such literati gatherings had inspired Han's portrayal of activities in Bamboo Hat Garden. But the development of Zhang Garden thereafter contrasted sharply with the decadent lifestyle in the fictional garden.

Zhang Garden was located by the road from the Settlement to Tranquility Temple and Fool Garden. Zhang Shuhe bought the property from a foreign merchant in 1882, expanded it, and opened it to the public as a commercial establishment in 1885. In the late 1880s, a visitor noted:

> It covers an immense area and has buildings that tower to the heaven. [The visitors] keep walking for dozens of yards and see delicate bridges and pavilions, meandering into a different heaven and earth. Below them are small boats floating in the pond; this scene makes visitors forget to return home. If [they] want to borrow this place for a party with courtesans, they are also welcome.
>
> (Chen [1887] 1996: 86)

The garden was famous for its enormous size, open space, and Western-style landscape and architecture. In 1893 a landmark building designed by English

Figure 6.14 A carriage accident in Zhang Garden.
Sources: *Dianshizhai huabao,* September 1893; Wu et al. 2001: 10.206.

architects was added to the garden. Exotically titled Arcadia Hall (Ankaidi), the building could accommodate the congregation of a thousand people and was then the city's tallest structure. The garden soon developed into a city away from the city, in which visitors not only enjoyed viewing the exotic landscape and architecture but also experienced a wide range of indigenous and Western-style interior spaces, such as a teahouse, restaurant, theater, storytelling house, exhibition hall, photo gallery, and sport and amusement facilities (Xiong 1996).

In 1893, *Dianshizhai huabao* reported that due to the Zhang Shuhe's successful management, those who had regularly visited Fool Garden now switched to Zhang Garden. The report illustrated an accident that a young man and his wife in a carriage fell into a pond in the garden and provided two observations: one considered it a lesson for those domestic women who ventured into public places; the other suggested that handrails be added to the pond so that no such accidents would happen again. The latter view not only accepted the presence of domestic women in public spaces but also implied that improvements had to be made to these spaces (Figure 6.14).

Around that time, visits of the garden by domestic couples were still rare, as most visitors were still courtesans and their patrons. In the late 1890s, the garden

Figure 6.15 Top: Western diplomats and merchants met in a British theater at Shanghai to discuss the blockade of the Wusong River. Bottom: Chinese and Western women of distinction met in the Arcadia Hall of Zhang Garden.

Sources: *Dianshizhai huabao,* October 1884, December 1897; Wu et al. 2001: 1.135, 15.43.

was paired with Fourth Avenue as the popular daytime and nighttime destinations of the pleasure tour. The city's star courtesans, such as Lu Lanfen, Lin Daiyu, Jin Xiaobao, and Zhang Shuyu, regularly visited the garden for tea. These courtesans displayed the latest fashions in the city. Copies of the tabloid *Youxi bao* with courtesan photos inserted were distributed free of charge to visitors in the garden (Xiong 1996: 35). The courtesans' glamour was most splendidly displayed in the garden but it was also their twilight, as they gradually lost the privilege of being the only type of women permitted in such public spaces.

More and more elite domestic women visited the garden and other public spaces in the city around the turn of the century. A milestone event in the garden was a meeting on December 6, 1897, when 112 Chinese and Western women of distinction congregated in Arcadia Hall to discuss establishing a women's school in the city. *Dianshizhai huabao* reported this event as the first ever in China's long history under the title "The Grand Meeting of Skirts." The meeting was led by the wife of the Shanghai Daotai (magistrate), and more than half of the participants were Western women. The illustration primarily featured Western women in ornate dresses while most Chinese women are shown in the background, except the two occupying the chair positions at the meeting table (Figure 6.15, bottom).

In depicting this unprecedented event, the artist (signed as Zhu Ruxian) copied the architectural interior and figural composition of a drawing of Wu Youru published in the same pictorial thirteen years earlier, which depicted a meeting of foreign merchants in a British theater in Shanghai (Figure 6.15, top). Imitations of Wu's drawings were quite common in illustrated guides and novels, usually reproducing same characters in the original, such as the courtesans. In this particular case, however, the artist not only copied the "democratic" roundtable and Western-style interior but also reproduced the gestures of the foreign men in the female figures. He could only imaginatively visualize the novel event by appropriating those elements pertaining to a Western-style meeting of men. This pictorial plagiarism seemed to have betrayed a fear of the male sojourner: the new type of Chinese women librated from their domestic quarters would behave like Western men in public. Indeed, the newly-gained freedom of these women paved the way for their participation in the city's capitalist production and consumption. Their appearances in the city's public spaces also signified the beginning of the end of the golden age of Shanghai courtesans.

Around the turn of the century, Zhang Garden was not only an entertainment complex that displayed the world's latest technological inventions but also a public arena where political speeches and meetings were regularly held to deliberate on the modernization of China and plot revolutions against the dwindling Qing Empire (Xiong 1996). This change of the garden reflected a larger change of Shanghai from merely a pleasure tour site for the sojourners to a cultural capital where modern consumerism and national politics were combined. The city sanctioned not only the public activities of courtesans and the new type of women but also a new generation of intellectuals with revolutionary agendas. The space of decadent pleasure, dominated by courtesans and their patrons, then transformed into a space of progressive and even radical movements.

Conclusion

When *Flowers of Shanghai* was published in book form in 1894 and *Dianshizhai huabao* ended its fourteen years' publication in 1898, China was on the brink of a series of revolutionary changes. China's humiliating defeat by Japan (1894–95) aroused an awakening sense of Chinese nationalism among the natives while the treaty of Shimonoseki opened the treaty ports to rapid industrialization. Shanghai soon developed into the "Paris of the Orient," a dream city of modern glamour and consumption. In the meantime, the imperial reforms (1898–1902), the founding of the Republic (1912), and the May Fourth Movement (1919) ended China's "stagnant" past and initiated a new era of modern progress. Shanghai also changed from the sojourners' pleasure city to a stronghold of leftist intellectuals and national center for anti-imperialist and revolutionary movements.

While these historical movements marked a radical break with the late Qing period, the city's everyday life had shown remarkable continuity with the past. Shanghai residents still dreamed a better home in the crowded neighborhoods, sought security amid wars and displacements, and eased their aguish and stress under the neon lights, if not in viewing "the sea of flowers." Even in the twenty-first century, the city's residents still experience painful relocations as the city's new modernization project transforms ageing working-class neighborhoods into transnational business districts. The same sense of alienation or displacement seemed to have marked the city's everyday life through these modern transformations.

While the sense of alienation is repressed in contemporary observers who welcomed such transformations as historical progress, nineteenth-century sojourners alleviated their anguish by perceiving similar changes in natural and mythic imageries. I have relied on these long-discarded perceptions in mapping a Shanghai modernity that was marked by the ever same commodity economy or "new nature" and the recurrences of mythical experience. Moreover, this modernity entailed a new consciousness of space and materiality and a new kind of visual experience. I have demonstrated that the colonial capitalist development ruptured the traditional spatial configuration of self-contained households, towns, and natural landscape in a continuous spread, while producing a new set of fragmented as well as fluid urban spaces. This transformation was generated from within the community of Chinese sojourners, who actively appropriated or domesticated new technology and products rather than passively reacting to Western influences.

In the *li* compounds jointly created by foreign landowners and native builders, visibility and openness marked a new kind of residential and commercial space. In these inclusive neighborhoods, the sojourners reinvented the courtesan house as a surrogate "home" in which they enjoyed a range of sensory and sexual pleasures, adopted a new kind of material culture, and built their romantic relationships and social networks beyond the traditional household lines. Their everyday life was increasingly mediated by commodity culture and commercial activities, which generated new distinctions and interactions between the elite and the lower class.

Beyond the *li*'s exclusively native space, the sojourners experienced exotic spectacles in a range of new public spaces. On the Bund the *yang fang* and the avenue seemed to have challenged the long-established ideal of heavenly creation, while in the native quarters these spatial types were readapted to stage the displays of female bodies and sensational events. A range of public interiors such as novelty shops, theaters, and storytelling houses offered more visual attractions that marked a departure from traditional folk culture. The deployments of these spaces blurred as well as redefined the old borderline between the elite and the commoners, and gradually forged the crowds of sojourners into a new urban public. The tension between the local and the colonial was also played out in these spaces, anticipating the conflict between nationalist and imperialist interests of the later periods.

This cognitive map of fin-de-siècle Shanghai I have reconstructed could indeed be compared to a natural landscape: it went through a transformation like a natural creation. Just as the literati lamented that old-style courtesans had disappeared from the city like ephemeral flowers, we would regret that there are hardly any physical traces of the world of nineteenth-century sojourners left in Shanghai today. The city's modernization and real estate boom in the early twentieth century erased almost all nineteenth-century urban forms. Today, as if history repeats itself, a new wave of modernization rapidly obliterates what is left of early twentieth-century Shanghai. As the city is repeatedly torn down and rebuilt, one might see this urban change either as a heroic process of mankind (or the nation) or just as part of natural obsolescence that resembles the mythic transformation of seas and fields. However historians or observers frame such changes, the capitalist transformation of urban spaces and the global flows of capital and resources continue to unfold.

Today, Shanghai is hosting World Expo 2010 and once again draws the world's attention not only to the city's reemergence on the international stage after the Maoist era but also to its unique modernization course in the last two centuries. At this moment of glory and glamour, we should also remember the decadent world of the sojourners and courtesans who had arguably created the first Chinese modern. Although indulging in opium smoking and other pleasures, they were still sober in presenting their modern world as a decadent one, probably because they occupied a moment and place that belonged neither to the patriarchal Confucian world nor to the heroic world of modernization. I hope that I have redeemed this "vantage" position of theirs in showing that the decay and decline as a spatial and material process is always part of modern life.

Glossary of frequently-used Chinese terms

cainü	talented lady
changsan	first-class courtesan
chuju	callout duty
daidang	with a share of investment
dajiao	(women with) big feet
fangli	residential ward
gongguan	(merchant) residence
guanren	courtesan
huayanjian	flower opium room/house
ji	courtesan
jia	home/family
jian	bay or basic spatial unit of a building
jiaoju	callout
jiaoshu	courtesan
jiuju	banquet party
kaipian	prelude song
keren	client or guest
ketang	reception hall
laoye	master (salute to the male customer)
li	neighborhood, residential compound
longtang	dead-end alley
mingji	famous courtesan
niangyi	married female servant
nütangguan	waitress
pipa	courtesans' music instrument
saihui	religious procession
shikumen	stoned portal entrance
shuyu	first-class courtesan
tang	hall
tang(zi)	second-class courtesan house/brothel
taoren	purchased daughter or courtesan
tian	sky/heaven/nature
tianrenheyi	the harmony of nature of man

tingzijian	back room
xianghao	courtesan lover/mistress
xiansheng	sir (salute to a courtesan)
xie	waterfront pavilion
xuan	pavilion
yangfang	foreign-style building
yao'er	second-class courtesan
yeji	streetwalker/pheasant
yeyou	hedonistic tour
yichang	foreign place
yu	apartment/temporary residence

List of Chinese characters

Adebao 阿德保
a'ge 阿哥
Ajin 阿金
Anhui 安徽
Ankaidi 安塏第
anmingtingzhi 安命聽之
Aqiao 阿巧

Bai Juyi 白居易
baiguan xiaoshuo 稗官小説
Baihua 百花
bailingtai 百靈台
Baishe zhuan 白蛇傳
baixiang 白相
baomu 鴇母
Baoshan jie 寶善街
baoxiandeng 保險燈
benbang 本幫
benjia 本家
biaofangjian 裱房間
biji 筆記
bijian jiaobi 比肩交臂
bingfangjian 並房間

cainü 才女
Caiyi jie 綵衣街
caizi jiaren 才子佳人
canghai sangtian 滄海桑田
Cangshan jiuzhu 蒼山舊主
chaguan 茶館
chalou 茶樓
Chang'an 長安
Changfu 長福

changsan 長三
Changzhou 常州
chayuan 茶園
Chen Xiaoyun 陳小雲
Chen Xingeng 陳辛庚
cheng 城
Cheng Jinxuan 程謹軒
chi shuangtai 吃雙台
chuanqi 傳奇
chuju 出局
Chunjiang xiaozhi 春江小志
cishi 詞史
Ciyuan xingshi lu 詞媛姓氏錄
cizhi 次之
Cui ping shan 翠屏山
cun 村

dacai 大菜
dacaiguan 大菜館
dachawei 打茶圍
dafangjian 打房間
Daguanlou 大觀樓
Daguanyuan 大觀園
daidang 帶檔
dajiao 大腳
Dajiaoyao 大腳姚
Damalu 大馬路
dan 旦
Dan'guiyuan 丹桂園
danhu 蛋戶
danzifang 彈子房
Daxing li 大興里
Daxue 大學

Dayishanren 大一山人
Dibao 邸報
dibao 地保
difangzhi 地方誌
Dingfeng li 鼎豐里
dingqingwu 定情物
Diyilou 第一樓

enke 恩客
erhuang xiaodiao 二黃小調

fancaiguan 番菜館
Fang Penghu 方蓬壺
fangli 坊里
fenghuo shanqiang 封火山牆
Fengliu guangda jiaozhu
　風流廣大教主
fengtuzhi 風土志
fenyun 紛紜
Fujian 福建
fumuguan 父母官
fushang 府上
Fuxian tang 富仙堂
Fuzhou Road 福州路

Gao Yabai 高亞白
Ge Zhongying 葛仲英
Gengshangyicenglou
　更上一層樓
Gong Zhifang 公之放
Gongbuju 工部局
gongguan 公館
Gonghe li 公和里
gongsuo 工所
gu 古
Guandi 關帝
Guangdong 廣東
Guanghushang zhuzhici
　廣滬上竹枝詞
guangyin 光陰
guanji 官妓
guanren 倌人
guhun 孤魂
guinu 龜奴
Guixin 桂馨

Guixin fangmei 桂馨訪美
guolairen 過來人

haisang 海桑
Haishang qishu 海上奇書
Haishang yin 海上吟
hangning 杭寧
He Guisheng 何桂笙
Hengdali yanghang 亨達利洋行
Hexin li 合信里
Hexing li 合興里
Hong Shanqing 洪善卿
hongbang 紅幫
Hongcun 宏村
Hongkou 虹口
Hongqiao 虹橋
Hongshun tang 洪順堂
Hu Shi 胡適
huabang 花榜
huafang 畫舫
huaguo 花國
Huaguxi 花鼓戲
hualou 畫樓
Huang Cuifeng 黃翠鳳
Huang Erjie 黃二姐
Huang Xiexun 黃協塤
Huangpu River 黃浦江
Huanying huabao 寰瀛畫報
huayang zaju 華洋雜居
huayanjian 花煙間
Huayeliannong 花也憐儂
huayuan 花園
Huayulou 花雨樓
Huazhonghui 華眾會
Huiban 徽班
huiguan 會館
Huifang li 薈芳里
Huifanglou 繪芳樓
huiye 匯業
Hushang pinghua lu 滬上評花錄
Hushang yanpu 滬上艷譜
hutong 胡同
Huzhongtian 壺中天

ji 妓

jia 家
Jiali 家禮
jian 間
Jiang Yueqin 蔣月琴
Jiang Zhixiang 蔣芷湘
Jiangnan 江南
jiangtou 匠頭
Jiangxi 江西
jiaofang 教坊
jiaoju 叫局
jiaoshu 校書
jiazhang 家長
jiazhupo 家主婆
jiefang 街坊
jiefangjian 借房間
jiefu 姐夫
jihu 機戶
jin 今
Jin Xiaobao 金小寶
Jinfeng 金鳳
Jing'ansi 靜安寺
Jingban 京班
Jingbao 京報
Jingbao 晶報
Jingkou 京口
Jin'guiyuan 金桂園
jingyou 境遊
Jinling shi'erchai 金陵十二釵
Jiu'an 久安
jiuju 酒局
jiulou 酒樓
Jixiang jie 吉祥街
Ju'an li 居安里
Jufengyuan 聚豐園
jupiao 局票
juren 舉人
Juxiu tang 聚秀堂

kaichawan 開茶碗
kaipian 開片
kejing ke'e kexi 可驚可鄂可喜
keren 客人
ketang 客堂
kezhan 客棧
Kuang'er 匡二

kuilei 傀儡
Kunqu 昆曲

Lai Touyuan 賴頭黿
Lai'an 來安
Lanfang li 蘭芳里
Lanting xu 蘭亭序
laobao 老鴇
Laoqichang 老旗昌
laoye 老爺
Le shuo 樂說
li 里
Li Heting 李鶴汀
Li Peilan 李佩蘭
Li Shifu 李實夫
Li Shufang 李漱芳
Li Zhuanhong 黎篆鴻
Liaozhai 聊齋
Liang Qichao 梁啟超
Liji 禮記
lilong 里弄
Lin Daiyu 林黛玉
Lin Sufen 林素芬
lingfangjian 領房間
Lishuitai 麗水台
Liu Jingting 柳敬亭
longtang 弄堂
Louxian 婁縣
lu 錄
Lu Lanfen 陸蘭芬
Lu Xiubao 陸秀寶
Lu Xiulin 陸秀林
lüli 閭里
Lun jiao wenda 論交問答
Luo Zifu 羅子富

Ma Guisheng 馬桂生
Ma Rufei 馬如飛
mache 馬車
Madiao 馬調
mafu 馬夫
maizhubao 賣珠寶
malu 馬路
Mantingfang 滿庭芳
Mao'erxi 貓/帽/毛兒戲

matouqiang 馬頭墻
Mei Xuanshi 梅宣史
Meijia jie 梅家街
Mianyunge 眠雲閣
mianzi 面子
Minbao 民報
mingji 名妓
mingjue 名角
mingshi 名士
Mingyuan 明園
mu 畝
muzuo 木作

Nanchengxin 南誠信
Nanking 南京
Nanzhoujin li 南畫錦里
nei 內
niangyi 娘姨
Ningbo 寧波
nüchangshu 女唱書
Nütanci xinyong 女彈詞新詠
nütangguan 女堂倌

paifang 牌坊
paiju 牌局
Pan Qiaoyun 潘巧雲
pintou 姘頭
pinxia 品下
Pinyulou 品玉樓
pipa 琵琶
Puqing li 普慶里

qi 奇
Qi Yunsou. 齊韻叟
Qian Xinbo 錢辛伯
Qian Zigang 錢子剛
Qianzhuang 錢莊
qiao 敲
qijia, zhiguo, pingtianxia 齊家,治國,
    平天下
Qin Yubo 秦裕伯
Qinghe fang 清和坊
Qingming 清明
Qingyuan li 清遠里
Qingyun li 慶雲里

qinlou chuguan 秦樓楚館
Qipan jie 棋盤街
qixi 七夕
qizuo 漆作

ren 人
renjiaren 人家人
renqiaoji er tiangong duo 人巧極而
    天工奪
Rixin 日新
rong-hua-fu-gui 榮華富貴

saihui (yingshen) 賽會(迎神)
san yimin 三異民
sanheyuan 三合院
se 色
shangdeng 上等
Shanghai xinbao 上海新報
Shangren li 尚仁里
shaolutou 燒路頭
shen 身
Shen Xiaohong 沈小紅
Shenchang shuju 申昌書局
sheng 生
shenjie quxiang 深街曲巷
Shenyuan 申園
shi 時
Shi Quan 石荃
Shi Tianran 史天然
Shi Xiu 石秀
Shiba mo 十八摸
shidafu 士大夫
shiji baijia 史記百家
shijian 時間
Shijie fanhua bao 世界繁華報
shijuzhibi, menxiangxiuzhi 室居櫛比,
    門巷修直
shikumen 石窟門
Shilu 石路
shimao 時髦
shiwai taoyuan 世外桃源
shizhai 實在
shizuo 石作
Shuangbao 雙寶
Shuangyu 雙玉

shuchang 書場
shuhuadeng 書畫燈
shuizuo 水作
shuodashu 說大書
shuxian 書仙
shuyu 書寓
shuyu tangchang 書寓堂唱
Sihaishengping 四海昇平
siju 私局
Sima Guang 司馬光
Simalu 四馬路
Siming suoji 四冥瑣記
Songjiang 松江
suli 俗例
Sun Sulan 孫素蘭
Suzhou 蘇州

ta 榻
taiji 台基
Taiping 太平
Taixi 泰西
Taixianhanqi 太仙韓奇
tang 堂
Tang Xiao'an 湯嘯庵
Tang Yu 唐瑜
Tangjia jie 唐家街
tangming 堂名
tangzi 堂子
taoren 討人
teng keren 騰客人
tian 天
Tianfuyuan 天福園
Tianhou 天後
tianjing 天井
tianrenheyi 天人合一
tianxia 天下
Tianxianyuan 天仙園
tingzijian 亭子間
Tonghe li 同和里
Tongqing 同慶
tongshi 通事
toumian 頭面
Tu Mingzhu 屠明珠
tudong 圖董
Tuhua ribao 圖畫日報

wai 外
waichang 外場
waiguo caiguan 外國菜館
Wang A'er 王阿二
Wang Guixiang 王桂香
Wang Liansheng 王蓮生
Wang Xizhi 王羲之
Wei Xiaxian 衛霞仙
Wen Junyu 文君玉
wenban 文班
wenyan gaogu 文言高古
Wu Xuexiang 吳雪香
Wucenglou 五層樓
wudai tongtang 五代同堂
wuji zhitan 無稽之談
wulun 五倫
Wumalu 五馬路
wusheng 武生
wushi 烏師
Wusong 吳淞
wuzhehui 無遮會

xiajiao yangqian 下腳洋錢
xiangbang 相幫
xianghao 相好
Xianghe li 祥和里
xianshen shuofa 現身說法
xiansheng 先生
xiaobao 小報
xiaojia biyu 小家碧玉
xiaojie 小姐
Xiaoliu'er 小柳兒
Xiaoshibao 小時報
Xiaotaoyuan 小桃源
Xiaoxiangguan shizhe 瀟湘館使者
Xidi 西遞
xie 榭
xiji 西妓
Xingren li 興仁里
Xinjie 新街
xinwenzhi 新聞紙
Xinyongqing li 新永慶里
Xixin li 西新里
Xiyuan 西園
xiyuan 戲園

Xizi 西子
Xu Maorong 徐茂榮
xuan 軒
xuanjuan 宣卷
xunhuan 循環
Xunhuan ribao 循環日報
xunzhang 尋丈

Yan Fu 嚴復
Yang 鶯
yangfang 洋房
yangguang huo 洋廣貨
Yangjing Creek 洋涇濱
Yangliu loutai 楊柳樓臺
yanguan 煙館
Yangzhou 揚州
yanjian 煙閒
Yanshi congchao 艷史叢鈔
yanta 煙榻
yanyi 演義
Yao Jichun 姚季絨
Yao Wenjun 姚文君
yao'er 么二
yao'er zhujia 么二住家
yecha 夜叉
yeji 野雞
yeshi 野史
Yeshilou 也是樓
yeyou 冶遊
Yeyou bilan 冶遊必覽
yi 易
yichang 夷場
yijian liangxiang 一閒兩廂
Yili 儀禮
Yiliyuan 一笠園
Yin Chiyuan 尹癡鴛
Yinghuan suoji 瀛寰瑣記
yinglian 楹聯
Yipinxiang 一品香
yiyang nüzi 異樣女子
yong 庸
Yongchang 永昌
youling 優伶
Youxi bao 遊戲報
yu 庽

Yu qingting 玉蜻蜓
Yu Xiushan 俞秀山
yuan 鴛
Yuan Sanbao 袁三寶
Yuan Yunxian 袁雲仙
Yuanyangting 鴛鴦廳
Yudiao 俞調
Yuelai kezhan 悅來客棧
Yuesheng Quanheng 悅生全亨
yuju 寓居
yuwen weisheng 鬻文維生
Yuxiu li 毓秀里
Yuyuan 豫園
Yúyuan 愚園

zabao 雜報
zaji 雜記
Zao'an li 早安里
Zhang Chuanshan 張船山
Zhang Huizhen 張惠貞
Zhang Shou 張壽
Zhang Shuhe 張叔和
Zhang Shuyu 張書玉
Zhang Xiaocun 張小村
Zhang Xiuying 張秀英
Zhangshi weichunyuan
    張氏味蓴園
Zhao Erbao 趙二寶
Zhao Puzhai 趙樸齋
Zhaofu li 兆富里
Zhaogui li 兆貴里
Zhaohua li 兆華里
Zhaorong li 兆榮里
zhen 鎮
Zhongtu 中土
Zhongyong 中庸
Zhou Fenglin 周鳳林
Zhou Lan 周蘭
Zhou Shuangzhu 周雙珠
Zhoujin li 晝錦里
Zhu Airen 朱藹人
Zhu Ruxian 朱儒賢
Zhu Shiquan 諸十全
Zhu Xi 朱熹
zhuang 幢

Zhuangzi 莊子

Zhufeng 珠鳳

zhugong 主公

zhujia 住家

zhuzhici 竹枝詞

Zhuzi meimaocai 朱子美茂才

zimingzhong 自鳴鍾

zu fangjian 租房間

zuo huoji 做夥計

zuo shengyi 做生意

Notes

Introduction

1 David Wang's concept of "repressed modernities" in late Qing fiction not only challenges the notion that Chinese modern literature took form after the May Fourth era but also broadens the scope of literary modernity to include various genres of fiction that were decadent and popular rather than moral and elite. Wang (1997: 19) asserts the late Qing's "capacity to generate its own literary modernity in response, and *opposition*, to foreign influences." This period produced a wide array of pursuits after the new and the innovative in the context of international literature. Though later "repressed" by the positivist tradition, such alternative voices in fact coexisted with it in the twentieth-century literary realm. By highlighting the continuity in the aesthetic forms of Shanghai literature, Des Forges (2007) also challenges the distinction between realist and modernist fiction of the 1930s and 1940s and earlier Shanghai narratives initiated by late Qing installment fiction. Wang's and Des Forges's studies are grounded in literary history and criticism but their arguments seem to have a broad applicability. In this book, I rely on literary but mainly non-fictional sources (such as travel notes and folk-style poems) in mapping the modernity of late nineteenth-century Shanghai.

2 The same impact was on European powers when the Mongolian conquest of Eurasia and the discoveries of the new trade routes ended the isolation of the great civilizations. The origin of capitalist development as a global process can indeed be traced back to the demise of the localized worlds in the late Middle Ages.

3 In his essay "These on the Philosophy of History," Benjamin (1968: 253) suggests enlisting the services of theology, which today has to keep out of sight, in historical materialism. His main point, as I understand, is that the past only becomes fully meaningful when it is put in (Messianic) relation to a later cataclysmic moment.

4 Paul Cohen (1984: 147–98) advocates a "China-centered" historiography; for a critique of it, see Dirlik 1996. Meng Yue's (2006) comparative study of eighteenth-century Yangzhou and Suzhou and nineteenth-century Shanghai is a recent example of the China-centered approach. Meng sees the rise of Shanghai as a result of the decline of the Qing Empire and its "inside-out" geographical shift, and remaps a macro-spatial "noncapitalist" history that nonetheless inherits the totalizing scope of the "capitalist" historiography she seeks to critique. By establishing causal links between the decline of Yangzhou and Suzhou and the rise of Shanghai, Meng constructs a chain of events that spread over a vast space and time. In this book I foreground the continuity between late-imperial Jiangnan and modern Shanghai not by constructing such links between real urban spaces in different times and places but by examining the persistence of traditional imageries (as represented in urban literature) in the spatial production of late Qing Shanghai. Moreover, in the city's everyday environment it is impossible to separate the "noncapitalist" from the "capitalist." Even if these binary concepts are valid,

we should examine their interaction and combination in the Chinese context rather than posit the one against the other as mutually exclusive.

5 This approach is influenced by Benjamin's (1968: 163) notions of *Erfahrung* and the archeology of modernity. For a detail discussion this methodology, see "Knowing historical experience" in Chapter 2.

6 In summer 2005, I reflected on major events featured in the media of those years: "When I started to write about early modern Shanghai in American academia, America was about one year after 9/11. In the course of the development of this project, everybody was talking about 'weapons of mass destruction.' This 'smoking gun' eventually lured American and British troops into Iraq. Soon Sadam Hussein was captured in a bunker a harmless, tired old man, but a few days later he reappeared with vigorous spirit, reiterating his earlier rhetoric. In the meantime, more and more American bodies are flown home while gas prices rise to a record high. George W. Bush speaks of spreading freedom to the world in a way similar to how Donald Trump speaks of cashing in his idea and inscribing his name on Manhattan landmarks. Considered to be retarded by the American public, Bush always manages to outsmart his rivals, while John Kerry plays a hero in a war he had earlier judged as wrong and is in turn judged by the American public as a wrong candidate. The state he represents is understood to be the one that backfires his campaign by endorsing gay marriage. The affair of the governor of New Jersey is not nearly matched by the steamy kiss exchanged between Madonna and Britney Spears during the MTV award. In the meantime, the Super Bowl is eclipsed by Janet Jackson's 'wardrobe malfunction,' while her brother Michael makes every court appearance a personal showing off so that he prophesies his acquittal like an emasculated messiah. The wages of Wal-Mart employees match with the prices of the store's cheap products made by Chinese rural migrant workers—whose wages can only match with their crowded factory dormitories or squalid tenements in coastal China—while Yao Ming earns millions of dollars playing for Houston Rockets and becomes a national hero back home. The awesome destructive power of the Asian Tsunami leaves us few unforgettable stories, as the survivors return home wordless, probably silenced by the home videos that capture the sublime power, by the flat TV screen that broadcasts the cataclysmic event as if it were the low-quality rendering of a video game or Hollywood special effect. I do not see much meaning, much destiny, in the order of these events as they have unfolded in this period when I spent many dreary hours reading the equally confused Shanghai literati, except that 'there moves the procession of creatures of which, depending on circumstance, Death is either the leader or the last wretched straggler' (Benjamin 1968: 97). I may have just succeeded in ignoring him" (Liang 2005: 3–4; text edited).

7 There are a great number of books on modern Shanghai architecture recently published in Mainland China; for examples, see Wang 1989; Wu 2008; and Zheng 1999. Recent studies in English language include Kuan and Rowe 2004 and Denison and Ren 2006.

8 Drawing on the same visual sources, Jonathan Hay (2001) surveys new developments in the built environment and painting of late nineteenth-century Shanghai. His study is grounded in aesthetic analyses of the visual materials and omits the social contents of the new urban environment as recorded in contemporary textual sources. His argument that "the [Shanghai] architects and painters . . . created the first fully modern Chinese visual culture" needs rethinking. The "architects," as I show in Chapter 4, were in fact compradors, carpenters, and other craftsmen, who were either nouveau riche or traditional lower class, very different from modern professionals (who were yet to arrive in Shanghai) and traditional painters (who belonged to the class of literary elite). In making an aesthetic connection between the built environment and painting, Hay overlooks their different social meanings.

9 The drawings also showed details, such as figures and interior settings seen through the windows of Chinese buildings (e.g. Figures 4.3, 5.4), which contemporary photographs could not reveal.

1   Fluid tradition, splintered modernity

1   This question of Shanghai's relation to modern China has been the core of a scholarly debate. Rhoads Murphey (1953) presents the Shanghai model as key to understanding modern China, but he later considers the city to be distinct from the rest of China (Murphey 1977). Marie-Claire Bergère (1981) also argues that Shanghai represents an economic and cultural model that resulted from its international status and was seen by Communist China and the world as atypical. Shanghai was indeed very different from the rest of China, precisely because its development brought together various immigrants or sojourners from all over the country in close interaction with an international array of imperial powers. The transformation of the cultural identities of these sojourners not only generated the meanings of the city's modernity, but also exemplified the interactions between various regional traditions and a modern cosmopolitan culture. The uniqueness of Shanghai in modern China does not mean it was more similar to the modern West than to the rest of the country, but rather that its modern urban culture had multiple facets and meanings that reflected the interplay of diverse regional and international sources of this cosmopolitan culture, and was perhaps more complex than that of any other region.

2   Though Buddhist and other popular cults were widely observed in China, they were essentially different from the dominant religious practices in the West. For the roles of those cults in Chinese society, see Yang 1961. The scholarly debate on their nature and function demonstrates that it is difficult to draw a clear line between the sacred and the mundane in Chinese society.

3   Jürgen Habermas (1989) considers that the "public sphere" was born during the Enlightenment and the Church and the court in pre-modern Europe cannot be considered to be public spheres.

4   This is not to say that in late imperial China there was no distinct urban identity; in fact, city walls and other civic structures were the conspicuous symbols of urban identity. Nonetheless, wealthy gentry families residing in a network of towns maintained close ties with the rural lands they owned. This intimate relation between different towns and villages was lost in the overgrowth of modern metropolises such as Shanghai. This transformation is discussed in detail in Chapter 5.

5   The courtesan tradition in Jiangnan, according to legends, began in the turmoil of the late Tang, which drove many court entertainers to the south. In the Song, there were public and private courtesans, who were owned by the government and rich households, and independent courtesans in the "floating world" (Bossler 2002). The latter seemed to be the predecessors of the commercial courtesans in Ming-Qing Jiangnan.

6   Dorothy Ko (1994: 256–61, 266–74) analyzes some similar features between gentry wives and courtesans. Susan Mann (1997: 121–42), while emphasizing the growing gap between elite women and courtesans under the puritanical policy of the High Qing, concludes that the lines between courtesans and respectable commoners were permeable and shifting.

7   Male sojourning took different forms. Scholars and officials went sightseeing and traveled to academies and examination halls, in addition to going on the routine circuits that took them to jobs all over the empire. Merchants, artisans, and common laborers migrated to conduct business and seek employment (Mann 1997: 35).

8   This lack of a clear borderline between gentry and merchants, in contrast to the situation in pre-modern Japan, had arguably prevented the formation of a distinct bourgeois class in late imperial China (Skinner 1977e: 553; Rowe 1989, 1984).

9   This was mentioned in the guidebooks of the 1910s and '20s; see Hershatter 1997: 36.

10   In his study of material culture in modern China, Frank Dikötter (2007: 7) uses the concept of appropriation to account for the emergence of material modernity, which he considers not just a set of givens imposed by foreigners but a repertoire of new

opportunities, by which the local was transformed as much as the global was inflected to adjust to existing conditions. Thus, inculturation rather than acculturation accounts for broader cultural and materials changes in late Qing and Republican China.

2 The convergence of writing and commerce

1 According to James Watson (1985), the orthopraxy rather than orthodoxy promoted by the Qing rulers succeeded in erasing regional differences and thereby creating a unified empire. For a reevaluation of Watson's influential idea, see Dutton 2007.

2 The concept of ever-changing, or *yi*, is embodied in the title of the ancient classic *Yijing* or *Book of Change*, while that of ever-the-same, or *yong*, in the title of *Zhongyong* (Mean and unchanging).

3 The concept of eschatology, just as that of the sacred origin, was also absent in the mainstream Chinese culture, against which, however, rebellious movements, such as the White Lotus Cult in the eighteenth century, often prophesied an impending destiny.

4 Dorothy Ko (1994) considers this period an age of "quantity printing"; commercial publishing then played a greater role than either private or official publishing in setting the trend of mainstream print culture (Shang 2003: 190).

5 Such newssheets were observed in major Chinese cities by Westerners in the nineteenth century (Britton 1933: 5–7). Popular newsprints were also produced during the Sino-French war in the 1880s (Wagner 2007b: 123). There is no reason to think that such newsprints did not appear earlier; in the Ming there were various non-official newspapers, such as *xiaobao* or *zabao* (Shang 2003: 191), which might be similar to the popular newssheets.

6 The court paper was called *Dibao* in the Ming; its content covered a wide range of gossip and sensational events, which in turn were republished in non-official newspapers, frequently quoted and paraphrased in literati notes, and eventually found their way into many literary miscellanies (Shang 2003: 191–92).

7 There is no accurate information about literacy in nineteenth-century Shanghai. A conservative estimate of 5 percent literacy would place the reading public at some figure around twenty million in the nation, or over ten thousand in Shanghai (Britton 1933: 2). Des Forges (2007: 10) gives more optimistic estimates, 60 percent adult males and 10–30 percent adult females, as provided in Yuan Jin (1998). Evelyn Rawski's (1979) estimates of basic literacy in the late Qing are 30–45 percent for adult males and 2–10 percent for adult females.

8 The *Shenbao* was printed in the form of small folded booklet, reminiscent of traditional books, on one side of thin bamboo pulp paper (Mittler 2004: 47). By contrast, *Shanghai xinbao* was printed in the broadsheet format on imported paper and could not cover its production cost and when it lowered its price in competing with the *Shenbao*.

9 In the next three decades, the *Shenbao* accommodated a wide range of conflicting voices: editorials on new topics but worded in traditional rhetoric, sensational tales masquerading as news reports, and advertisements repackaging foreign products for Chinese consumers (Mittler 2004: 55–86, 118–72, 315–22; Huntington 2003).

10 In August 1886, a *Shenbao* editorial said that there were previous examples of the court hearing from below and that the paper followed this established practice rather than importing a Western model (Xu and Xu 1988: 38–39). The editorial sought to legitimate the paper's new practices by referring to historical precedence.

11 In the paper's first thirty issues, seven editorials were about introducing to Shanghai and China new technologies, such as railway, steamboat, modern mine, and water supply; six editorials criticized current practices in the local community, such as heavy trade tax, bridge fare, opium addiction, foot binding, prostitution, and the government's unsuccessful prohibition of prostitution; other editorials advocated traditional practices

and values, such as the imperial examination, a person's predetermined fate, and thrifty (Xu and Xu 1988). In the next three decades, the paper's editorials continued to cover a broad array of topics, including moral polemics, comments on new phenomena, travel notes, and the readers' opinions (Mittler 2004: 69–86, 330–43).

12 Wu left the pictorial around 1890 and published his own pictorial, titled *Feiyingge huabao* (Flying-shadow-pavilion pictorial), until 1893. His best works in these pictorials were late collected into *Wu Youru huabao* (Treasures of Wu Youru painting, 1908). For an exhaustive study of Wu and other illustrators for *Dianshizhai huabao*, see Wagner 2007b: 126–45; see also Ye 2003: 12–13; Reed 2004: 95–96.

13 The pictorial's "lowbrow" depiction of the courtesans would contrast with the *Shenbao*'s deliberations on social and moral issues related to the courtesans and lower-class sex workers (March 21, 1879; October 25, 1887; May 25, 1888; January 12, 17, 1897).

14 The *Shenbao* press also reprinted books for preparing the imperial civil service examinations and vernacular novels that had previously been prohibited. Major opened a Chinese bookstore, Shenchang shuju, to sell these books.

15 Huang Shiquan ([1883] 1989: 126) considers *Haizou yeyou lu* the best of Shanghai courtesan literature; he also mentions *Chunjiang xiaozhi* by Xiaoxiangguan shizhe, *Haishang yin* by Yuan Zuzhi, and *Ciyuan xingshi lu* by Zhuzi meimaocai as the second-class works, and dismisses *Hushang yanpu*, *Hushang pinghua lu*, *Yeyou bilan*, and *Guang hushang zhuzhici* as those which "the book merchants made profit with by abusing [the materials], and which should not be read at all."

16 Dianshizhai was a lithographic press that specialized in reproducing paintings, calligraphies, and rare books. For a detailed discussion of lithography presses as Sino-Western hybrids in nineteenth-century Shanghai, see Reed 2004: 88–127.

17 Nineteenth-century *Shenbao* published quite a few articles about courtesans and many poems dedicated to them. The paper's reports about courtesans mentioned by Hershatter (1997: 17–18, 136, 230–36) are from the 1870s, while those about common prostitution are from the 1920s and 1930s.

18 Henriot (2001:15) also admits that he did not have full access to the archival sources and had only what was given to him by the staff in charge of the archives.

19 All citations to *Flowers of Shanghai* are to Han [1894] 1998, given parenthetically by chapter and page number.

20 As advertised in the *Shenbao*, a novel cost about ten cents; the guidebooks would have cost about the same.

21 For a discussion of the righteous man and the maternal male, see Benjamin 1968: 103–104.

22 Similarly Yu Huai's ([1654] 1992) memory of the glamour of late Ming courtesans would have consoled his desolate life in the alien dynasty that had decimated native heroes. When Cao Xueqing set out to write about a few "extraordinary women," he was also protesting against his own fate: "Finding myself useless in the world, and unable to accomplish anything, and recognizing moreover, upon reflection, that in point of conduct my female companions of earlier days were all superior to me, and that my beard and manliness were not equal to their feminine dress and adornments, I was grieved indeed. Grief, however, was idle and of no avail, and my case appeared hopeless in the extreme" (Cao and Gao 1971: 1; trans. Cao 1968–70). The real purpose of this passage was not to extol female superiority but to show the author's disillusionment with a world in which the sage seemed to be dead and his family was in decline. It is also worth noting that Wang Tao's father died in 1849 when he was only twenty and his young wife died in the next year. Yeh (1997: 432–33) gives a different interpretation of Wang's powerlessness in playing the role of "flower protector."

23 Scholars in two disciplines have examined this novel. Social historians of courtesan culture show interest in studying it but fall short of providing in-depth analyses (see Hershatter 1997: 417; Yeh 1998: 47, 2006: 254). More detailed analyses are found in literary studies, which can be traced back to the discovery by Lu Xun (1981) and

Hu Shi ([1926] 1983) of the novel as a literary masterpiece in the early twentieth century. The novelist Eileen Chang (Zhang Ailing) has translated it into Mandarin and English (Han 1983, [1894] 2005). Stephen Cheng (1979, 1984) has analyzed its narrative techniques. David Wang (1997: 89–101) sees it as a transitional moment within the genre of the courtesan novel and discusses ethical issues such as the tension between desire and virtue. Keith McMahon's "Fleecing the Male Client" describes the peculiar powers that the novel's "prostitute-yakshas" exercise over their male clients; his main theme is "to demonstrate how the male customer seeks self-definition through his relationship with the prostitute, and how he in fact finds pleasure in the aura of control that the prostitute exerts over him" (McMahon 2002: 2). But the novel does not present "fleecing" (*qiao*) the client as the dominant practice in the courtesan houses. McMahon overemphasizes the courtesan's control over her client, overlooking that such control was probably mutual and balanced by romantic sentiments. Chloë Starr (2007: 87–89, 176–87) examines the novel's textuality, narrative, and characterization in the context of late Qing "red-light" fiction. Alexander Des Forges (2007) considers the novel to have initiated a tradition of modern Shanghai novels. His insightful and exhaustive analyses of the aesthetic features of referentiality (to specific dates and real places in the city), simultaneity, disruption, excess, and mediating subjectivity in the novel and late Qing fiction in general demonstrate the ways in which fiction reading might have shaped the discursive constructs of Shanghai identity and modernity.

24 Patrick Hanan (1998: 346) considers *Fengyue meng* the first Chinese city novel rooted in a specific locality, namely Yangzhou, and argues that the novel constitutes the main literary context within which *Flowers of Shanghai* was written and should be read.

25 Many guidebooks also borrowed authority from the *guolairen*; see Baiti guolairen [1894] 1973; Ge [1876] 2003: 206–14.

26 Lu Xun (1981: 338–39) considers the novel's realism a transitional form between idealized portrayals in early courtesan novels and condemnations in late ones.

27 Quoted in Hu Shi's ([1926] 1983: 9–10) preface for the 1926 edition of the novel. According to Hu, two short articles by Han's friend Lei Jin in *Xiaoshibao* (1925) are the only biographical sources of Han Bangqing.

28 The descriptions of the fine sky, beautiful land, and virtues people are quotations from *Lanting xu*, a well-known essay by the fourth-century calligrapher Wang Xizhi.

3 Ephemeral households, marvelous things

1 For example, Zhou Shuangzhu always urges Hong Shanqing to come back soon (3.294, 32.453), and Shen Xiaoshang also worries about which place Wang Liansheng is leaving for (4.302).

2 Some guidebooks explained this kind of establishment under the entry *tangming*, which appeared earlier than the *yu*. One guide said that many *tang* first appeared in the walled city and then moved to Chessboard Street (Qipan jie) in the British Settlement in 1860–61 (Huayu 1895: 6.3). The *yu*, *shuyu*, and *tang* could all be generally referred to as *tangzi*.

3 Whereas the courtesan house (*yu*, *zhujia*, or *tang*) was indeed different from a low-class sex establishment, it is hard to draw a clear line between the courtesan business and the open sex trade in nineteenth-century Shanghai. The situation was made more confusing by the various terms coined for the new types of entertainment and sex services, including *tangming*, *zhujia*, *siju*, *changsan*, and *shuyu* (Huayu 1895: 6.3–4). A main task of the guidebooks was to explain these terms and put them in a clearly defined order, but they were hardly successful. For example, *zhujia* is an ambiguous term explained in different ways: it usually means a small establishment (like the *yao'er zhujia*) of a lower standard than the *yu*, but sometimes a *zhujia* in decline was very similar to the *yeji* (streetwalker) house, which solicited customers from the street. Some sources

explain that *zhujia* is a general term for any small homelike establishment that could also be a *yu* (Huayu 1895: 3–4; Wang [1878] 1992b: 5689). In this book, I borrow "courtesan house" as a convenient, if imprecise, term from Western languages to refer mainly to the (*shu*)*yu* and occasionally to the *zhujia* and *tang*.

4 This was the typical way of naming the sons of a family; daughters often went without formal names.

5 Mann (1997: 139) notes that surrogate and blood kin groups in courtesan quarters of eighteenth-century Jiangnan were matrilineal, and that tokens of matrilineal descent hint at the ways in which the courtesans' all-female communities mimicked even while they subverted the kinship structure of the respectable family.

6 On the issue of who had more control in the courtesan house, Hershatter (1997: 70) thinks the clients made the rules, whereas Yeh (1998: 2–3) argues that the courtesans benefited from them. McMahon's (2002) reading of the novel supports Yeh's argument. Narrating many intriguing affairs between the courtesans and their clients, the novel presents their rather similar situations. While there is no strict equality between them, and each case varies, their relations are more or less balanced.

7 Shanqing makes his observation while helping his friend Wang Liansheng settle a dispute with Shen Xiaohong, who has been upset by Liansheng's new relationship with Zhang Huizhen. Xiaohong's *niangyi* disputes Shanqing's remark by pointing out that Xiaohong is loyal to Liansheng and has no other customer, and that Liansheng has promised to pay off her debt. Apparently some of the more committed *xianghao* relationships go beyond the aloof liaison described by Shanqing, who himself indeed has such a relationship with Zhou Shuangzhu.

8 In the novel, the merchant Li Zhuanhong once requests that each of his guests call four courtesans to a party he hosts. Since each courtesan also brings her attendant (*niangyi* or *dajie*), there are more than fifty people in this party held in a courtesan boudoir (15.358).

9 McMahon's (2002: 19) analysis of this episode notes Liansheng's promise to pay off Xiaohong's debt and not to visit Huizhen again, but does not mention Xiaohong's request for a banquet, about which her *niangyi* drops subtle hints. There are many subtexts in the conversations in Wu dialect and in Han Bangqing's layered narrative: when Liansheng vows that he will not visit Huizhen again, Xiaohong knows that promise is empty. So she insists that he host a banquet right away, but does not want him to pay off her debt right away (perhaps because the debt is not yet due).

10 According to Henriot (2001: 252–54), who provides a financial analysis of banquets or dinners in courtesan houses, a dinner cost 12–13 yuan in the late Qing period.

11 Comparing Han Bangqing's narrative with realism in nineteenth-century European fiction, David Wang (1997: 72) writes, "[Han] made even the most glamorous banquets and the most sensuous rendezvous sound like familiar and familial routines." This literary realism seems to reflect a historical fact: the courtesans and their clients really made these banquets look like routine familial gatherings.

12 The introduction of Western coins was important to trade development in Shanghai, where the traditional weighting of silver had been complicated and unreliable. The silver coins, or yuan, used in the settlements were mostly Mexican dollars. A yuan valued slightly less than a tael or traditional unit of silver. For a discussion of currency in late Qing Shanghai, see Lanning and Couling 1921: 392–400.

13 The task of the guidebooks was mainly to explain these rules and practices that regulated a new type of social intercourse—from introduction into a courtesan house to lengthy courtship to a possible love affair—and the social and financial behaviors of courtesans, customers, madams, and maids/servants (Yeh 1998: 15–16). Never before had the courtesan literature presented a similarly standardized practice with clear rules governing the courtesans' and clients' financial and social behavior. Yeh is right to observe that many of these rules were unique in China's history; but it is worth noting

that some terms—such as *tangming* and *dachaiwei* (tea parties)—were also used earlier in Yangzhou pleasure quarters, as seen in the novel *Fengyue meng* (preface dated 1848; Hanshang 1991). Also, by labeling them as "ritualized regulations" Yeh neglects the difference between business etiquette and traditional rites.

14 A year was divided into three business seasons that started and ended on the major festivals in the lunar calendar: New Year's Eve, the Dragon Boat Festival (the fifth of the fifth month), and the Mid-Autumn Festival (the fifteenth of the eighth month).

15 For example, in the novel Zhang Huizhen and Wu Xuexiang call each other "Xuexiang A'ge" and "Huizhen A'ge" (5.308).

16 McMahon's (2002: 15) analysis of this episode emphasizes Xuexiang's control of Zhongying. But the bantering between the two also reveals their genuine emotional attachment.

17 McMahon (2002: 18) writes: "Once [Zifu] becomes her favored customer, it is as if he becomes her subject and as such subjects himself to what a prostitute does to a man: she 'fleeces' him." But this relationship cannot be taken as typical of others in the novel. For example, Xuexiang's "control" of Zhongying had nothing to do with fleecing. They and various other courtesan characters cannot be reduced to the generalized figure of "prostitute-yaksha."

18 In a modern or bourgeois nuclear family, this certain mature woman is his mother; but in a traditional communal household, it seems to me, she could be his nurse or just a woman of daily intimate contacts in his childhood.

19 Applying Freudian theories to reading Qing erotic and romantic fiction, McMahon's (1995) analysis of the polygamous household is mainly concerned with its "sex economy," in which the gender privilege of the male polygamist does not necessarily make him superior to his women. But Freud's (1961) concept of "sex" is not just the force that drives men and women into coitus; it is also the more basic force of life and death. Explaining male–female relations solely (or mainly) in terms of sexual behavior or *ars erotica* would reduce human lives into programs predetermined by the sexual drive, and neglect that sexual behaviors are always conditioned by emotion, marriage practice, business, and other social factors. For example, the miser and shrew—the characters with the *innate* habits of "retention" and "splashing" in McMahon' analysis—could in reality have developed these habits *secondarily* from childhood traumas or simply from an arranged *teenage* marriage. In this marriage, the first wife, estranged from her husband, becomes a shrew, a doting mother, or anything in-between, while the husband, if he is not henpecked, becomes either the promiscuous wastrel or the miser, whose preservation of the "vital essence" is merely an indication of his failure in finding love and subsequent withdrawal to a world of self-love.

20 A slightly revised version of this poem was later incorporated in the novel, as this "romance" is reenacted in a witty play between Yin Chiyuan and Gao Yabai, the literati characters probably modeled after Han and Shi Quan (33. 455).

21 She would also be outperformed by the male courtesans (opera actors) in Peking where the court prohibited female entertainers; see the late Qing novel *Pin hua baojian* (Chen 1984) and David Wang's (1997: 61–71) analysis of it.

22 Benjamin (1999: 101–19, 388–404) highlights this feature of modern consumer culture in his study of nineteenth-century Paris; for an interpretation of his unfinished work, see Buck-Morss 1989. Paola Zamperini's recent study of fictional representations of fashion and identity in late Qing Shanghai emphasizes the departure from the past to an embrace of new Western-style "*wenming.*" Though she cautions that "this reading is just as problematic because it reduces this tangled web of representations to teleological Western modernity as the manifested destiny of China" (Zamperini 2003: 323), she does not spell out the "ever-the-same" features of this tangled web or note that the fashionable clothes, however fancifully represented in fiction, were commodities rather than pure symbols or "bodies." The commercial, material aspect is missing in her analysis.

23 Explaining this phenomenon under the entry "*maizhubao*" (selling jewelry), a guide-book comments that such peddlers usually overcharged the courtesan houses (Huayu 1895: 6.13); see Banchisheng 1891: 3.11–12, 4.9; Hershatter 1997: 81.

24 In explaining the term *shimao*, a guidebook author was uncertain about its precise meaning and mentioned that a courtesan would not like to be called a *shimao guanren* (Huayu 1895: 6.14).

25 Yeh's (2003: 400) analysis of these materials shows a transformation of the courtesan image from the traditional to the new and cosmopolitan, from the emblem of an ideal-ized world order to the representative of Shanghai's aggrandizing and fascinating but also quite disturbing urban lifestyle. Though her account is broadly true, her picture of a linear transformation oversimplifies the actual tangle of various genres of courtesan images alternating and coexisting with one another. For example, the courtesan por-traits she considers to be in the traditional and elite style were in fact sold to a popular audience (Huayu 1895), while what she sees as popular materials, like those mocking courtesans' indiscreet behaviors in public, were in fact from more serious publications such as *Dianshizhai huabao*—at least more highbrow than the guidebooks.

26. In the novel, the courtesan Zhou Shuangbao fights with Zhou Shuangyu for a precious silver pipe as the indication of her rank in the house (17.368).

27. The modern Chinese word for time, *shijian*, was in fact borrowed from the Japanese lexicon. The traditional character *shi* refers to hour rather than time.

28. For example, Luo Zifu stores his treasure chest behind Huang Cuifeng's bed (59.589). The novel also mentions that Cuifeng uses the chamber pot behind the bed (8.324). The traditional-style bed went out of fashion in the early twentieth century, when courtesans used Western-style beds and divided their boudoir into a guest room and a bedroom in which female sexuality was no longer so mysterious.

29. To boost their fame as the *cainü* or *jiaoshu*, some courtesans liked to hang some dedi-catory *yinglian* given by their clients, which were often of obscure literary quality according to Huang Shiquan ([1883] 1989: 120).

4   The meeting of courtyard and street

1 Cultural and architectural historians have explored the social contents and architec-tural forms of the *lilong*, focusing on the twentieth century and the extant structures. They have not paid adequate attention to the genesis and social contents of nineteenth-century *li*, which can only be known through contemporary writings and drawings. Important studies of the subject in Mainland China include Wang and Chen 1987; Luo 1991; Luo and Wu 1997; and Luo and Sha 2002. For studies of the *lilong* in the West, see Lu 1999 and Zhao 2004. Today, most surviving *lilong* houses are in dilapidated condition, soon to be demolished and rebuilt into commercial or residential high-rises, while a few others are preserved as the city's revolutionary and cultural heritage; for discussions of this transformation in relation to the Chinese revolutionary legacy, see Liang 2009, 2008b.

2 The document was a joint product of the British Consul George Balfour and Shanghai Daotai; for its English and Chinese versions, see Lu and Xu 1999: 543–50.

3 A different figure, 500,000 to 600,000, is given in Lu and Xu 1999: 91. The official esti-mate of the population of the settlements and Chinese city combined was 1 to 1.5 million around that time (De Jesus 1909: 233).

4 According to the censuses of the International Settlement, its population, mostly Chinese, was 92,884 in 1865, 110,009 in 1880, and 245,679 in 1895 (Lu and Xu 1999: 119). The figures of the 1865 census were 90,000 natives in the Settlement, 50,000 in the (French) Concession, and 5,589 foreigners (De Jesus 1909: 233).

5 A *jian*, about 4–5 meter wide, was the standard spatial unit in traditional Chinese archi-tecture; a building was usually a linear alignment of three, five, or seven *jian*.

6 Some scholars suggest that the row-layout of the *li* was an imitation of terrace houses in England (Lu 1999; Zhao 2004). But no historical record indicates any conscious copying of that model in Shanghai.

7 The revision deleted the stipulations in the original Land Regulation that prohibited the landowners to let houses to Chinese tenants, to acquire a lot of land larger than ten *mu*, to acquire land for pure speculation instead of building houses, and to arbitrarily determine the rents of their properties (Lu and Xu 1999: 551–52).

8 This comment was made during Alcock's brief revisit of Shanghai on his way to a new diplomatic mission in Japan in 1859. Alcock probably felt that he himself had also just escaped the jaws of death three years after his consulship in Shanghai when the city was in an imminent danger of being overtaken by the Taiping rebels.

9 Two other poems by the same poet were about the works of the stone guild (*shizuo*) and paint guild (*qizuo*). These guilds reflected the traditional divisions of construction work.

10 The compradors were also responsible for constructing the earliest Western-style buildings on the Bund; see "Marvels on the Bund" in Chapter 5.

11 "*Shijuzhibi, menxiangxiuzhi,*" quoted from an unidentified historical source in Dong et al. 1982: 18. Wang Tao ([1878] 1992a: 5700) also used *lüli* to refer to the *li* compounds in the settlements.

12 Twentieth-century *lilong* houses adopted Western-style *shikumen*, decorated with Classical columns and Roman arches.

13 These two arrangements were called *zu fangjian* and *zuo huoji*, which were mentioned in Hong Shanqing's inquiry of Zhang Huizhen's move to a new house (4.299); see below.

14 In the novel, the servant Adebao beats the secret lover of his wife in a *longtang* (41.498).

15 The family come to Shanghai to bring Zhao Puzhai home. They first stay in a hostel and then want to stay in the city rather than returning home. As they run out money, a friend of their hometown neighbor lets them stay in this house in Qinghe fang for free. One night, Puzhai returns home late and notices that every house except theirs in the *longtang* has a bright glass lamp at the entrance (31.443). Obviously this is a courtesan neighborhood.

16 See note 3 in Chapter 3. Recent scholars have debated the idea of "the hierarchy of Shanghai prostitution," which Hershatter (1989) first proposes in examining the different kinds of sex workers from 1870 to 1949. Henriot (1996: 134–36) opposes this idea and its implication of a rigid system and suggests alternative terms such as "categories," "types", and "lower ranking categories." Hershatter (1997: 35) later states that "the hierarchy of prostitution was a shared imaginary," though "courtesans were 'really' divided into distinct grades." Yeh (1998, 2006) also considers the complicated "hierarchy" of nineteenth-century courtesans as one of the "rituals" stipulated in the guidebooks.

5 Ultimate ingenuity, amorphous crowds

1 Revisiting Shanghai in 1859, Sir Rutherford Alcock (1863: 28, 35) wrote: "Fifteen years ago, corn, and rice, and cotton covered the ground, now entirely occupied for more than a mile square with foreign buildings; – mansions, for the foreign merchants, and pack-houses of corresponding extent for merchandise." He also noted: "Behind [the Bund], – away in the midst of cornfields and Chinese hamlets, – was the beginning of a Missionary settlement, supposed far enough in the country never to be overtaken by the all encroaching and mundane pursuits of commerce. It was difficult in 1859 for me to find my way through a very labyrinth of streets and houses, to where the once isolated missionary village looked out on the open country." De Jesus (1909: 27–28) also depicted a "rustic landscape which greeted the eyes of the founders of the settlement as at the sunset of on the 9th of November 1843." He wrote: "The locality chosen was

then mostly under cultivation, intersected by several small creeks, with a quiet hamlet nestled here and there among its shady trees, while far and wide the turf heaved in many a mouldering heap over generations of peasants there resting for ever on the very scene of their former toils. Along the foreshore lay the dilapidated towing path of old, where a cheering throng used to urge on the immense fleet of tribute-laden junks as each glided down the river. But for the bustle on such occasions, the future Bund lay undisturbed save by some lonely fisherman with his net or some busy boatman scouring his sampan at the outskirt of verdant fields, where rice, corn, and cotton were grown."

2 In fact, a few wonders featured in this guide, such as the City Temple garden and the Hall of Learning, were located in the walled city. The preface's neglect of these old wonders probably reflected Earnest Major's emphasis on the settlements in the joint production of this guide with his Chinese employees.

3 Of course, this contrast also indicated that the artists imitated or copied Western prints in depicting the *yangfang* while continuing to render Chinese houses in the traditional pictorial style.

4 Dikötter (2007: 155–67) seems to have overlooked this dual character of the Chinese house in showing that in the Republican period, the modernization of dwellings led to a "gradual sealing off of the house," as new building materials created more rigid boundary with the outside world.

5 A bamboo poem depicted the Chinese guilds that specialized in constructing Western-style buildings: "Among those who work as carpenters in Shanghai,/ The craft of the *hongbang* is superbly delicate;/ Imagining after the Western craft and imitating its method,/ They build high mansions and naturally earn huge profit" (Yi'an [1906] 1996: 168).

6 These ideals advocated by Western religious and secular thoughts were not shared by indigenous Chinese cultures. This situation was well put by Shanghai Daotai (magistrate) Wu Xu in an address to the British Consul: "You remarked to me that the Chinese, being actuated by a common feeling, none of them would be willing to come forward [as witness against a fellow Chinese]...You entirely ignore the circumstance that the Chinese people have never been influenced by any common feeling. Further, in the [street], people from every part of China are mixed together, owing to which, no one cares for the sorrows and ills of another" (Great Britain, Public Record Office, FO 228.274, 1859; quoted in Goodman 1995: 1).

7 Recently scholars posit apologetic views of the new crowd composed of all classes, of men and women. It took shape in a democratizing commercial culture and the individual in the crowd is considered to be the imaginative glue in the making of a mass audience, a new public, an "imagined community" of right-feeling (Shaya 2004: 60; Schwartz 1998). Nonetheless, distinction should be made between individual experiences and reflective actions. Precisely by erasing this distinction, the totalitarian state advocates the mindless crowd as the new public of solidarity.

8 For a classical study of the death instinct in living life, see Freud 1961.

6 The mingling of magnates and masses

1 According to late nineteenth-century guidebooks, these entertainment spaces, along with the teahouse (*chaguan* or *chalou*) and the courtesan house (*tangzi*), were the top eight destinations of Shanghai's pleasure tour.

2 After being humiliated by the courtesan Wei Xiaxian (see Chapter 3), Yao's wife forbids Jichun to visit Xiaxian again. Through some connections, she finds a "safe" courtesan, namely Guisheng, for Jichun to visit.

3 For a discussion of lesbians and modernity, see Benjamin 2003: 55–58.

4 Liu Jingting in the Ming was considered the father of storytelling art. Yudiao created by Yu Xiushan around 1820 was a melody style produced with the instrument *pipa*. Madiao created by Ma Rufei around 1860 was a singing style similar to talking, usually used in storytelling (Ge [1876] 2003: 155; Huang [1883] 1989: 115).

5 This passage and the following quote from Chi were reprinted in turn-of-century guides (Meihua 1894: 1.3; Huayu 1895: 6.3). These guides and travelogues did not provide a detailed chronology with precise dates of the evolution of storytelling in late nineteenth-century Shanghai. They only gave a general picture of the evolution.

6 Some *shuyu* performed in their private residences, where visitors could ask them to perform at the cost of two yuan per song. This business was called *shuyu tangchang* (Meihua 1894: 2.12).

7 The author of this report W. MacFarlane was probably from Walter MacFarlane & Co., Glasgow. An advertisement of the company's products, including electrical light pillars and brackets, electrical wire ways, and glass enameled drain and soil pipes, in *North China Herald* (May 2, 1898) was reprinted in Ge [1926] 2003: 100.

8 The private box cost 1.2 yuan, the pit seat 0.8 yuan, and the rest from 0.5 to 0.3 yuan (Yeh 2005: 82).

9 Different characters for *mao* were used to refer to this opera genre, which could be translated as Cat Opera, Chic Opera, or Hat Opera. The genre was said to have originated from courtesan houses in Yangzhou and Suzhou (Wang [1860] 1992a: 5650; Meihua 1894: 2.12).

10 Actors were luxury goods traded between the elite in the late Ming and early Qing. Not only individual actors but entire troupes were sold, bestowed upon friends, and bequeathed upon relatives (Volpp 2002: 949).

11 Translation revised from Ye 2003: 191–92; for descriptions of similar events in Shanghai, see Wang [1860] 1992a: 5644; Huang [1883] 1989:110–11; Ge [1876] 2003: 63.

12 Literati authors described these shows in exhaustive details but offered no reflective reading of them (Mao 1877; Huang [1883] 1989: 104, 114–15, 138–39). Such alien spectacles were sensational distractions rather objects of contemplation or respect; for the sojourners, they were merely a different kind of show from those in the theaters and storytelling houses.

13 Bryna Goodman's (2000) in-depth study of this event sees it as a stage of power plays between the native guilds and the "semicolonial" power. But she has not sufficiently considered the spatial conditions under which the parade was staged or analyzed the visual discourses of the parade.

14 Alcock (1863: 39) recorded a scene of the city's muddy roads before the modern streets were built: "When it rains in Shanghai, it… reduces the roads to a sea of mud, hardly passable except on stilts…"

15 *Dianshizhai huabao* alone reported over a dozen carriage-related accidents. In addition to Figures 1.2, 5.5, 6.12, and 6.14 in this book, see Wu et al. 2001: 1.219, 1.234, 3.40, 3.80, 3.323, 4.131, 6.192–93, 14.98, 14.196.

16 Erbao's insight regarding the pleasure of the fallen characters does not prevent herself from being lured by it. During this visit, she has been invited to theaters and restaurants and becomes attracted to the city (29.434–31.444). The family stay in the city and Erbao eventually becomes a courtesan (35.464). See note 15 in Chapter 4.

17 The park's regulations also prohibited dogs entering it. In the next century, the myth of an imaginary sign "No Chinese or dogs allowed" in the park was widely circulated as the evidence of national humiliation under the colonial rule (Bickers and Wasserstrom 1995). In the late nineteenth century, however, there was no strong or widespread protest against the regulations among the sojourners. Des Forges (2007: 21, 165) points out that the park was relatively unimportant to the natives and did not register in any significant way in the Shanghai fiction.

18 The 1884 guide portrayed the "blue-eyed Western couples hand in hand" (Wu 1884: 2.29). A bamboo poem also depicted a public view of Western couples: "Western men and women do not know shame,/Hand in hand walking together on streets;/Their licentious words and obscene noises ignored by others,/Who can only hear the birds' gibberish" (*Shenbao* 1874; Gu 1996: 50).

References

Historical sources

Alcock, Sir Rutherford. 1863. *Capital of the Tycoon: A Narrative of a Three Years' Residence in Japan*, 2 vols. London: Longman, Green, Longman, Roberts & Green.

Baiti guolairen 白隄過來人. [1894] 1973. "Yeyou zihui wen" 冶遊自悔文 (The self-confession of a courtesan patron). In Meihua, 1.5–6.

Banchisheng 半癡生. 1891. *Haishang yeyou beilan* 海上冶遊備覽 (A complete guide of touring Shanghai), 4 juan. Shanghai: n.p.

Cao Xueqin 曹雪芹. 1968–70. *The Dream of the Red Chamber [Hong Lou Meng]*. Trans. E. C. Bowra. In *The China Magazine*. Hong Kong: Noronha & Sons.

Cao Xueqin and Gao E 高鶚. 1971. *Hong lou meng* 紅樓夢 (The dream of the red chamber), 4 vols. Hong Kong: Zhonghua Shuju.

Chen Qiao 辰橋. [1887] 1996. *Shenjiang baiyong* 申江百詠 (One hundred poems about Shanghai). In Gu, ed., 79–92.

Chen Sen 陳森. 1984. *Pin hua baojian* 品花寶鑒 (The precious mirror for appreciating flowers). Taipei: Guangya chuban gongsi.

Chi Zhicheng 池志澂. [1893] 1989. *Huyou mengying* 滬遊夢影 (Dream images of touring Shanghai). In Ge, Huang, and Chi, 153–67.

Chongtianzi 蟲天子, ed. 1992. *Xiangyan congshu* 香艷叢書 (Anthology of fragrances of beauties), 20 vols. Beijing: Renmin wenxue chubanshe.

Dianshizhai huabao 點石齋畫報 (Point-stone-studio pictorial). 1884–1898. Shanghai.

Fang Yingjiu 方迎九, ed. 2002. "Han Bangqing yishi yiwen gouchen" 韓邦慶佚诗佚文钩沉 (Essays and poems of Han Bangqing). *Ming Qing xiaoshuo yanjiu* 明清小说研究, 2: 227–40.

Feiyingge huabao 飛影閣畫報 (Flying-shadow-pavilion pictorial). 1890–1893. Shanghai.

Ge Yuanxu 葛元煦. [1876] 2003. *Huyou zaji* 滬遊雜記 (Miscellaneous notes on visiting Shanghai), 4 juan. Reprint, in *Zhongguo fengtu zhi congkan* 中國風土志叢刊 (Anthology of China local culture records), vol. 44. Yangzhou: Guangling shushe.

Ge Yuanxu, Huang Shiquan, and Chi Zhicheng. 1989. *Huyou zaji, Songnan mengying lu, Huyou mengying*. Shanghai: Shanghai guji chubanshe.

Gu Bingquan 顾炳权, ed. 1996. *Shanghai yangchang zhuzhi ci* 上海洋场竹枝词 (Bamboo poems of the Shanghai settlements). Shanghai: Shanghai shudian chubanshe.

Han Bangqing 韩邦庆. [1894] 1998. "Haishang hua liezhuan" 海上花列传 (Flowers of Shanghai). In Muzhenshanren and Han, 267–619.

——. [1894] 1984. "Sing-song Girls of Shanghai." Trans. Eileen Chang. In Liu Ts'un-yan, ed., 95–110.

———. [1894] 2005. *Sing-song Girls of Shanghai*. Trans. Eileen Chang and Eve Hung. New York: Columbia University Press.

Han Ziyun 韓子雲 [Han Bangqing]. 1983. *Haishang hua* (Flowers of Shanghai), trans. Zhang Ailing 张爱玲. Taibei: Huangguan.

Hanshang mengren 邗上蒙人. 1991. *Fengyue meng* 风月梦 (Dream of wind and moon). Ji'nan: Jilu shushe.

Huang Ruijie 黄瑞節, ed. 1341. *Zhuzi cheng shu* 朱子成書 (The book of Master Zhu). Reprint, in Ebrey 1991a, 184–212.

Huang Shiquan 黄式权. [1883] 1989. *Songnan mengying lu* 淞南梦影录 (Record of dream images of Shanghai). In Ge, Huang and Chi, 80–152.

———. 1992. *Fenmo congtan* 粉墨叢談 (On powder and ink). In Chongtianzi, ed., vol. 17: 4847–905.

Huang Xieqing 黄燮清. [1857] 1996. "Yangjing zhuzhi ci" 洋泾竹枝词 (Bamboo poems of the Yangjing Creek). In Gu, ed., 349–51.

Huayu xiaozhu zhuren 花雨小築主人. 1895. *Xinji haishang qinglou tuji* 新輯海上青樓圖記 (Illustrated record of Shanghai courtesan houses, the new edition). 6 juan. Shanghai: n.p.

Jingying xiaosheng chuji 鏡影嘯聲初集 (Mirror images and flute sounds, the first collection). 1887. Tokyo: n.p.

Legge, James, trans. 1966. *The Four Books*. New York: Paragon.

Lei Jin 雷瑨. [1922] 1987. "Shenbao guan zhi guoqu zhuangkuan" 申報館之過去狀況 (The early conditions of the *Shenbao* press). In *Zuijin zhi wushi nian: Shenbao wushi nian zhou jinian* 最近之五十年: 申報五十周紀念 (The recent fifty years: fiftieth anniversary of *Shenbao*). Reprint. Shanghai: Shanghai shudian.

Li Dou 李門. [1795] 2003. *Yangzhou huafang lu* 揚州畫舫錄 (Record of the painted boats of Yangzhou). Reprint, in *Zhongguo fengtu zhi congkan*, vols. 28, 29. Yangzhou: Guanglin shushe.

MacFarlane, W. 1881. *Sketches in the Foreign Settlements and Native City of Shanghai*. Reprinted in *Shanghai Mercury*.

Mao Xianglin 毛祥麟. [1870] 1985. *Mo yu lu* 墨餘錄 (Records of leftover ink), ed. Bi Wanchen 畢萬忱. Shanghai: Shanghai guji chubanshe.

Meihua anzhu 梅花盦主. 1894. *Shenjiang shixia shengjing tushuo* 申江時下勝景圖説 (Illustrated grand views of contemporary Shanghai). 2 juan. Shanghai: n.p. Reprint, *Folklore and Folk literature Series of National Peking University and Chinese Association for Folklore*. 1973. Taipei: National Peking University.

Muzhenshanren 慕真山人 and Han Bangqing. 1998. *Qinglou baojian* 青楼宝鉴 (The precious mirror of pleasure quarters). Beijing: Huaxia chubanshe.

North China Herald. 1850–1900.

Penghua Sheng 捧花生. [1817] 2003. *Qinhuai huafang lu* 秦淮畫舫錄 (Record of the painted boats of Qinhuai). Reprint, *Zhongguo fengtu zhi congkan*, vol. 31. Yangzhou: Guanglin shushe.

Shenbao 申報 [Shanghai daily]. 1872–1900.

Sun Yusheng 孙玉声. 1995. "Tuixinglu biji" 退醒庐笔记 (Notes of retreat-wakening hut). In *Minguo biji xiaoshuo daguan* 民国笔记小说大观 (Anthology of note-novels from the Republican period), vol.1. Taiyuan: Shanxi guji chubanshe.

Wang Tao 王韜. 1880. *Taoyuan chidu* 弢園尺牘 (The letters of Wang Tao), 12 juan. Shanghai: n.p.

———. 1985. "Manyou suilu" 漫遊隨錄 (The record of my wandering). In Wang Xiqi 王錫祺, ed., *Xiaofanghuzhai yudi congchao* 小方壺齋輿地叢鈔 (Collection of geographical works from the Xiaofanghu studio), vol. 62. Hangzhou: Hongzhou guji shudian.

——. [1887] 1987. Songbin suohua 淞濱瑣話 (Miscellaneous talks on the coast of Shanghai). Changsha: Yue lu shu she.

——. [1875] 1989. Yinruan zazhi 瀛壖杂志 (Maritime and littoral miscellany). Shanghai: Shanghai guji chubanshe.

——. [1860] 1992a. *Haizou yeyou lu* 海陬冶遊錄 (Record of visits to the distant corner at the sea). In Chongtianzi, ed., vol. 20: 5633–84.

——. [1878] 1992b. *Haizou yeyou lu fulu* 海陬冶遊錄附錄 (Addendum to the record of visits to the distant corner at the sea). In Chongtianzi, ed., vol. 20: 5685–785.

——. [1878] 1992c. *Haizou yeyou lu yulu* 海陬冶遊錄餘錄 (Extra to the record of visits to the distant corner at the sea). In Chongtianzi, ed., vol. 20: 5787–810.

——. [1878] 1992d. *Hua guo jutan* 花国劇談 (Dramatized talk on the flower country). In Chongtianzi, ed., vol. 19: 5247–318.

Wu Youru 吳友如. 1884. *Shenjiang shengjing tu* 申江勝景圖 (Illustrated grand views of Shanghai). 2 juan. Shanghai: Dianshizhai.

——. [1908] 2002. *Wu Youru huabao.* 吳友如畫寶 (Treasures of Wu Youru painting), 4 vols. Shanghai Wenruilou. Reprint. Shanghai: Shanghai shudian chubanshe.

Wu Youru et al. 2001. *Dianshizhai huabao: Daketang ban* 点石斋画报: 大可堂版 (Point-stone-studio pictorial: Daketang edition), ed. Zhang Qiming 张奇明, 15 vols. Shanghai: Shanghai huabao chubanshe.

Yang Jingting 楊靜亭. [1864] 2003. *Dumen jilüe* 都門紀略 (Brief records of the capital). Reprint, *Zhongguo fengtu zhi congkan*, vol. 14. Yangzhou: Guanglin shushe.

Yi'an zhuren 頤安主人. [1906] 1996. *Hujiang shangye shijing ci* 滬江商業市景詞 (Poems about Shanghai commerce and markets), 4 juan. In Gu, ed., 93–182.

Yu Huai 余懷. [1654] 1992. *Banqiao zaji* 板橋雜記 (Miscellaneous notes of Banqiao). In Chongtianzi, ed., vol. 13: 3637–72.

Yuan Zuzhi 袁祖志. [1876] 1996. *Haishang zhuzhici* 海上竹枝詞 (Bamboo poems of Shanghai). In Gu, ed., 1–27.

Zhuquan jushi 珠泉居士. 1784. *Xu Banqiao zaji* 續板橋雜記 (Sequel to the miscellaneous notes of Banqiao). In Chongtianzi, ed., vol. 18.

Zizhu shanfang zhuren 紫竹山房主人. 1892. *Haishang qinglou tuji* 海上青樓圖記 (Illustrated record of Shanghai courtesan houses). Shanghai: n. p.

Scholarly literature

Benjamin, Walter. 1968. *Illumination: Essays and Reflection*, ed. Hannah Arendt. New York: Schocken Books.

——. 1977. *The Origin of German Tragic Drama*, trans. John Osborn. London: NLB.

——. 1999. *The Arcades Project*, trans. Howard Eiland and Kevin McLaughlin. Cambridge, MA: Harvard University Press.

——. 2003. "The Paris of the Second Empire in Baudelaire." In *Selected Writings*, ed. M. W. Jennings, vol. 4: 3–92. Cambridge, MA: Harvard University Press.

Bergère, Marie-Claire. 1981. "'The Other China': Shanghai from 1919 to 1949." In *Shanghai: Revolutions and Developments in an Asian Metropolis*, ed. Christopher Howe, 1–34. Cambridge: Cambridge University Press.

Betta, Chiara. 2000. "Marginal Westerners in Shanghai: The Baghdadi Jewish Community, 1845–1931." In Bickers and Henriot, eds, 38–54.

Bickers, Robert, and Christian Henriot, eds. 2000. *New Frontiers: Imperialism's New Communities in East Asia, 1842–1952*. Manchester: Manchester University Press.

Bickers, Robert, and Jeffrey Wasserstrom. 1995. "Shanghai's 'Dogs and Chinese Not Admitted' Sign: Legend, History and Contemporary Symbol." *The China Quarterly*, 142: 444–66.

Bossler, Beverly. 2002. "Shifting Identities: Courtesans and Literati in Song China." *Harvard Journal of Asiatic Studies*, 62.1: 5–31.

Bray, Francesca. 1997. *Technology and Gender: Fabric of Power in Late Imperial China*. Berkeley, CA: University of California Press.

Britton, Roswell S. 1933. *The Chinese Periodical Press, 1800–1912*. Shanghai: Kelly & Walsh.

Buci-Glucksmann, Christine. 1994. *Baroque Reason: The Aesthetics of Modernity*, trans. Patrick Camiller. London and Thousand Oaks, CA: Sage.

Buck-Morss, Susan. 1989. *The Dialectic of Seeing: Water Benjamin and the Arcades Project*. Cambridge, MA: MIT Press.

Chaffee, John W. 1985. *The Thorny Gates of Learning in Sung China: A Social History of Examinations*. Cambridge: Cambridge University Press.

Chen Bohai and Yuan Jin. 1993. *Shanghai jindai wenxueshi* (History of modern Shanghai literature). Shanghai: Shanghai renmin chubanshe.

Cheng, Stephen. 1979. "*Flowers of Shanghai* and the Late-Ch'ing Courtesan Novel." Ph.D. dissertation. Harvard University.

——. 1984. "*Sing-song girls of Shanghai* and Its Narrative Methods." In Liu Ts'un-yan, ed., 95–110.

Cohen, Paul. 1974. *Between Tradition and Modernity: Wang T'ao and Reform in Late Ch'ing China*. Cambridge, MA: Council on East Asian Studies, Harvard University.

——. 1984. *Discovering History in China: American Historical Writing on the Recent Chinese Past*. New York: Columbia University Press.

De Jesus, C. A. Montalto. 1909. *Historical Shanghai*. Shanghai: Shanghai Mercury.

Debord, Guy. 1970. *The Society of the Spectacle*. Detroit: Black and Red.

Denison, Edward, and Guang Yu Ren. 2006. *Building Shanghai: The Story of China's Gateway*. Chichester: John Wiley and Sons.

Des Forges, Alexander. 2003. "Building Shanghai, One Page at a Time: The Aesthetics of Installment Fiction at the Turn of the Century." *Journal of Asian Studies*, 62.3: 781–810.

——. 2007. *Mediasphere Shanghai: The Aesthetics of Cultural Production*. Honolulu, HI: University of Hawaii Press.

Dikötter, Frank. 2007. *Things Modern: Material Culture and Everyday Life in China*. London: Hurst.

Dirlik, Arif. 1996. "Reversals, Ironies, Hegemonies: Notes on the Contemporary Historiography of Modern China." *Modern China*, 22.3: 243–84.

Dong Jianhong et al. 1982. *Zhongguo chengshi jianshe shi* (History of Chinese urban construction). Beijing: Zhongguo jianzhu gongye chubanshe.

Du Li. 1983. "Yapian zhanzheng qian Shanghai hanghui xingzhi zhi shanbian" (Changes in the nature of trade associations before the Opium War). In *Zhongguo zibenzhuyi mengya wenti lunwenji* (An anthology of papers concerning the sprouts of capitalism in China), ed. Nanjing daxue lishishi, 141–71. Nanjing: Nanjing daxue.

Dutton, Donald S. 2007. "Ritual, Cultural Standardization, and Orthopraxy in China: Reconsidering James L. Watson's Ideas." *Modern China*, 33.1: 3–21.

Ebrey, Patricia B., trans. 1991a. *Chu Hsi's Family Rituals: A Twelfth-Century Chinese Manual for the Performance of Cappings, Weddings, Funerals, and Ancestral Rites*. Princeton, NJ: Princeton University Press.

——. 1991b. *Confucianism and Family Rituals in Imperial China: A Social History of Writing about Rites*. Princeton, NJ: Princeton University Press.

Feuchtwang, Stephan. 1974. *An Anthropological Analysis of Chinese Geomancy*. Vientiane, Laos: Vithagna.

Freud, Sigmund. 1953. "The 'Uncanny.'" In *The Standard Edition of the Complete Psychological Works of Sigmund Freud*, ed. and trans. James Strachey, vol. 17: 219–55. London: Hogarth Press.

——. 1961. *Beyond the Pleasure Principle*, trans. J. Strachey. New York: Liveright.

Furth, Charlotte. 1999. *A Flourishing Yin: Gender in China's Medical History, 960–1665*. Berkeley, CA: University of California Press.

Ge Gongzhen. [1926] 2003. *Zhongguo baoxue shi*. (A History of Chinese Journalism) Shanghai: Shanghai guji chubanshe.

Gentz, Natascha. 2007. "Useful Knowledge and Appropriate Communication: The Field of Journalist Production in Late Nineteenth Century China." In Wagner, ed., 47–104.

Golas, Peter G. 1977. "Early Ch'ing Guilds." In Skinner, ed., 555–80.

Goldstein, Joshua. 2003. "From Teahouse to Playhouse: Theaters as Social Texts in Early-Twentieth-Century China." *Journal of Asian Studies*, 62.3: 753–79.

Goodman, Bryna. 1995. *Native Place, City, and Nation: Regional Networks and Identities in Shanghai, 1853–1937*. Berkeley, CA: University of California Press.

——. 2000. "Improvisation on Semicolonial Theme, or, How to Read a Celebration of Transnational Urban Community." *Journal of Asian Studies*, 59.4: 889–926.

Habermas, Jürgen. 1989. *The Structural Transformation of the Public Sphere: An Inquiry into a Category of Bourgeois Society*, trans. T. Burger. Cambridge, MA: MIT Press.

Hanan, Patrick. 1998. "*Fengyue Meng* and the Courtesan Novel." *Harvard Journal of Asiatic Studies*, 58.2: 345–72.

Hanssen, Beatrice. 1998. *Water Benjamin's Other History: Of Stones, Animals, Human Beings, and Angles*. Berkeley, CA: University of California Press.

Harvey, David. 1982. *The Limits to Capital*. Chicago, IL: University of Chicago Press.

——. 2000. *Spaces of Hope*. Edinburgh: Edinburgh University Press.

——. 2001. *Spaces of Capital: Towards a Critical Geography*. Edinburgh: Edinburgh University Press.

Hay, Jonathan. 2001. "Painting and the Built Environment in Late Nineteenth-century Shanghai." In *Chinese Art: Modern Expressions*, eds. Maxwell Hearn and Judith Smith, 60–101. New York: The Metropolitan Museum of Art.

Henriot, Christian. 1996. "'From a Throne of Glory to a Seat of Ignominy': Shanghai Prostitution Revisited, 1849–1949." *Modern China*, 22.2: 133–63.

——. 1999. "Courtship, Sex and Money: The Economics of Courtesan Houses in Nineteenth- and Twentieth-Century Shanghai." *Women's History Review*, 8.3: 443–65.

——. 2001. *Prostitution and Sexuality in Shanghai: A Social History, 1849–1949*. Trans. Noël Castelino. Cambridge: Cambridge University Press.

Hershatter, Gail. 1989. "The Hierarchy of Shanghai Prostitution, 1870–1949." *Modern China*, 15.4: 463–98.

——. 1996. "'From a Throne of Glory to a Seat of Ignominy': Shanghai Prostitution Revisited, 1849–1949: A Response." *Modern China*, 22.2: 164–67.

——. 1997. *Dangerous Pleasures: Prostitution and Modernity in Twentieth-Century Shanghai*. Berkeley, CA: University of California Press.

Hu Shi. [1926] 1983. "*Haishang hua liezhuan* xu" (Preface to *Flowers of Shanghai*). In Han Ziyun, 7–18.

Hugo, Victor. 1881. *Le Misérables*. In Victor Hugo, *Oeuvres complètes*, novels, vol. 8. Paris.

Huntington, Rania. 2003. "The Weird in the Newspaper." In Zeitlin and Liu, eds, 341–96.

Huters, Theodore. 2005. *Bring the World Home: Appropriating the West in Late Qing and Early Republican China*. Honolulu, HI: University of Hawaii Press.

Ji, Zhaojin. 2003. *A History of Modern Shanghai Banking: The Rise and Decline of China's Finance Capitalism*. Armonk, NY: M.E. Sharpe.

Johnson, Linda Cooke. 1995. *Shanghai from Market Town to Treaty Port, 1074–1858*. Stanford, CA: Stanford University Press.

Kim, Nanny. 2007. "New Wine in Old Bottles? Making and Reading an Illustrated Magazine from Late Nineteenth-Century Shanghai." In Wagner, ed., 175–200.

Knapp, Ronald G. 1999. *China's Living Houses: Folk Beliefs, Symbols and Household Ornamentation*. Honolulu, HI: University of Hawaii Press.

——. 2000. *China's Old Dwellings*. Honolulu: University of Hawaii Press.

——. 2005. *Chinese Houses: The Architectural Heritage of a Nation*. Boston: Tuttle.

Ko, Dorothy. 1994. *Teachers of the Inner Chambers: Women and Culture in Seventeenth-Century China*. Stanford, CA: Stanford University Press.

——. 1997. "The Written Word and the Bound Foot: A History of the Courtesan's Aura." In Widmer and Chang, eds, 74–100.

Kuan, Seng, and Peter G. Rowe. 2004. *Shanghai: Architecture and Urbanism for Modern China*. Berlin: Prestel.

Lanning, G., and S. Couling. 1921. *The History of Shanghai*. Shanghai: Kelly & Walsh.

Leach, Neil. 1997. *Rethinking Architecture: A Reader in Cultural Theory*. London: Routledge.

Lee, Leo Ou-fan. 1999. *Shanghai Modern: The Flowering of a New Urban Culture in China, 1930–1949*. Cambridge, MA: Harvard University Press.

——. 2000. "The Cultural Construction of Modernity in Urban Shanghai: Some Preliminary Explorations." In *Becoming Chinese: Passage to Modernity and Beyond*, ed. Wen-hsin Yeh, 31–61. Berkeley, CA: University of California Press.

Lefebvre, Henri. 1991. *The Production of Space*, trans. Donald Nicholson-Smith. Oxford: Basil Blackwell.

Lemière, J. 1923. "Sing Song Girl: From a Throne of Glory to a Seat of Ignominy." *Chinese Journal of Science and Art*, no. 1: 126–34.

Liang, Samuel Y. 2003. "The Fluctuation of Yin Yang: A Sex Model in Chinese Philosophy and Medicine." *APA Newsletters*, 2.2: 17–21.

——. 2005. *Ephemeral Households, Splintered City: Mapping Leisure in the Sojourners' Shanghai, 1870–1900*. Ph.D. dissertation. Binghamton, NY: Binghamton University.

——. 2007. "Ephemeral Households, Marvelous Things: Business, Gender, and Material Culture in *Flowers of Shanghai*." *Modern China*, 33.3: 377–418.

——. 2008a. "Where the Courtyard Meets the Street: Spatial Culture of the *Li* Neighborhoods, Shanghai, 1870–1900." *Journal of the Society of Architectural Historians*, 67.4: 483–504.

——. 2008b. "Amnesiac Monument, Nostalgic Fashion: Shanghai's New Heaven and Earth." *Wasafiri*, 23.3: 47–55.

Liang Yunxiang [Samuel Y. Liang]. 2009. "Shanghai longtong de gemin yu huaijiu: Cong zhonggong 'yida' huizhi dao Xintiandi" (The revolution and nostalgia of Shanghai long-tang: From the CCP first congress memorial to Xintiandi). *Taiwan shehui yanjiu jikan* (Taiwan: A Radical Quarterly in Social Studies), 76: 393–416.

Liu Ts'un-yan, ed. 1984. *Chinese Middlebrow Fiction: From the Ch'ing and Early Republican Eras.* A Rendition Book. Hong Kong: Chinese University of Hong Kong Press.

Lu, Hanchao. 1995. "Away from Nanking Road: Small Stores and Neighborhood Life in Modern Shanghai." *Journal of Asia Studies*, 54.1: 93–123.

———. 1999. *Beyond the Neon Lights: Everyday Shanghai in the Early Twentieth Century.* Berkeley, CA: University of California Press.

Lu Wenda and Xu Baorun, eds. 1999. *Shanghai fangdichan zhi* (History of Shanghai real estate development). Shanghai: Shanghai shehui kexueyuan chubanshe.

Lu Xun. 1981. "Zhongguo xiaoshuo de lishi de bianqian" (The transformation of the history of Chinese fiction). In Lu Xun, *Lu Xuan Quanji*, vol. 9, Beijing: Renmin wenxue chubanshe.

Luo Suwen. 1991. *Shikumen: Xunchang renjia* (Shikumen: Ordinary homes). Shanghai: Shanghai renmin chubanshe.

Luo Xiaowei and Sha Yongjie. 2002. *Shanghai Xintiandi: jiuqu gaizao de jianzhu lishi, renwen lishi yu kaifa moshi de yanjiu* (Shanghai Xintiandi: research on architectural history, humanity history, and development model of district renovation). Nanjing: Dongnan daxue chubanshe.

Luo Xiaowei and Wu Jiang. 1997. *Shanghai Longtang* (The alleyway of Shanghai). Shanghai: Shanghai renmin meishui chubanshe.

Mann, Susan. 1997. *Precious Records: Women in China's Long Eighteenth Century.* Stanford, CA: Stanford University Press.

Marx, Karl. 1983. *The Portable Karl Marx*, ed. Eugene Kanmenka. New York: Viking Press.

Marx, Karl, and Frederick Engels. 1976. *Collected Works*, vol. 6, Marx and Engels: 1845–48. London: Lawrence and Wishart.

McAleavy, Henry. 1953. *Wang T'ao: The Life and Writings of a Displaced Person.* London: The China Society.

McElderry, Andrea Lee. 1976. *Shanghai Old-Style Banks (Ch'ien-Chuang) 1800–1935.* Ann Arbor, MI: Center for Chinese Studies, University of Michigan.

McMahon, Keith. 1995. *Misers, Shrews, and Polygamists: Sexuality and Male-Female Relations in Eighteenth-Century Chinese Fiction.* Durham, NC: Duke University Press.

———. 2002. "Fleecing the Male Customer in Shanghai Brothels of the 1890s." *Later Imperial China*, 23.2: 1–32.

Meng Yue. 2006. *Shanghai and the Edges of Empires.* Minneapolis, MN: University of Minnesota Press.

Mittler, Barbara. 2004. *A Newspaper for China? Power, Identity, and Change in Shanghai's News Media, 1872–1912.* Cambridge, MA: Harvard University Asia Center.

Mote, F. W. 1973. "A Millennium of Chinese Urban History: Form, Time, and Space Concepts in Soochow." *Rice University Studies*, 59.4: 35–65.

———. 1977. "The Transformation of Nanking, 1350–1400." In Skinner, ed., 101–53.

Murphey, Rhoads. 1953. *Shanghai, Key to Modern China*, Cambridge, MA: Harvard University Press.

———. 1977. *The Outsiders, The Western Experience in India and China.* Ann Arbor, MI: University of Michigan Press.

Qin Shao. 1998. "Tempest over Teapots: The Vilification of Teahouse Culture in Early Republican China." *Journal of Asian Studies*, 57.2: 1009–41.

Rawski, Evelyn Sakakida. 1979. *Education and Popular Literacy in Ch'ing China.* Ann Arbor, MI: University of Michigan Press.

Reed, Christopher A. 2004. *Gutenberg in Shanghai: Chinese Print Capitalism, 1876–1937.* Vancouver: UBC Press.

Rowe, William T. 1984. *Hankow: Commerce and Society in a Chinese City, 1796–1889.* Stanford, CA: Stanford University Press.

———. 1989. *Hankow: Conflict and Community in a Chinese City, 1796–1895.* Stanford, CA: Stanford University Press.

Schwartz, Vanessa R. 1998. *Spectacular Realities: Early Mass Culture in Fin-de-Siècle France.* Berkeley: University of California Press.

Shang Wei. 2003. "*Jin Ping Mei* and Late Ming Print Culture." In Zeitlin and Liu, eds, 187–238.

Shaya, Gregory. 2004. "The *Flâneur*, the *Badaud*, and the Making of a Mass Public in France, circa 1860–1910." *American Historical Review*, 109.1: 1–60.

Shiba Yoshinobu. 1970. *Commerce and Society in Sung China*, trans. Mark Elvin. Ann Arbor, MI: Center for Chinese Studies, University of Michigan.

Simmel, Georg. 1997. "Bridge and Door." In Leach, ed., 66–69.

Skinner, G. William, ed., 1977a. *The Cities in Late Imperial China*, Stanford, CA: Stanford University Press.

Skinner, G. William. 1977b. "Introduction: Urban Development in Imperial China." In Skinner, ed., 3–31,

———. 1977c. "Introduction: Urban and Rural in Chinese Society." In Skinner, ed., 253–73.

———. 1977d. "Cities and the Hierarchy of Local Systems." In Skinner, ed., 275–351.

———. 1977e. "Urban Social Structure in Ch'ing China." In Skinner, ed., 521–53.

Starr, Chloë. 2007. *Red-light Novels of the Late Qing.* Leiden: E. J. Brill.

Twitchett, Denis. 1968. "Merchant, Trade and Government in Late T'ang." *Asia Major*, n.s. 14, part 1, 63–95.

Volpp, Sophie. 2002. "The Literary Circulation of Actors in Seventeenth-Century China." *Journal of Asian Studies*, 61.3: 949–84.

Wagner, Rudolf. 1995. "The Role of the Foreign Community in the Chinese Public Sphere." *The China Quarterly*, 142: 423–43.

———. ed. 2007a. *Joining the Global Public: Word, Image, and City in Early Chinese Newspapers, 1870–1910.* Albany, NY: State University of New York Press.

———. 2007b. "Join the Global Imaginaire: The Shanghai Illustrated Newspaper *Dianshizhai huabao*." In Wagner, ed., 105–74.

Wang, David Der-wei. 1997. *Fin-de-siècle Splendor: Repressed Modernities of Late Qing Fiction. 1849–1911.* Stanford, CA: Stanford University Press.

Wang Shaozhou. 1989. *Shanghai jindai chengshi jianzhu* (Shanghai modern architecture*).* Nanjing: Jiangsu kexue jishu chubanshe.

Wang Shaozhou and Chen Zhimin. 1987. *Lilong jianzhu* (Alleyway house architecture). Shanghai: Shanghai kexue jishu wenxian chubanshe.

Wang Shunu. [1933] 1988. *Zhongguo changji shi* (History of Chinese courtesans). Shanghai: Sanlian shudian.

Watson, James L. 1985. "Standardizing the Gods: The Promotion of T'ien-hou ('Empress of Haven') along the South China Coast, 960–1960." In *Popular Culture in Late Imperial China*, eds. David Johnson, Andrew J. Nathan, and Evelyn S. Rawski, 292–324. Berkeley, CA: University of California Press.

Widmer, Ellen, and Kang-i Sun Chang, eds. 1997. *Writing Women in Late Imperial China.* Stanford, CA: Stanford University Press.

Wu Hung. 1999. "Tian'anmen Square: A Political History of Monuments." *Representations*, 35: 84–117.

Wu Jiang. 2008. *Shanghai bainian jianzhu shi 1840–1949* (One hundred years history of Shanghai architecture, 1849–1949). Second edition. Shanghai: Tongji daxue chubanshe.

Xiong Yuezhi. 1996. "Zhangyuan: wanqing Shanghai yige gonggong kongjian yanjiu" (Zhang Garden: a research on a public space in late Qing Shanghai). *Dang'an yu shixue* (Archive and history), 12, 31–42.

Xu Yinong. 2000. *The Chinese City in Space and Time: The Development of Urban Form in Suzhou*. Honolulu: University of Hawaii Press.

Xu Zaiping and Xu Ruifang. 1988. *Qing muo sishi nian Shenbao shiliao* (Historical materials from *Shenbao* in the forty years of late Qing). Beijing: Xinhua chubanshe.

Yang, C. K. 1961. *Religion in Chinese Society: A Study of Contemporary Social Functions of Religion and Some of Their Historical Factors*. Berkeley, CA: University of California Press.

Ye, Xiaoqing. 2003. *The Dianshizhai Pictorial: Shanghai Urban Life, 1884–1898*. Ann Arbor, MI: Center for Chinese Studies, University of Michigan.

Yeh, Catherine. 1996. "Creating a Shanghai Identity – Late Qing Courtesan Handbooks and the Formation of the New Citizen." In *Unity and Diversity: Local Cultures and Identities in China*, eds. Tao Tao Liu and David Faure, 107–23. Hong Kong: Hong Kong University Press.

——. 1997. "The Life-style of Four *Wenren* in Late Qing Shanghai." *Harvard Journal of Asiatic Studies*, 57.2: 419–70.

——. 1998. "Reinventing Ritual: Late Qing Handbooks for Proper Customer Behavior in Shanghai Courtesan Houses." *Late Imperial China*, 19.2: 1–63.

——. 2003. "Creating the Urban Beauty: The Shanghai Courtesan in Late Qing Illustrations." In Zeitlin and Liu, eds, 397–447.

——. 2005. "Where is the Center of Cultural Production?: The Rise of the Actor to National Stardom and the Peking/Shanghai Challenge (1860s–1910s)." *Late Imperial China*, 25.2: 74–118.

——. 2006. *Shanghai Love: Courtesans, Intellectuals, and Entertainment Culture, 1850–1910*. Seattle, WA: University of Washington Press.

Yuan Jin. 1998. *Zhongguo wenxue guannian de jindai biange* (The modern reform of Chinese literary ideals). Shanghai: Shanghai kexueyuan chubanshe.

Zamperini, Paola. 2003. "On Their Dress They Wore a Body: Fashion and Identity in Late Qing Shanghai." *Positions*, 11.2: 301–30.

Zeitlin, Judith T., and Lydia H. Liu, eds. 2003. *Writing and Materiality in China: Essays in Honor of Patrick Hanan*. Cambridge, MA: Harvard University East Asian Center.

Zhao, Chunlan. 2004. "From Shikumen to New-Style: A Rereading of *Lilong* Housing in Modern Shanghai." *Journal of Architecture*, 9.1: 49–76.

Zheng Shiling. 1999. *Shanghai jindai jianzhu fengge* (The style of Shanghai architecture in modern times). Shanghai: Shanghai jiaoyu chubanshe.

Zou Yiren. 1980. *Jiu Shanghai renkou bianqian de yanjiu* (Research on population change in old Shanghai). Shanghai: Shanghai renmin chubanshe.

Index

accidents 134–6, 141, 173, 178, 203n15
Adebao 58, 201n14
Ajin 58, 106
Alcock, Sir Rutherford 88–90, 118, 201n8, 201n1, 203n14
alleys (*long*) 58–9, 69, 84, 86–7, 93, 97–8, 100, 105–6, 110,119,122–3, 158
Aqiao 105–6
architecture 6–7, 193n8; function 100–1; interior/interiority 76–80, 84, 137, 145–9, 159–60; openness 97–8, 137
authorship 29–30, 38

back rooms (*tingzijian*) 81, 93, 102, 106
Bai Juyi 104
balconies 98, 105, 119–20, 122–3, 125–7
bamboo poems (*zhuzhici*) 31, 36, 38, 47, 92, 95, 101, 105, 119–20, 122–3, 126–8, 130, 140–1, 149–50, 154, 156, 161–2, 177, 201n9, 202n5, 203n18
Banqiao zaji 32, 37, 58
banquet parties 60–3, 73–4, 86, 102–3, 198n8, 198n10
Benjamin, Walter 3–5, 15–16, 27, 30, 34, 41, 130, 134–6, 140, 152, 165, 192n3, 193n6, 196n21, 199n22, 202n3
Bergère, Marie-Claire 194n1
Bickers, Robert 203n17
bourgeoisie 14–16, 24, 194n8, *see* capitalism
Bray, Francesca 18
brawls 42, 98, 105, 130, 132–3, 137–8, 159, 175–6
Britton, Roswell S. 32–6, 195n5, 195n7
Buci-Glucksmann, Christine 3
Buck-Morss, Susan 16, 199n22
Bund 118–21, 166–7, 169–71, 174, 201n1

Cantonese: courtesans 145–6; goods 141; guilds 157; merchants 166–7; parade 169–70; restaurants 145–6; sex workers 85
Cao Xueqin 31, 155, 177, 196n22
capitalism: and print media 32–3; development 2, 4, 13–16, 20, 26–7, 70–1, 131, 163, 180–2; housing production 88–92; spatial strategy 14–15
carriages 70, 92, 115, 128–9, 132–3, 171–3
catharsis 156, 158, 165, 169
Chang'an 88, 93–4, 100
Changfu 110–11
changsan 49, 55, 62, 81, 86, 107, 109–11, 126, 197n3
Chen Qiao 37–8, 55, 101, 126–8, 130, 154, 177
Chen Xiaoyun 53, 69
Chen Xingeng 33
Cheng Jinxuan 91–2
Chessboard Street (Qipan jie) 107, 109, 121–5, 197n2
Chi Zhicheng 23, 37, 62, 76–7, 129, 132, 149, 151–3, 163, 171, 175, 203n5
chuju (outcall) 61–2, 64, 148
City Temple 23, 74, 164, 174, 202n2
civil service examination 21, 44, 47
civil society, *see* public sphere
Cohen, Paul 33, 44, 47, 192n4
colonial authority 4, 87–90, 131, 136, 169–70, 203n17
commodity: and body 139–40; fetishism 72–3, 76; soul 140
compradors 6, 24, 33, 91–3, 118–19, 121, 201n10
Confucianism, *see* neo-Confucian
convicts 130–1, 150, 164–5
courtesan: and modernity 24; as allegory 43, 72–3, 111; as natural imageries 72–3, 123–4; biographies 38, 109; categories and hierarchy 109, 197n3,

201n16; culture 24–5, 39–42, 84; dress codes 72; fashionable and chic 75–6; gifts 71; historical 21–2, 32, 151, 194n5; iconic images 24–5, 39, 200n25; in carriages 132–3, 171–3; in gardens 175, 178, 180; in restaurants 148; in storytelling houses 151–4; in the walled city 44–5; in Wang Tao 44–7; marriage 57, 60, 64–5, 75, 81–2; personae 65–6; physical appearances 72–3; portraits 38; relationship with client, *see xianghao*; services 25
courtesan houses: architectural settings 101–6; as entrepreneurial business 77; as home 53; at Chessboard Street 121–2; beds 79; boudoir interiors 76–83; business activities 60–4; business seasons 63, 103, 199n14; couches 79; dressers 79–20; gender relations 64–71; integrated pleasure and living 78–80; material culture 71–83; neighborhoods 107–12; signs 101–2; social relations 56–60; sorrow and death 82–3; terms adopted 48–9; types of 54–5; violence and destruction 81–2; visual representations 77
courtesan novels 7, 39–40, *see Flowers of Shanghai*
courtesan guides 38–43, *see* guidebook
courtyards 88, 127; layout 93; spatial type 28–9, 97, 158
courtyard-hall 31, 93, 103, 105–6, 157
crowds, urban 127–9, 134–8, 141, 159, 161, 164, 167, 175–6, 202n7
currencies 198n12

dajie (maids) 57–9, 63, 105–6, 111, 137–8, 148, 198n8, 198n13
Damalu, *see* First Avenue
De Jesus, C. A. Montalto 88, 118–19, 200n3, 200n4, 201n1
death 48, 68–70, 82–3; instinct 136, 202n8; scenes 45–6, 117, 134, 174, 193n6; world of deceased 164–9
decadent lifestyle 24–6, 48, 177, 182
Des Forges, Alexander 7, 39–40, 50, 143, 172–4, 177, 192n1, 195n7, 197n23, 203n17
Dianshizhai huabao (Point-stone-studio pictorial) 6–7, 13, 36–7, 50, 56, 59, 70, 77–8, 96, 98, 108, 110, 122, 125, 127–8, 130–9, 141–2, 144–8, 150, 153, 155–61, 166–70, 172–3, 178–81, 196n12, 200n25, 203n15

Dibao 195n6
Dikötter, Frank 4, 194n10, 202n4
domestic women 147–8, 68, 107, 110, 156, 161, 178, 180
Dong Jianhong 94, 201n11,
dream and reality 16, 48, 49
Dream of the Red Chamber, *see* Cao Xueqin

Ebrey, Patricia B. 18–19, 29–30

family (household) 18–19, 21, 28–31, 100; of courtesan house 56–60, 103
Family Rituals (*Jiali*) 29–31
Fang Penghu 177
fangli (residential ward) 88, 93–4
feminist critiques 5
feng shui 19, 95, 114, 117, 127
Fengyue meng 85, 197n24, 199n13
First Avenue 108, 140–3, 150, 168–70, 174
Flowers of Shanghai (*Haishang hua liezhuan*) 7, 39, 42, 49–83, 99, 101–11, 137–9, 141–5, 148, 171, 173–7, 197–200
flower opium houses (*huayanjian*) 104, 107–8, 149
Fourth Avenue 47, 101, 106–7, 125–33, 137, 140, 143–5, 148, 153, 158, 173–5, 180
Freud, Sigmund 66, 68, 199n19, 202n8

gambling parties 63, 78
Gao Yabai 54, 176, 199n20
gardens 23, 77, 120–1, 174–80
Ge Yuanxu 38, 49, *see Huyou zaji*
Ge Zhongying 55, 65, 73–4, 141–3, 199n16, 199n17
gender 5–6, 20, 58, 64–71, 148, 151–6, 178–80; reversal of traditional role 68, 70; maternal male 46, 152, 196n21
geography: imaginative 19, 27, 35, 116–17; urban 6, 11, 97, 107, 112
Goldstein 158, 161
Goodman, Bryna 113, 157, 168–70, 203n13
Great Learning (*Daxue*) 28–9
Gu Bingquan, *see* bamboo poems
guidebooks 30, 38, 42–3, 49, 109, 197n3, 198n13
guilds (trade association) 22, 113, 156–7; of construction 91–2, 201n9

Habermas, Jürgen 113, 194n3
Haizou yeyou lu 37, 23, 43, 45–6, 75, 85–6, 95, 196n15, 203n9, 203n11

Han Bangqing 42, 49–52, *see Flowers of Shanghai*
Han Ziyun, *see* Han Bangqing
Harvey, David 14–15
Hay, Jonathan 193n8
He Guisheng 47–8, 51, 177
Hegelian dialectics and teleology 14–16
Henriot, Christian 24, 40–2, 60, 63, 72, 77, 101, 151, 156, 196n18, 198n10, 201n16
Hershatter, Gail 24–5, 40–2, 60, 77, 194n9, 196n17, 198n6, 200n23, 201n16
historical experience 40–3
historical materialism 4, 15
historicism 1–5; anthropocentric 15–16
history: as redemption of the past 5; fragments of 41; humanist 2; methodology 41–2; natural 16; progress 2–3; sacred 2–3; Sino-centric 4–5, 192n4; sources of 40–3
Hong Shanqing 53, 55, 60, 69, 102, 106–7, 109–10, 143, 197n1, 198n7, 201n13
hoodlums, *see* thugs
households: space 18–19; ritual 18, 29–30, 53; *see* family
Hu Shi 197n23, 197n27
huabang (flower list) 155–6
Huaguxi (Flower Drum Opera) 162–3
Huang Cuifeng 57–8, 65–6, 71, 73–5, 200n28
Huang Erjie 57–8, 65, 74
Huang Shiquan 37, 47–8, 163; *see Songnan mengying lu*
Huang Xiexun, *see* Hang Shiquan
Huangpu River 11, 23, 85, 115, 118, 171
Hugo, Victor 130
Hujiang shangye shijing ci 92, 140–1, 201n9, 202n5
hutong 94
Huyou mengying 37–8, *see* Chi Zhicheng
Huyou zaji 38, 49, 100–1, 107, 121, 125, 140–1, 146, 149, 162–3, 171, 173, 197n25, 202n4, 203n11

immigrants 11–13, 24, 100, 194n1, *see* sojourners
imperialism (imperial powers) 2–3, 88, 115, 117, 121, 131, 170, 194n1
illustrators/artists 36–7, 167–8, 180; *see* Wu Youru

Jiang Zhixiang 47
Jiang Yueqin 72, 99
Jiangnan 6, 11, 17, 22, 25, 84–5, 87, 93, 96, 151, 192n4, 194n5, 198n5

Jin Xiaobao 180
journalism 33–7, 47, 91
journalists 43, 66–7; *see* literati-journalists

Knapp, Ronald 88, 96, 114
Ko, Dorothy 6, 21, 30, 194n6, 195n4
Kuang'er 76, 100–1
Kunqu 162

Lai Touyuan 42, 63, 82
Lee, Leo Ou-fan 2, 11–12
Lei Jin 47, 54, 197n27
li compounds 84, 86–112, 126, 130, 141, 182
Li Dou *see Yangzhou huafang lu*
Li Heting 54
li houses 93, 97–8, 100–6
Li Peilan 76
Li Shifu 54, 104, 110–11, 137–9
Li Shufang 82–3
Li Zhuanhong 75, 102, 198n8
Liang Qichao 2, 25, 27, 40, 47
lilong 12, 84, 200n1, 201n12
Lin Daiyu 172, 180
Lin Sufen 75
literacy 195n7
literati (scholar-officials): historical 16–18, 21; in *Flowers of Shanghai* 54, 176, 199n20
literati-journalists 24, 33–5, 43, 47–9, 69, 154–6, 177
lithography: printing 37–8; press 196n16
longtang 93, 97–8, 105–8, 201n14, 201n15
love affair, secret 57–8, 61, 70, 81, 105–6, 111, 147, 164
Lu, Hanchao 12, 101, 107, 200n1, 201n6
Lu Lanfen 172, 180
Lu Xiubao 60–1, 77
Lu Xiulin 73, 77
Lu Xun 39, 196n23, 197n27
Luo Suwen 93, 101, 200n1
Luo Xiaowei 88, 107, 200n1
Luo Zifu 65–6, 69, 106, 199n17, 200n28

Ma Guisheng 143, 148, 202n2
MacFarlane, W. 158–60, 162, 203n7
madam (*laobao*) 55–9, 65, 68–9, 74, 102–3, 111, 137–8, 198n13; *see* Huang Erjie, Zhou Lan
Major, Earnest 33–7, 47, 91, 196n14, 202n2
Mann, Susan 6, 71, 194n6, 194n7, 198n5
Mao Xianglin 89–91, 203n12
Mao'erxi 163
marriage 66–7; *see* courtesan marriage

marvelous (*qi*) contents: in fiction 31; in journalism 34–6
Marx, Karl 14–16, 72, 74, 140
masses, modern 42, 132–6, 144, 151, 154
McMahon, Keith 67, 76, 197n23, 198n6, 198n9, 199n16, 199n17, 199n19
Meng Yue 192n4
merchants 16, 22–4, 48, 194n8; friendship and networking 62; residences 53–4, 100; Western (landowners) 88–92, 100
missionaries 2, 32–4, 201n1
Mittler, Barbara 33–4, 36, 195n8, 195n9, 196n11
mixed residence (*huayang zaju*) 1, 11, 87, 89–90
modernity: as decay and disintegration 26; hybrid/multifaceted 4, 13, 17; in China/Shanghai 1–4, 6, 16–17, 19, 27, 113, 181; in the West 11–16; positivist 17
Murphey, Rhoads 194n1
mythic imagery 118–19, 124, 129

Nanking 21, 31, 32, 81–2, 84, 155
nationalism 131, 136, 170, 181
nature 3–4, 21, 29, 32, 72–3, 79, 114, 118, 129–30
nature-man harmony/unity 2–3, 29, 114–5, 123
neighborhoods 62, 75, 86–7, 103, 106–11, 123
neo-Confucian: classics 27–30; ideology 16–20; learning 28; orthopraxy 28–9; social hierarchy 95, 109; space 18–19
new (material) nature 4, 15–16, 27, 73, 78, 181
newspapers 33–6; editorials 34–6, 195n9, 195n11; readership 34
newssheets 33, 195n5
niangyi 57–9, 63, 69, 105–6, 150, 161, 176, 198n7, 198n8, 198n9
North China Herald 33, 169–70, 203n7
nostalgia 25, 32, 42–3, 48, 55, 66, 77, 80, 173,
nouveaux riches 24, 72, 91–2, 129, 146, 149, 172

opera: actors 70, 81, 106, 161, 163–4, 176, 203n10; genres 162–3; performances 102–3, 156, 161; troupes 162
opium houses 104, 108, 137–9, 148–50
opium smoking 48, 51, 78–9

parades 164–70
parks 174, 203n17

patriarchal order 18–19, 53, 59
peddlers 75, 137–40, 143, 149, 158, 200n23
Peking 21, 38, 51, 94, 158, 162, 199n21
Peking Gazette (*Jingbo*) 33, 35–6
Peking Opera 63, 152–3, 158, 162–4
Peking Road 91, 108
photographic evidence 7, 193n9
pictorial representation 6–7, 37, 167–8, 180, 202n3
pictorials 36–7, 196n12; *see Dianshizhai huabao*
pleasure quarter: in Jiangnan 21–2, 32, 67, 84–5, 199n13; in Shanghai 38–9, 50–1, 85–7, 101–11, 121–8
police 70, 108, 130, 137, 150, 167–9, 176
prelude songs (*kaipian*) 62–3, 152, 163
print culture, Ming-Qing 30–2
print media, Shanghai 32–40, 113
prostitution 24–5, 40, 195n11, 201n16; *see* sex trade
public sphere 19, 32, 113

Qi Yunsou 176–7
Qian Xinbo 47, 51
Qian Zigang 54, 66–7
Qin Yubo 164

real estate 88–92, 102
reception hall (*ketang*) 20, 88, 93, 98, 102–3; *see* courtyard-hall
religion: and modernity 2–4; beliefs 20, 165, 194n2; festival events 103, 156–7, 164–8
restaurants 144–8; Cantonese 145–6; Western-style 146–8
rickshaws 96, 106, 129, 173–4
Rowe, William T. 113, 194n8
rural-urban continuum 20, 115, 194n4

sages 3–4, 27–9, 44–5, 48, 80–1, 152, 196n22
saihui see parade
Sassoons 90–2
secularization 2–3, 14, 16
sedans 59, 103, 105–6, 126, 129, 171
servants: male 58–9, 76, *see* Adebao, Kuang'er, Zhang Shou; female, *see niangyi, dajie*
sex trade 48, 62, 67, 71, 101, 109–10, 197n3; *see* prostitution
sex workers: as "flowers" 123–8; low-class 109–11, *see yeji*
sexuality, female 66, 71–2, 124, 151

Shang Wei 30, 195n5, 195n6
Shanghai: British Settlement 11; French
  concession 11, 13, 107, 121, 129, 150,
  162, 200n4; foreign settlements 11,
  23, 53, 86–92, 114–18, 150; historical
  background 11; International Settlement
  11, 108, 150, 169, 174, 200n4; Land
  Regulations 87, 89; population 200n3,
  200n4; urban environment 51–2; walled
  city and suburb 22–3, 85–6, 117, 162,
  202n2
Shanghai xinbao 33–4, 195n8
Shen Xiaohong 61–2, 70, 80–1, 106, 176,
  198n7, 198n9,
Shenbao 33–6, 40, 42, 47, 49–52, 69, 95,
  105, 119–20, 122–3, 150, 154, 156, 158,
  161–2, 175, 177, 195n8, 195n9, 195n10,
  196n12, 196n14, 196n17, 196n20,
  203n18
Shenjiang shengjing tu 38, 114–18, 125–6,
  128–9, 171, 174–6, 203n18
Shenjiang shixia shengjing tushuo 23,
  77, 114, 146, 148, 153, 203n5, 203n6,
  203n9
Shi Quan 71, 199n20
Shi Tianran 81–2
Shi Xiu 70
shikumen (stone portals) 93, 95–8, 101,
  105, 107–8, 110, 122, 126, 141, 144,
  158, 201n12
shops 95, 100, 140–3
shuyu 55, 62, 107, 109–11, 151–6, 197n3,
  203n6
Sima Guang, 18
Simalu, *see* Fourth Avenue
Simmel, Georg 127
Skinner, G. William 17, 20, 22, 94, 115,
  194n8
Small Sword Rebellion 1, 11, 44–5, 87
Smith, Edwin M. 90–1
sojourners 11, 22, 31, 53, 55, 70, 66–7, 80,
  87, 100, 121–4, 168, 194n7
Songnan mengying lu 37, 43–4, 47–8, 76,
  85–7, 92, 112, 119–20, 137, 142, 149,
  154, 161–3, 169, 171, 173, 196n15,
  200n29, 202n4, 203n11, 203n12
space: cosmological order 28; disruption/
  rupture 4, 19–20, 27; everyday 4;
  exclusivity 144; fragmentation 15, 17, 19;
  hierarchy 95, 97; in literary production 27;
  in journalism 34–5; interiority 84;
  production 14–15: public 12, 19, 113,
  134, 150, 177; walled 19, 32, 95–6, 132
spectatorship 132–4, 154–5, 161

storytellers 27, 30–1, 34, 50, 62–3, 134,
  151–4, 202n4
storytelling houses 62, 134, 151–5, 162
streets 32, 85–7, 94–5, 97, 111–12, 124,
  131–2, 165, 171; as forests 129–30;
  events and spectatorship 132–4; names
  86, 95–6; *see* Chessboard Street, First
  Avenue, Fourth Avenue
syncretism, culture 20, 29–30
Sun Sulan 63
Suzhou 32, 75, 85, 94, 100, 109, 118, 166,
  192n4, 203n9

taiji 110
Taiping Rebellion 1, 11, 44, 121, 124–5,
  201n8
tea parties 63–4, 103
teahouses 110, 123–5, 127–9, 132, 134–5,
  137–40, 175
theaters: commercial 158–63; guild 156–7;
  local festival 156; stages 156–7, 161–2
thugs (hoodlums) 42, 58–9, 63, 81–2,
  104–5, 111, 130, 158–9
time: and clock 79; in journalism 34–5;
  linear consciousness of 2; secularization
  of 3
tingzijian, *see* back rooms
traditionalism 4, 12, 16–17
travel: ideal 114; literature 31–2
tour boats (*huafang*) 32, 84–5, 171–2
Tu Mingzhu 75–7, 99, 102

vernacular: architecture 6, 84, 93, 96,
  119, 126, 141; language 49; literature
  (romance) 21, 30–1, 50; street/alley 97,
  165; townscapes 115–16
visual: display 73, 77–8, 80, 140, 143, 150;
  experience 7, 123, 138, 151–2

Wagner, Rudolf 36, 113, 195n5, 196n12
Wang A'er 104
Wang, David Der-wei 7, 39, 192n1,
  197n23, 198n11
Wang Liansheng 54, 61–2, 69–70, 73, 77,
  79–81, 103, 105–6, 109, 143, 175–6,
  197n1, 198n6, 198n7, 198n9
Wang Shaozhou 87, 93–4, 107, 200n1
Wang Tao 23, 33, 37–8, 40, 43–8, 55, 69,
  72, 75, 77, 85–6, 95, 116, 118, 122, 124,
  153–4, 155, 161, 163–5, 196n22, 198n3,
  201n11, 203n9, 203n11
waterways 22, 32, 85
Watson, James L. 195n1
Wei Xiaxian 67–8, 103–5, 202n2

Wen Junyu 177
Western influences 1, 11–13, 16–17, 20
windows 97–8, 110, 119–23, 126–8, 132–3, 141
Wu Xuexiang 65, 73–4, 105, 110, 141–3, 199n15, 199n16, 199n17
Wu Youru 37–9, 180, 196n12

xianghao 60, 64, 69–71, 198n7
Xiaoliu'er 70, 81, 106, 176
Xinji haishang qinglou tuji 39, 55, 62, 77, 80–1, 103, 197n2, 197n3, 200n23, 200n24, 200n25, 203n5
Xu Maorong 111

Yan Fu 2
yangfang (Western-style buildings) 13, 92, 107, 118–24, 127, 137, 141, 144, 175–6, 178, 201n10, 202n5
Yangzhou 82, 85, 192n4, 197n23, 199n13, 203n9
Yangzhou huafang lu 31, 37
Yao Jichun 54, 67, 148, 202n2; wife of 67–8, 143, 148, 202n2
Yao Wenjun 42, 63
yao'er 49, 55, 60, 62, 73, 81, 107, 109–11, 121, 197n3
Ye, Xiaoqing 36–7, 43, 166–7, 196n12, 203n11
Yeh, Catherine 7, 24–5, 38, 40, 42–44, 48, 155–6, 163, 172, 174, 196n22, 198n6, 198n13, 200n25, 201n16, 203n8
yeji (streetwalkers) 104, 108, 110–11, 137–40, 150–1, 197n3

yeyou (pleasure tours) 114, 124, 171–2, 174, 180, 202n1
Yin Chiyuan 54, 176, 199n20
Yu Huai 32, 196n22
Yu Yuan (West Garden) 22–3, 174
Yuan Sanbao 63
Yuan Yunxian 152, 154
Yuan Zuzhi 37–8, 47–8, 111–12, 177, 196n15

Zhang Ailing 73, 197n23
Zhang Garden (Zhangyuan) 177–80
Zhang Huizhen 61–2, 66, 73–4, 77, 80–1, 99, 103, 105, 109–10, 175–6, 198n7, 198n9, 199n15, 201n13
Zhang Shou 58, 104, 106, 110
Zhang Shuhe 177–8
Zhang Shuyu 180
Zhang Xiaocun 54, 61, 104, 107–8, 111
Zhang Xiuying 82
Zhao Erbao 58, 71, 77, 81–2, 105, 174, 203n16
Zhao Puzhai 54, 58, 60–1, 101, 104–8, 111, 173–4, 201n15
Zhou Fenglin 163
Zhou Lan 57–8, 99, 102, 106
Zhou Shuangbao 57, 200n26
Zhou Shuangyu 57, 102, 200n26
Zhou Shuangzhu 53, 57, 66, 109, 197n1, 198n7
Zhu Airen 75
Zhu Ruxian 180
Zhu Shiquan 104, 110
Zhu Xi 29